darlie koshy

indian design edge

strategies for success in the creative economy

foreword by ratan tata

LOTUS COLLECTION
ROLI BOOKS

Lotus Collection

This edition published in 2008
The Lotus Collection
An imprint of Roli Books Pvt. Ltd.
M-75, G.K. II Market, New Delhi 110 048
Phones: ++91 (011) 4068 2000, 2921 2271,
2921 2782, 2921 0886, Fax: ++91 (011) 2921 7185
E-mail: Info@rolibooks.com; Website: rolibooks.com
Also at
Bangalore, Chennai, Jaipur, Kolkata, Mumbai, Varanasi

Design: Supriya Saran
Production: Naresh Nigam & Kumar Raman

ISBN: 978-81-7436-670-2

Typeset in Gill Sans by Roli Books Pvt. Ltd. and
printed at Gopsons Papers Ltd. in India

contents

to my mother

who stands tall by being a living example of steely resolve and pragmatism with a will to succeed against heavy odds, inspiring me to overcome many obstacles in my life's journey.

How precious also are your thoughts towards me, O God! How great is the sum of them! (If) I should count them they are more in number than the sand; when I awake, I'm still with you.

Psalms

acknowledgements

In my view, every book is a collective effort although the author is in the forefront. Many colleagues, friends, well-wishers and sometimes even acquaintances contribute to the development of thoughts and ideas with or without one's knowledge. My long stay in the textile and handloom industries and then in fashion and retail, and later in the area of design, from 1977 onwards until now has resulted in a large number of associates and friends who consider me as someone who has innovated and pioneered many initiatives for India's fashion and retail sectors and in recent years spearheaded the design movement in India. I am humbled by the respect and recognition I have received and I extend my heartfelt thanks to all those who have directly or indirectly helped in my journey so far. I must thank especially the young practising designers who have provided illuminating case studies for this book investing their precious time: Sanjeeb Chatterjee and Anjalee Wakanker, Michael Foley, Abhijit Bhansod, Sridhar Marri and friends like Armando Branmchini and my colleagues at the National Institute of Design or NID, Dr Deepak John Mathew and Vijai Singh Katiyar who helped me with the photographs.

My long stint as director of the NID since June 2000 has afforded an opportunity to meet men and women of substance and they have all in some way or the other played varying roles in my development and growth. During my stints, over the years, on the board of International Council of Societies of Industrial Design, or ICSID, I have interacted with a wide spectrum of leading designers and thought leaders in most parts of the world including Europe, the US, China, Africa, and Southeast Asia.

During my years at the NID, one important visitor to the institute, who specially left an indelible impression on my mind owing to his genuine modesty, humility, good humour and greatness: Ratan Tata. I am so happy that this book is uniquely privileged by his generous Foreword despite pressures on his time. I owe sincere thanks to him especially as I do recognize that while he is a tall business leader, he is also a 'Designer' with a big 'D' at heart.

Over the years, I have also been closely involved in founding and organizing the CII-NID Design Summit, the *Businessworld*-NID Design Excellence Awards and initiating the National Design Policy. Innumerable meetings and discussions left me richer as I not only met and interacted with Mr Kamal Nath, Union Commerce and Industry minister, and many senior officers in the Ministry of Commerce and Industry, the Department of Industrial Policy and Promotion, Science and Technology, Planning Commission, but also came in direct contact with iconic leaders and doyens of the industry.

Residing in Ahmedabad has brought me in touch with many leading lights from all walks of life within the campus and outside. NID's Governing Council has always had luminaries as its chairmen and members and I have had the privilege of working closely with several in the last decade and the interactions have added great value.

When I took over as director of the NID, there were several 'design gurus' among the faculty and I learnt invaluable lessons from each of them and my gratitude therefore goes out to them, as also the alumni and students of NID.

My frequent travels in India and overseas, presentations, speeches, long working hours and the writing of books have all taken a toll on my family life and cannot ever be fully compensated. I have a sense of guilt in this regard and my special thanks to my caring wife, Roshini, son, Arun and daughter, Alika for always being there as good shoulders to lean on.

The unwavering commitment of my staff in helping me put this book together needs special mention. Padmavati Bet, senior research assistant, toiled tirelessly on the manuscript, typing and carrying out innumerable corrections. My dependable executive secretary, Chanda Naidu of over eight years and the Research & Publications team at NID have also put in substantial efforts in this endeavour.

Every effort has been made to trace the copyright holders of the material used in this book and to get their written consent. We thank all those who have so generously allowed me to quote from their books, refer to their case studies and pictures. However, in case I have overlooked any inadvertently, then I owe them both an apology and a thanks!

My editor Sudha Sadanand, from Roli Books who said at my first ever meeting that I am on a 'dentist's chair', till the book is really done, has put in painstaking efforts and my thanks are due to her! A big thank you to Priya Kapoor of Roli Books, who took upon herself to see the book through.

A still from an animation film *The Rain Dance* by NID student Vijay Kumar Arumugam.

foreword

These are exciting times for India in many spheres and design is one such prominent area with potential and future promise. As an architect, I have always been conscious of India's rich heritage in the substantial pool of human talent in design and the immense entrepreneurial possibilities of leveraging that talent on a global stage.

The NID is among the most prominent repositories of India's talent and knowledge in design and I have had the privilege of several productive discussions with its staff and students over the years. I have also been following the institute's initiatives into new areas like transportation and automobile design and its endeavour to transform itself into an internationally-acclaimed multi-campus institute.

Dr Darlie Koshy has had a ringside view of the evolution of Indian design over the years and I can well appreciate his need to communicate the power of design not only to the converted but to practically every one as designs affects every body, in some way or the other. His book traces the development of Indian design, beginning with its deeper roots in our culture and traditions and concluding on a note of how to unleash the competitive edge of Indian design to improve the quality of life for many more people. As this book is also the result of the author's research for India's first National Design Policy which came out in 2007, there are also several policy facets underlying the discussions in the book.

The main argument running through the book is the need to become a 'creative manufacturer' or innovative provider of services in a cross-section of national human endeavours. To simplify matters somewhat, the book's call is to create a movement towards realizing the dream of 'Designed in India, Made for the World'.

For Indian industry, whether in services or in manufacturing, whether as a large unit or as an SME (small and medium enterprise), the book identifies new opportunities for creating a 'design enabled' India. It also lists certain focus growth areas and sketches a roadmap on how to use design elements to craft global Indian brands in those areas. The book argues that design as a source of intellectual property needs to be fully explored and utilized by Indian industry since the international market place is increasingly being dominated by creators of intellectual property.

Design, the book emphasizes, can have a major role to play in shaping and upgrading many aspects of India's civil life. Manmade urban environments, products and services is just one of the many areas where the author calls for 'societal innovation' to use design to empower people and improve their quality of life and creates what he calls a 'design democracy'.

For the many who place a premium on design and innovation, this book will be an inspirational read and I am honoured to have been asked to write this foreword. I trust and hope this book will be the precursor to more such endeavours by the author.

Ratan Tata. Chairman, Tata Sons

introduction

Let's celebrate the fact: India is on a sustained path of growth and that is manifested, amongst several other things, in its vibrant economy, a strong presence of youth power and a credible position in the global arena. As is expected, this unprecedented growth is a result of 'change' in the larger perspective of a nation, and like in any other sphere, change automatically impacts the world of design. There's no doubt that design and innovation, as also several other factors, are the new enabling forces that can unleash the power and potential of a country like India which has a heritage spanning nearly 5000 years. This book is an attempt to trace and touch upon the evolution and growth of Indian design while unveiling the connections which make it possible for design to add and realize value and to create brands in the new age economy.

As a starting point, design establishes itself purely through cultural and emotional connections and in the final process sustains itself in a market as a commercial entity.

Therefore, if on the one hand ancient crafts and design form a great recipe for preserving our roots and values in a rapidly changing global world, management philosophies, science and technology are the tools which provide the impetus for creating wealth and maintaining a quality of life. The initial chapters in the book examine these linkages while placing crafts as the foundation for design innovation from the point of view of skills, materials, techniques and innate human creativity and people centricity. There is no gainsaying the fact that Indians are creative people and this is not a generic statement but amply exemplified by some of the grass-roots innovations, as is evident in this book. The innovation and creativity of those at the 'bottom of the pyramid' is an important factor in the coming years as India is not only a huge market in the making but also a reservoir of tacit knowledge and design power.

Today, it is the 'context' that defines and redefines designs as they conceptualize products, systems and arbiters' culture and emotions. Therefore, it is not just about marrying technology and design or humanizing technology but also about ensuring that designs conform with the inner core of the customers. The human-centricity of designs has become the central focus of new design thinking. More than 'design' as a noun, 'design/ing' as a verb focuses on the processes, as they are often more critical, than just outcomes. The paradigm shift, as it were, is about the manner in which form, function, and image converge with the help of technologies to offer 'experiences' through products and services. The world over, economies are now more focused on creative industries, as was seen in UK, with a great amount of emphasis on design-led and other allied creative industries. 'The Rise of the Creative Class' has led to new concepts like creative cities and design capital and economies are increasingly being described as 'innovation economy', 'creative economy' and the like by trying to capture that fleeting 'zing' which provides a different texture and character to the emerging ecosystems of innovation and design. In a nutshell, in creative economies ideas rule the roost, and the litmus test is the speed with which ideas are converted to marketable products and services. In this context, an interesting turn of phrase is 'creative destruction' which has become the norm of the day and those who design change and interpret change with the help of new products, systems and ideas are bound to be winners.

Although India is on an upsurge now, in the past the country was rather content being a protected economy and by and large gave creativity, innovations and original designs a miss. Even the most precious heritage of Indian crafts, handlooms and handicrafts, have languished and been ignored. Although I do say, as I have earlier, that at an individual level the Indian people are creative but as a collective whole, there's been a failure to protect Indian ideas and discoveries in the global arena. It is rather strange that India's very own ancient traditions and philosophies of yoga, herbal treatments, and hundreds of culture specific products and recipes have been exported elsewhere to create wealth while India has remained a mute spectator espousing the 'used apple policy' through reverse engineering and screw-driver technologies. There has been a general apathy towards spaces, environments, architecture, roads, infrastructure, gardens, and museums and this has had an impact not only on the health of the nation but there has been a gradual but severe degradation in manual skills and creative talent too.

One of the most stark examples of the deterioration of the visual culture in India is: its cities are devoid of any aesthetic appeal and ambience with the exception of perhaps a few. Given the situation, can India discover the 'Design Edge', and become a 'Creative Manufacture', rather than being a 'Factory to the World' which is how I feel China is positioning itself? For instance, in garments, can India move from being a 'Tailor to the West' to becoming a 'Brand Creator'? How come a smaller country like Italy which had no design schools till 1985 is able to capture 27 per cent of the world luxury market and several dozens of world beating brands; or, for that matter Korea which was known for slipshod products till mid-eighties turn the tables to have today in its kitty world beating brands like LG and Samsung? How small countries like Sweden have been able to realize top designed products and brands, like SAAB, Volvo, Ericsson and Ikea, and Finland which has successfully created great mass brands like Nokia.

Other pertinent questions are: is there a way to re-establish an 'Indian idiom in Design'? How do we decode the design identity and enable the industry to compete on 'Design Edge'? Why is it that despite the presence of NID since 1961, design education in the country did not receive sufficient patronage from either the government or the industry to multiply and scale-up, like the Indian Institute of Management (IIM) or the Indian Institute of Technology (IIT). Let us not forget that these institutes were set up as post-independent India's iconic temples of learning, as part of the Nehruvian vision, almost at the same time.

By and large due to lack of an expansive view, for a long time design failed to dovetail either strategy or technology and could only register its presence at the end of the process chain; merely confined to form and colour changes or just packaging and aesthetics. Some graphics were added in good measure at best. However, today design precedes product creation through an in-depth research focusing on consumer's 'ethnographic' or 'psycho-aesthetic' needs. For instance, the culture specificity of Korean products indicates the ability of design to bring forth emotion, culture and values by encoding these efficiently. There was a time when products were designed by a group of designers and domain experts as they were technology enabled. Today, services are technology enabled and they need to be designed more or less like products. Spaces, products, images, and services merge seamlessly and converge as experience often delivered through and held devices on the move. Therefore undoubtedly, design has a major challenge, as seen through the examples of Apple's incredible holistic designing process which combines the product and an ecosystem around it including the retail system, in taking a great leap forward towards designing 'experiences' for the users. This has been a paradigm shift and a strategic success by design.

Many high growth sectors hold the key to India's emergence as a design power. As I have said earlier and also reiterate in the book, the skills, traditions, and decoding of ancient handlooms and crafts of India cannot be overlooked to create new lifestyles and luxury goods for tomorrow. Similarly, India is exploding with 'mobility', automobiles and communication devices will call for tremendous design interventions as the future unfolds. Customized design for the media and entertainment industry along with the burgeoning world of Bollywood and animation films require a gamut of talented designers for world-class output.

However, I feel there is a severe crunch of talent in the country and Indian design scene is a classic example of what is termed as the 'National Design Deficit'. The number of designers required in tandem with the number of technologists fall far below the requirements. It is time design education in India, led by NID over the last five decades, once again 'shift orbit' to create a critical mass of quality designers with generic design capabilities, indepth domain expertise and a 'glocal' outlook. Afterall NID's repositioning and transformational turnaround at the beginning of the twenty-first century is a significant case study as the institute emerged as one of the top design schools in the world as reported by the *Businessweek*, US in 2006 and 2007, consecutively. As a milestone in the history of Indian design, NID pitched hard for the first National Design Policy of India to be formulated and it came to fruition in February 2007.

The first National Design Policy is a landmark simple and flexible document that could provide necessary impetus as it leaves enough room for improvement by those whom I would like to call stakeholders. The policy creates a direction and environment for accelerating growth of design-led industries and design practices including expansion of much neglected design education. The world reacted to the policy document

The GenNext Experience: Young designers at NID's PG campus, Gandhinagar.

with unprecedented enthusiasm as for the first time it galvanized India's fragmented design community. There is great anticipation about branding Indian design, promoting a design movement and most importantly, an unwavering commitment from the industry to use design strategically by setting up its own design studios and hiring more Indian and international designers as is evident from Tata Motors, Titan Industries, Mahindra and Mahindra, Bajaj and other handful of companies who are rapidly realizing the value of design and innovation.

At a micro level, there has been a transformation as well and Indian design practice is changing rapidly. Many small design studios are growing at a hectic pace to achieve critical mass and size. Some of them are in the mode of mergers and acquisitions. Some have become 200-designers strong design factories. A vision for design leadership is being now envisaged through many local initiatives in Pune, Goa, Mumbai and Bengaluru.

From the days of iconic designers and prima donnas, design is now entering a period driven by participation and teamwork; which I have termed as 'Design Democracy'. The best example for democratic design is one involving services and there are numerous examples of empowering consumers through this. For example, the digital devices and mobiles in India which have ushered in a period of greater interactivity and empowerment of choice. This is a time for making Indian design stand up and get noticed in both manufacturing and service sectors. This book is an attempt to create a vision for India to assume leadership in the world of design to make 'Designed in India, Made for the World' the new mantra to reverberate around the globe in the not too distant future.

evolving design

indian mind: a design powerhouse

Redefining work and living spaces: Display of furniture and interior design ideas by Chitra Sarwara, an NID graduate.

Facing page: *Kamas*, a car designed by NID student Ramesh Gound for a design contest by Pininfarina, Torino, Italy.

Indian mind is a storehouse of creativity and represents the heritage of the millennia. The ancient craft traditions of India manifest great diversity and creativity as they evolved through vicissitudes of time and various external influences. Oral traditions, fascinating and unique to the country, have also played a major role in capturing the essence of India's traditions over time immemorial and passed on seamlessly from one generation to another. The Indian intellect has many firsts to its credit – from the ancient fields of yoga, the art of love and love making, Ayurveda, statecraft as also literature, economics, medicine and to the more recent Information Technology and life sciences. As is apparent, with the gradual transition of Indian economy from being a purely agrarian to service-driven knowledge economy, India has a unique chance of becoming a design-led creative powerhouse in the twenty-first century. One of the primary reasons for this is definitely the obvious shift from disparate individual efforts to a

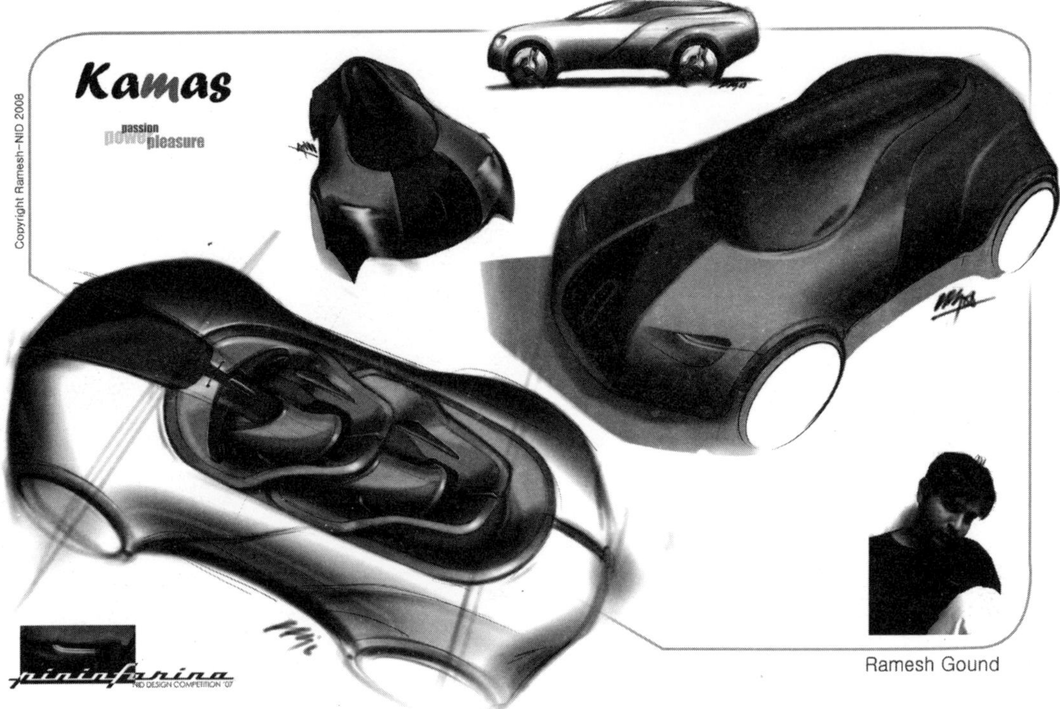

collective endeavour by a country as diverse and futuristic as India.

One of the most significant capabilities of the human mind is to dream, visualize, and to express in words. This faculty makes human beings the first among equals and is, therefore, exclusive in nature. Some scholars attribute this unique human capability to the peculiar structure of the human spine and the fact that human beings are vertically stationed – as they are on two legs. The average length of the vertical column in males is about 71 cms while in females it is 61 cms. The human neck, at any given point, can only turn forty degrees on either side and therefore the eyes cannot see what is at the back. This, some thinkers opine, has also been a major contributing factor in the evolution of communication and formation of social groups.

With specific reference to what is the Indian 'mind', it has been argued time and time again that it may have been perhaps somewhat on a higher plane when compared with other civilizations. Of course, Indian mind has certain distinct characteristics, when compared to other ancient civilizations like the Greek, Egyptian or Aztec. However, if we consider the sheer 'power' of mind, then the singlemost distinctive factor is the 'world forming faculty of the mind', which is the ability to dream, visualize and create the hitherto unknown. That is truly creativity in quintessence.

As mentioned earlier, Indian collective memory was primarily created through oral traditions prevalent in India. Most of India's knowledge was not in written form but existed in tales, poems, songs, music and folkloric art and this tradition has seeped into the minds of its people. The Indian mind can memorize and retain a lot. As is well known, some of the people's relative position in society was determined by how many Vedas they could memorize and recite: honorifics like Dwivedi, Trivedi, or Chaturvedi, now used as second names, were the result of the capacity of

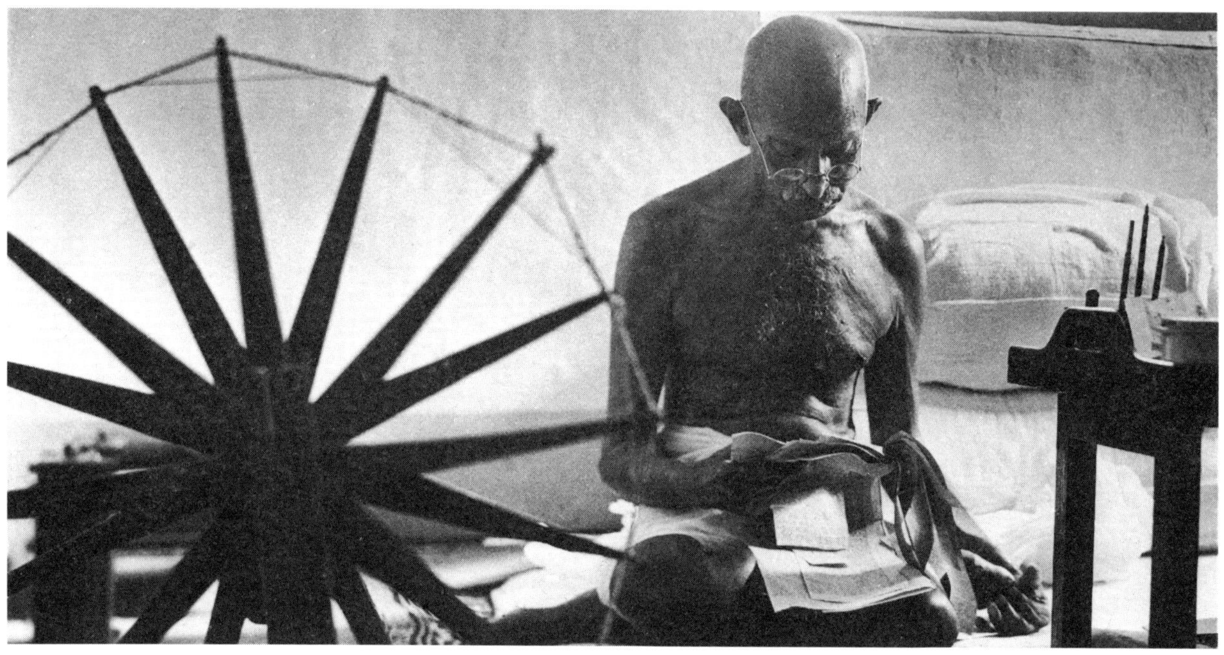

Mahatma Gandhi used visual symbols like the *charka*, spectacles or the utilitarian wooden footwear to convey his philosophy and direction.

reciting either two, three or four Vedas. The storytelling traditions are so interlinked to the Indian mind that like S. Balaram, author of *Thinking Design* observes, the Indian concern to some extent has not only been with reality but also about transcending the reality. The two great epics, the Ramayana and Mahabharata and the collection of fables, the Panchatantra have assumed larger than life proportions over a period of time. Panchatantra, in fact has its roots in the *Kathasaritsagar*, which has been a true ocean of stories and tales. (Somadeva's *Kathasaritsagar*, composed around the sixteenth century AD, is a collection of ancient tales that extols social values.)

However, like I have said in the Introduction to this book, change is a necessity and in this context this complete dependency on oral transfer of knowledge, although unique and exciting, has proven to be inadequate in the current knowledge-driven-economy scenario. The reason: while other countries increasingly focused on the creation of Intellectual Property Rights (IPR) through documentation, India lost out considerably as tacit knowledge remained largely confined to oral traditions. However, there is no doubt that Indian crafts are linked to the very origin of the dawn of time. As ancient legends have it, the Devas and Asuras churned the primal ocean to extract *amrut* or nectar. Having got their nectar, they needed a vessel to store it, and Viswakarma moulded an earthern pot for them. (Viswakarma is the god of India's arts and crafts. He is said to have had five sons: Manu who worked in iron, Maya in wood, Toshtwa in brass, copper, alloys, Shilpy in stone and finally Viswajna, who was gold and silversmith). In all these fields that the 'divine' beings were so adept at, India has had a rich tradition of original creativity which cuts across 360 craft clusters with an estimated workforce of over thirty million artisans.

The awe-inspiring contribution of the Indian mind is not just confined to cold figures but has been well documented by some of the greatest thinkers and philosophers. As the world renowned American historian,

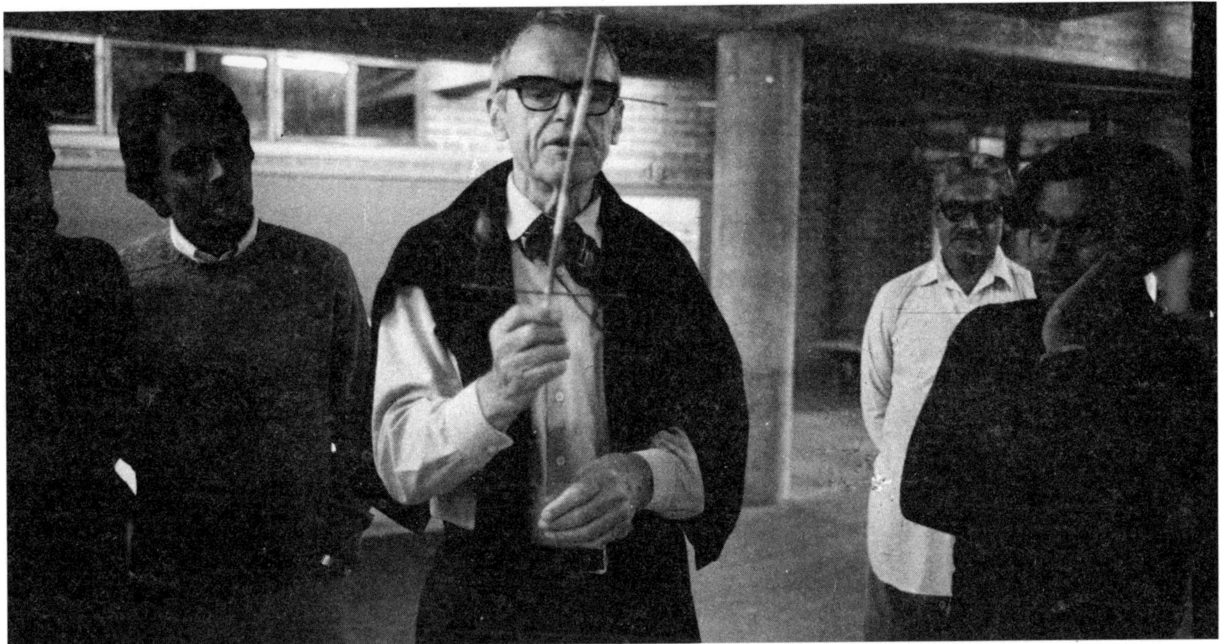

Charles Eames contributed to the seminal document, *The India Report* which resulted in setting up a design institute in India.

Will Durant said: 'India was the mother of our philosophy; mother of much of our mathematics; mother, through the Buddha, of the ideals embodied in Christianity; mother, through the village community, of self-government and democracy. Mother India is in many ways the Mother of us all ...' Or as Max Mueller put it succinctly: 'If I were asked under what sky the human mind has most fully developed the choicest gifts, has most deeply pondered on the greatest problems of life, I should point to India.'

Extolling India's virtues, Sri Aurobindo said: 'India of the ages is not dead nor has spoken her last creative word; she lives and has still something to do for herself and the human peoples ... India is the guru of the nations, the physician of the human soul in its profounder maladies; she is destined once more to now-mould the life of the world, and restore the peace of the human spirit.'

The Indian mind is seen to be timeless as the past, present and the future are considered to be cyclical with creation followed by stability and then destruction or *srishthi, sthithi, samharam,* and in that seamless order. In fact in design this is a key principle to understand and imbibe as 'cradle to grave' sustainability driven approach advocated by eco-design proponents. The Indian mind is the outcome of the innumerable years of ancient traditions and legacies, which present an organic and comprehensive worldview. Amongst other things, it strives to attain wisdom, seek truth and hold self-renunciation and sacrifice as sacrosanct.

The aberrations in history or the tides of time have not fully robbed the enchanting diversity, rich landscape, eclectic fusion and beauty of Indian crafts. The aesthetics of India, reflected through the crafts and its forms, shapes and its colour pallets are almost like its food reflecting great diversity and varied tastes. The multitude of hues and forms seen in the shandys and melas of India tell the stories of hundreds of crafts that belong to a vast and diverse country – with 18 major and 1,600 patois and dialects, 6 major religions, 6 major ethnic groups, 52 major tribes, 6,400 castes and sub castes, 29 major festivals and over a billion people. This diversity is really the core for understanding an Indian idiom in design and design always blooms in diversity.

The Indian freedom movement saw the emergence of several creative minds at work. Mahatma Gandhi, for one, influenced generations of Indians in being one of the perfect examples of this. According to S. Balaram, the Mahatma used visual symbols and semiotics to great effect as popular expressions for shaping a mass movement. The spinning-wheel or the *charka*, his spectacles or the utilitarian wooden footwear, all these elements of design conveyed a great deal about his philosophy and direction. Gandhiji was also very conscious of design's communication capabilities and its lasting impact on the masses. He was probably the first one to have organized a design competition in India and that too for the designing of *charka* with an attractive prize! When Gandhiji wanted to increase the mechanical efficiency of the *charka*, a German friend of his, called Herman Kallenbach, designed an eight-spindle spinning wheel which increased the productivity many times. Yet Gandhiji rejected the design saying that it looked complex and hence would not be acceptable to the common people. Gandhiji believed in people-centric design, especially for the rural folk in India's villages.

Guru Kalamandalam Gopi, Kathakali artist performing a dance recital organized by Spic Macay at the NID.

Amongst several other things, the most iconic of Indian designs, according to Charles Eames, the world renowned American designer of the century, and someone who along with his wife, Ray actually laid the foundation of NID, is the *lota*. He was very impressed with it and thought the *lota* to be one of the most evolved of all designs. In a way, the *lota* is linked to the very origin of Indian crafts. In his much acclaimed *India Report* of 1958, Charles Eames elaborated on the concept of indigenous design through the powerful symbolism of *lota* – how it could be placed on the head stacked or held at the hip by a woman drawing water from village wells and ponds to carry to great distances; the ease with which village womenfolk carry the vessel on the head and walk with both hands free. One of the most beautiful designs to have emerged from India, is the mystical six yards of an unstitched garment – the sari – which undoubtedly represents the most versatile of all designs. Chantal Boulanger, a French anthropologist who spent many years in India studying the art of draping, has recorded more than a hundred different ways of draping a sari. Despite changing fashions and a desire to be 'comfortable' in other clothes, the sari brings out the best in a woman and drapes well on all sizes of women and requires no customization. The other and one of the most fascinating symbols for people elsewhere in the world is the *bindi* and its organic form *sindoor*, which captures Indian design's fascination for round-shaped objects rather than geometrical shapes. Indian design is more organic in nature and has continuity, a cyclic rhythm as mentioned earlier. Indian music also embodies continuity and the difference in musical notes of an instrument like the sitar and the guitar is quite symbolic of this essential difference. All forms of Indian art essentially revolve around the nine *rasas* or emotions and Indians do have an exaggerated sense of the *rasas*. Whether in music or in sheer taste, these *rasas* are very different from what is perceived in the West. The nine *rasas* which represent various emotions like love, pleasure, anger and the grotesque find no parallel elsewhere and are an integral part of all Indian dance forms like the Kathakali, Kathak and Bharatanatyam.

Moving away from the traditional forms of art, even in the field of mass entertainment, India has made great strides whether in popular film music or Bollywood movies. The acceptance of Indian films in English, particularly addressing the diaspora, are increasingly showcasing the Indian visual language in moving images earlier initiated by masters such as Satyajit Ray, Mrinal Sen, Ritwik Ghatak, Shyam Benegal, and Adoor Gopalakrishnan. Yet another yardstick to measure India's uniqueness in creating a niche so far as its time-tested traditions is concerned has to do with the rising popularity of Indian food – as zany and interesting as Indian pop music! The rise of Indian authors in English, of course, has already captured the world's imagination with an Indian winning the prestigious Booker Prize. Yet another significant factor is the linguistic skills which today dictate the world trade movement especially in the knowledge economy. Prof Uday Karmarkar of UCLA, once said in an article in *Harvard Business Review* that off-shoring and outsourcing of work as in software and design are going to be dictated by linguistic conformity and India scores high because of its felicity with the widely used English language.

With the arrival of the twenty-first century and the morphing of knowledge economy to innovation-led creative economy, it is clear that one sure source of competitive advantage is going to be ideas. India's contribution to the invention of *shunya* (zero; though some dispute this) and the concept of 'infinity' have probably helped Indians to understand the language of software viz, binary language better. However, creativity and innovation are not given importance in many developing economies including India. If India has to compete on value, it should put a premium on innovation. As Dr APJ Abdul Kalam, said in his book *Envisioning an Empowered Nation*, society and economic growth are interlinked as we move from the agrarian to industrial and then to an information society followed by a knowledge economy. The demand for products reflecting information and knowledge increases as the society undergoes rapid transformation.

Shyam Benegal, one of the modern masters of Indian cinema.

It is also imperative for design to humanize technology with culture and emotion. This is going to be the crucial differentiator in an overcrowded marketplace. If design does not marry technology, the hiatus between the physical and the virtual will widen further to the detriment of the people. In a knowledge economy, closed minds are as dangerous as closed technology. Open minds discover new frontiers.

Dr Kalam in a speech in Hyderabad in December 2006 poignantly pointed out, that . . . although we are a country of 1.1 billion, we behave on many occasions as a country of a mere million, More than anything else, I feel it is our mindset which often comes in the way of bigger achievements. But in recent years, there's been a ray of hope as Indian corporates have started to dream and think big which are positive signs of change. It is quite clear that Indian mind inherently has great potential. To convert it into a powerhouse, there needs to be collective will for 'cohesive vision', and 'timely and purposeful action'. From an individualistic mindset, India needs to move to a collective endeavour. We also need to clearly align promise and delivery, vision and action. Design with its user centricity has the 'magic' to help in making a visible difference to the lives of people around the world.

design for development

NID Heritage Campus in Ahmedabad is one of the foremost multi-disciplinary institutions of design education and research.

It is to the credit of the visionary political leadership of India that technology, design and management were given rather equal attention in the post-independent period. The first IIT was set up in Kharagpur in West Bengal in 1950 while the first NID was set up in Ahmedabad in Gujarat in 1961. Yet another first, the IIM was established in 1962, also in Ahmedabad. That the golden triangle of technology, management and design were put in place within almost a decade-and-a-half after Independence indicates the forward looking vision of a nascent democracy. It is another fact that these visions did not fully materialize and design, in particular, languished till economic liberalization began.

The preoccupation of NID, till the last few years of the twentieth century, was primarily with design for development and rightly so, given the developmental stage of the country's economy and the social fabric. As a premier national education institution, NID through its chequered history has been continuously striving and struggling not only to achieve excellence in design education, but also for bringing design to the forefront of national and international agenda for development.

The design for development thrust was supposed to get a new fillip with the 1979 UNIDO-ICSID or the International Council of Societies of Industrial Design conference held at NID. The Ahmedabad Declaration made at this conference is historically significant as it proposed even at that time a need for a 'Design Policy and Promotion' and had indicated a blueprint for the industry to become design driven. Unfortunately, either it was ahead of its times or the stakeholders could not come together to push the same forward. Both the declaration and the call for collective action on design unfortunately failed to take off and the fragmented Indian design fraternity, speaking in different voices at critical junctures, hampered the progress of design in the country. Many other less developed countries saw the declaration as a tool for development.

However, in India the development march of design did not receive any traction and stumbled along between mostly inaction and chaos until the dawn of the twenty-first century. Amongst several other things, institutes are often recognized for endeavouring to produce collective vision relevant to its time and beyond and by doing that are remembered and hence the 1979 declaration in which NID played a key role was a historic milestone.

The Ahmedabad Declaration is an important document which reflects the journey of design as it moved through the pangs of industrial society through 'design for development' and 'design for personal statements, and variety' thus evolving to the current focus on sustainable design. The text indicates the vision, and most importantly provides pointers towards the comprehensive role of design in shaping our world, especially for the developing and less developed parts and provides the backdrop for later developments towards the first National Design Policy announced in February 2007. Some excerpts:

> The Meeting for the Promotion of Industrial Design in Developing Countries convened by the United Nations Industrial Development Organization (UNIDO) in close cooperation with the International Council of Societies of Industrial Design (ICSID) and the Indian National Institute of Design in January 1979, in line with the Lima Declaration and Plan of Action and in pursuance of the Memorandum of Understanding signed between UNIDO and ICSID on 26 April 1977 to accelerate jointly industrial design activities in developing countries in order to satisfy the urgent needs in this field, and to carry out as extensively as possible the promotional activities necessary to alert developing countries to the advantage of including industrial design in their planning processes.

Some of the measures as excerpted from the Declaration envisaged at that time were:

- Developing countries are encouraged to consider the establishment of design institutions, design centres and/or other design-practising and promotional institutions to spread design methodology, awareness and consciousness.
- These institutions should develop close and sustained links with industrial activity in government and in the private sector, at every level including heavy industries, medium-scale industries, small-scale, rural and craft industries, as well as with educational and research institutions, and with people who are ultimate users of design.
- These institutions must work to establish a priority for industrial design through the creation of a national design consciousness. They must hasten the awareness that in all areas of public expenditure, the integration of design in the planning process can ensure optimum quality and utilization of resources. They must communicate that industrial design is concerned with the improvement of our environment through the appropriate use of raw materials, increased productivity, with the protection of health, human safety, natural and cultural resources, with the enhancement of working environments, and with expanding work opportunities and earnings at all levels, including exports. Therefore design considerations should be incorporated in plans for national development.

The Ahmedabad Declaration also made some major recommendations for the promotion of industrial design. Some of those were:

- There is a definite need in many lands for an official statement of policy on industrial design which could provide a basis for a national understanding of this profession. Unless such a national consensus is achieved, it will be difficult for the industrial design movement to be quickly accepted and to move ahead with speed.

- Each developing country would first need to establish its own design objectives before it can select or innovate design policies and programmes appropriate to its needs.
- Industrial design is involved with creating not only material but also spiritual values. While the loss of cultural identity and values can seldom be restored, a sweep towards a general culture within a shrinking world is obvious. The industrial designer can help to link a people's aesthetic with modernization, and thus serve as a force for confidence and identity, both individual and collective.
- The education system with industrial design centres should be geared to bring out job creators and not mere job fillers, resource generators and not mere resource users. The training of trainers must be the first priority for countries introducing industrial design to their economies.
- Promotional strategies are particularly important for service to craft and small-scale industries which are often unable to afford their own full-time designers. These strategies will require constant innovation and understanding of the importance of appropriate design, and the application of marketing skills is basic to this exercise.
- Industrial designers in many developing countries will need to ensure that the requirements of medium- and large-scale industries are not overlooked in the effort to serve the widely dispersed design requirements of the small-scale sectors.
- In countries with rich craft traditions, the production of handicrafts and the thoughtful mastery of the experience of form accumulated through centuries should be utilized by the industrial designer as a prime resource, integrating the benefits of contemporary technology.

The portions excerpted here are relevant for two reasons. First, the background of the National Design Policy, reinitiated by NID starting 2001, has its roots in this document which finally led to the first National Design Policy of India. Second, the complete text also brings out the manner in which the industry actually 'missed the bus' in creating a strong nexus with designers, and how designers failed to connect with industry proactively and how institutions laboured under the limitations while developing an ecosystem for innovations. And this shows up time and again so far as the expectations of the Indian consumer is concerned. The industry seems ill-equipped in fully realizing the aspirations of the country's large population wanting affordable and well-designed products. Blaming it on obsolete technology doesn't always work as access to technology alone has never satisfied people. In the past, there have been several examples of how outdated technology, run-of-the-mill designs, incorrect usage of local raw materials etc. have led to a debilitating effect on the entire industrial sector which is now gradually showing signs of rejuvenation and competitive capabilities. Finally, consumer is king, say a lot of experts who analyze markets and trends but generally speaking, the Indian consumer often ends up getting products which are not necessarily suitable to his or her culture, lifestyle and economic standards but is forced to use them due to a lack of an alternative. Indian industry has to assimilate this clearly. The call for use of design for small and medium enterprises has also not been paid any attention.

Ignoring these very basics, there is one trend which has emerged recently and an example of that is how in virtually every seminar, the topic of discussion unfortunately veers around a comparison with China. Even when the design of the newest range of Titan watches is created in India, the same being manufactured in Hong Kong, tells the story of a new manufacturing and cost/time-based competency required to marry design successfully with production. Design and innovation have to play a defining role in reinventing the manufacturing sector to give it a competitive edge as is beginning to happen in the service sector. Success is possible if design can be used to interface with technology more imaginatively and in a humane and time efficient manner. India has to take a leadership role to leverage its creative edge in design; innovation and creativity undoubtedly provide the trump cards for India.

emergence of design

World history is often criticized for its euro-centricity while Asia has been rather conspicuous by its absence. This is even more so in case of design history. Despite the abundance of information – the twenty-first century is also termed the 'information age' – one is not likely to find enough information on design in Asian countries with the sole exception of Japan. One of the many contributing reasons for this could be the region's preoccupation with survival needs in the process of development. The other is the image of design which projected itself as the renowned industrial designer, Raymond Loewy's superficial streamlining, American architect, Louis Sullivan's self-conscious form following function, the rebellious extravaganza of the Memphis Group, or the creations of the enfant terrible of design, Philippe Starck. Around the late 50s and early 60s, Asian leaders did recognize the significance of design along with management and technology as catalysts in the process of industrialization. Many design and technology institutions were founded and infrastructure established. However, the realization of full potential of design did not occur till the winds of globalization began to blow in the late 80s and early 90s. This meant a twenty to thirty year hiatus, and Asia is now eager to bridge the gap in the fastest possible manner. There is no gainsaying that Asia's race for development recently has been faster than all other regions of the world. Not surprisingly, the future of global enterprise is expected to depend significantly on the present rate of rapid modernization of Asian countries.

However, it may not be that easy as Asia is not a unified entity. It has more diversities than commonalities. It is a vast region covering diverse cultures and ethnicities; different national histories and unique deep-rooted cultures. In terms of the size of human population alone, Asia outweighs the rest of the world. With rapid economic development in recent years, Asian countries have developed a relationship of interdependence and mutual influence on each other's society and culture. This relationship is further accelerated by Information Technology and the internet revolution.

A glimpse of the design developments in some of the Asian countries reveals that the countries, which were turning to the West in the twentieth century for inspiration and leadership, are now turning towards each other for mutual collaboration because they are more conscious of their cultural identities, similarities in developmental advancements and strengths. The profession of design has now started to show signs of maturity.

The economic, social and cultural realities of many Asian countries with their sizeable chunks of population faced with poverty, illiteracy, and a lack of infrastructure, calls for an attitudinal check on the part of those who seemingly fashion the new world, and for them to be sensitive and responsive to the needs of the people, conditioned as they are by their social, economic, cultural and environmental demands, which are varied and specific to individual and regional conditions. Design must be culturally relevant and acceptable to different communities within nation states. Yet another thing to remember is that design is an important step in the process of transition. When technologies change at a rapid pace and the resulting aspirations create an imbalance in social and cultural patterns, 'design process' can be harnessed to create harmony between technology, cultures and environment. Design has the capacity to humanize technology and harmonize cultural hiatus. Designers and design educators have an added responsibility especially in Asian countries in creating appropriate products and services which aid in economic prosperity, social transformation and environmental and cultural harmony.

If we take a look at the developments in the Asian design scenario, it reveals the urge to 'design for need' while responding to what is 'design for greed or desire'. This is a consistent pattern in almost all the Asian countries. The Changi Airport, for instance, in Singapore is a visual metaphor for the country and its design situation – conspicuously clean, hi-tech and efficient – speaks for the country's aspiration towards a technological future. But aesthetically, it is self-conscious and imposed. Amongst the Asian countries, however, for a long time Singapore stood out as the one to have recognized design as a major differentiating factor. The country went all out to participate in various trade fairs organized around the world and included the 1984 design promotion as an important activity of the Singapore Trade Development Board to provide various support systems to the industry. The 'Design Singapore' initiative, a sequel to that beginning, clearly articulates a plan and places Singapore as an entry point for both India and China. Further, the 'Design Singapore' initiative is yet another milestone and has ushered in a major transformation involving several major architects and designers of the world. Singapore is now also gearing up to host the 2009 ICSID Design Congress.

Singapore is indeed a shining example in the Asian design fraternity and a lot of praise is owed to its government which, amongst other things, also encourages and facilitates overseas design firms and manufacturers to design products locally. Singapore is a trading port where change by design becomes imperative and the government insists on it. More than a decade-and-a-half ago in 1990, Singapore started a series of biennial international design forums, which were very popular. In the same year, Singapore launched the Young Designers Award for students aged between thirteen and seventeen to make the young aware of design and to encourage them to get interested in design. In restrospect, this was indeed a laudable initiative because as said earlier, design can flourish only in a design-educated society. Therefore, what Singapore is doing is to build indigenous design capability on the one hand while trying to preserve its cultural identity on the other and the newly constituted Ministry for Information, Technology, Communication & Arts (MICA) and 'Design Singapore' are working towards the same. Singapore has decoded what is perhaps of prime importance – understanding of diasporic bent towards design, especially for countries with considerable migrant ethnic population.

Malaysia's geographical location between the Indian Ocean and the South China Sea is perhaps a factor in its history of continual influences of both the West as well as the East. After its independence from Britain in 1957, the country developed rapidly and is today considered as one of the most attractive investment destinations in Asia. Soon after its independence, the country recognized the key role design could play in industrial development and by 1971 a new economic policy was introduced to encourage local manufacturers to use design as a creative tool in the application of new technology in order to reduce the nation's dependence on imported products. By the 1990s, Malaysia succeeded in becoming a major exporter of manufactured products from being a low value commodity exporter.

How the above was possible is self-evident; formal design education in Malaysia started in the late 1960s, just a few years after its independence, with teachers from the neighbouring Thailand as well as Australia. To begin with, it adopted the British model of design education and today Malaysia is looking at establishing its own design identity. This, like in the case of Singapore, would not have been possible without the government's support which continuously allocated funds and formulated policies to encourage local design and brands. In 1994, the Malaysia Design Council was established under the department of Science and Technology for design promotion and design awareness which recognizes outstanding designs by conferring the Good Design mark for products and services. However, despite all these efforts, the Malaysian industry somehow lagged behind in its indigenous product innovations, and needs to do a lot more for securing a place in the globalized future.

As mentioned earlier, in 1958, Charles and Ray Eames,, projected the *lota*, a traditional Indian vessel, as an inspiring example for the emerging Indian design profession to follow. India's design story is quite similar to that of other colonized countries except for its long history of over 5,000 years of artistic sensibility and aesthetic explorations of design through various forms. In 1961, when India's first professional design training commenced with the setting up of the NID, the founders studied the world's best design schools, such as Bauhaus, ULM, Royal College of Art, and Allgemeine Gewerbeschule Basel, taking into account an eclectic overview to evolve their own kind of design education. The overall result: few other design schools followed suit; the impact of design on Indian industries still remains inadequate. While on the one hand the excellence of design education produced professionals of international standard, on the other, design in India badly lacked both promotional and policy support.

Post the Charles Eames *India Report* of 1958, half a century has gone by but India has only just recently announced its first National Design Policy, which hopefully may catapult Indian design to its deserving position in the country's economic progress and social development. Although as a result of global competition and the opening of markets, a few Indian industries were forced to innovate and focus on indigenous design, as recommended by the Eames, these were just a handful of exceptions. One of the major hindrances in this entire scenario is due to structural deficiencies which bears simultaneous presence of large scale, small scale, craft, and cottage level outfits. Therefore, promotional efforts lead by institutions and individuals have been sporadic and unsustainable. One of the major initiatives, to tide over some of the hindrances in the Indian design scenario, was the first UNIDO-ICSID meeting on Design for Development (1979), which led to the most significant Ahmedabad Declaration signed by thirty-seven countries. The Golden Eye project of the 1980s is yet another innovative design experiment, which focused on the revival of the Indian crafts industry; it can certainly be called an industry, as it employs more than thirty million people. Eminent designers from around the world such as Ettore Sottsass, Mario Bellini, Milton Glaser, Ivan Chermayeff, and Frei Otto, were invited to India to work with Indian master craftsmen and design unique craft products. The Festivals of India of the 1980s also brought about a design revival in the craft sector. There have been other major and positive efforts also – the setting up of Techno-design Interface Group in 2001 by the Department of Science and Technology; the collaborative efforts of CII-NID in holding annual design summits since 2001; and, the setting up of India's first modest design display centre, the NID-ITPO Showcase Design in 2002. The Statement of Intent signed by educators from twenty-seven countries brought out at the end of the International Conference at NID in March 2005 was also an important milestone in mainstreaming the Indian design movement and in connecting the issues given the global context.

There are some other interesting design examples in Asia. Korea, for instance, is a country which in the past used to function as a conduit for Chinese, Mongol and Japanese influences. Now, while it cannot help admiring and emulating Japan for its economic and commercial progress, it also

Charles Eames showed confidence in India's inherent strengths and capabilities.

would like to be distinct from Japan, as it was invaded and ruled by the same from 1910 to 1945. Korea's economy largely operates through what is known as the chaebol or the massive conglomerates. The chaebols, literally business groups in Korean, initially grew by imitating Zaibatsu (giant corporations) of Japan and by copying Japanese and German products. But gradually Korea began to look for its distinctive identity. This process of 'rediscovery' holds great significance for the Korean people and these days one hardly finds any foreign vehicles on Korean streets except Korea's very own brands like Hyundai or Daewoo. While its old guard designers were educated in Korean schools, often by Japanese teachers, the young generation is educated in the west and acutely aware of the international developments in technology and design. The credit for this could once again be attributed to the Korean government which took a keen interest in design as a tool for economic prosperity and rapid industrialization and gave it a great thrust in the first five-year plan for industrial promotion (1993-97) resulting in a significant growth of designers and design firms. Korea faced an economic crisis in 1997 which further forced the need for accelerated design and innovation strategy. The second five-year plan cleverly included design and infrastructure provision and public awareness for the same started at a national level. Korea has targeted to elevate the quality of her design to almost a hundred per cent in comparison to other advanced countries. In 2001, Korea set up one of the world's largest and comprehensive design centres where facilities include a design innovation centre, a business incubator apart from large convention and exhibition halls. It is, therefore, not surprising that for a country of Korea's size, thousands of students are enrolled annually in design programmes and the country's design competitiveness has started worrying even developed countries.

Lately, the third Korean Design Policy has further accelerated the design movement in Korea and several brands from Korea are now leading in the world. The key factor in the Korean success story seems to be the undivided focus on user-centric designs with both an eye for detail and emotional appeal.

Despite the terrible losses sustained in 1945 at the end of the Second World War, Japan rose to strength in design, manufacture and as a major economic power in the world. The country set a fantastic example for the world in going about achieving what may have seemed incredible for many and is now considered the first industrialized country in Asia. Japan occupies a unique position in the world as it applies its traditional and somewhat strict disciplined work culture to modern day manufacture and marketing strategies. The country began its industrialization process by copying the best-selling products abroad and exported them at unbeatable prices. It soon got over this phase and sought to find its distinct character in the global market. Under its Ministry of Trade & Industry, it established the good design 'G' mark as early as 1957, followed by Japan Industrial Promotion Organization in 1969 and the Japan Design Foundation in 1981. Its activities include constant information exchange, regular design competitions and design promotion through exhibition and conferences.

In order to better understand Japan's overall design philosophy, we need to revisit the 1970 world exposition held at Osaka, where the theme was 'Design for Every Being'. In most Japanese creations, invention strongly dominates designs. Japanese products, ranging from Toyota's automobiles to Sony's Walkman, are distinguished for their miniaturized grace, focusing as it were on the reality of the ever-present squeeze on domestic space. But in recent years, a trend towards 'larger' products has been noticed in Japanese designs, perhaps as a metaphor for affluence. While keeping its indigenous and traditional design culture intact, Japan has always been conscious of its presence in the international arena considering more than half of its corporate identity programmes are run by foreign designers such as Saul Bass for Minolta, Chermanyeff and Geismar for Nissan. The adage 'local at home and global outside of it' neatly summarizes the Japanese attitude to design.

Thailand, yet another emerging player in Asia, supports

the preservation of its culture in its entirety through education, research, animation and development as an important tool for socio-economic and political development of the country. Therefore, the role of industrial design in this regard is well accepted in Thailand. Leading universities offer design as part of their regular educational curricula; as part of its policy to promote and support the development of product design for export as well as indigenous designers. The Department of Export Promotion of Thailand organizes design contests and conferences through its Product Development Centre. In all, an honest and earnest attitude towards encouraging good design culture in the country and in Asia.

As regards design, Australia is yet another interesting story to emulate and follow. A multicultural country, Australia established the Industrial Design Council in 1958 with the aim of promoting design and improve the quality of Australian manufactured products. In 1975 with the creation of Commonwealth statutory authority under the Australian Council Act, Australian design got a fantastic impetus. Recognizing education and awareness as key aspects of progress in the country's industrial and economic growth, Australia established design education in art schools following the British model. For instance, the Design Institute of Australia founded in 1958 was set up to serve professional designers practicing as private consultants or staff designers. The institute acts like a design council and maintains a standard of professional competence and ethical conduct amongst Australian designers. In 1984, in order to encourage young talent, the institute commenced designer awards and student designer awards followed by an exhibition of award-winning entries. In general, Australia believes in the concept of well-designed products as a criterion for commercial visibility, technical competency and human factors, which include aesthetic, ergonomic, environmental and economic considerations. 'Standards Australia' which has been organizing the Australian Design Awards for the last several years, have rechristened the awards as 'Australian International Design Awards' from 2008. With the first award function held on 30 May 2008 in Sydney, over 840 invited guests included ICSID Board members thus marking a major shift in the orientation and import.

While reviewing the design scene in Asia, China does need a special mention as the country is undoubtedly the focus of world's attention – the 'waking dragon' which is now unleashed and growing rapidly under one party State patronage. A country where one quarter of the earth's population resides, China is already producing mass quality products at incredibly cheap prices by organizing its enormous labour force. Chinese design educators are presently concerned about marketability, sustainability, and aesthetics of its products. In the words of Jim Kaufman, Education Committee Chair, Industrial Designers Society of America or IDSA: 'When they (the Chinese) move from a manufacturing source to a product development position, they will truly have a product design presence in the world.' Despite a fantastic reputation, China has recently set up a design and brand policy ministry to specially focus on design and establishing its various brands.

As an overall perspective, Asian countries are by and large still agrarian though many of them are rapidly industrializing. China, India, Thailand, the Philippines, Malaysia, Pakistan or Sri Lanka are no different in this regard. The urge to use design interventions for hastening industrial progress, economic prosperity and societal development is present in varying degrees in all. The Southeast Asian tigers and other developing countries in Asia are increasingly using the power of design to increase the per capita GDP, unit value realization of products by the industry and most importantly to project national cultures and identity. The true test of Asian design will, however, lie in the ability to transform from local to global while addressing both the challenges concerning 'design for need' and 'design for (greed) desire' and managing the diversities the region embodies. Among Asian countries, India being the largest democracy and a fertile ground for creativity, diversity and an enormous talent pool can emerge as the 'dancing elephant' of the region in all its grandeur and impact.

defining and exploring design

Defining design is not easy but design can certainly be seen, understood and enjoyed. Simply put, design is the opposite of chaos, ugliness and complexity. Creating simplicity out of complexity through a creative process resulting in aesthetics, safety, eye appeal, comfort and several such benefits form the core of design. Some of the important definitions are given below:

> Design is a huge deal not because it makes things beautiful or garners awards, but because in our rapidly changing, customization oriented, service-added, software-added, intangibles-oriented business environment, design is a critical focus for knowing what a product is, what a customer is, and what an organization is. – Tom Peters

> Design is very much a part of our lives, it is found in nature as well as in our manmade environment. Shapes, forms, colours and textures all combine to become a unified whole which is commonly called 'a design'. In design, the elements are the things we work with, the principles are what we do with them.
> – Dorothea C. Malcolm

> Product design input contributes 60 per cent to its wealth generation (value addition), as well as influences 50 per cent of the inbuilt quality of its value chain and thereby contributes significantly to the competitiveness of the product.
> – Dr APJ Abdul Kalam

As is evident, there are numerous explanations about design but few aspects and characteristics are clear. Design is a word, which enthuses, inspires, baffles and confounds even the most knowledgeable. The origin of the word design is from the Latin word *designare*, which means, 'to express'. The Italian word for the same is *desegno*, which is to 'to draw a sketch', and the French word *dessin* means 'to draw a sketch for painting'. Literal meanings notwithstanding, the stages involving planning and finding creative solutions is what makes design resourceful and further, creating and enabling opportunities where often none exists is what makes it a critical strategic tool. In reality, the word design has outgrown these activities and concepts and in several contexts today has become a prefix or suffix which generally goes beyond 'planning or laying out'. The word design has become an extremely comprehensive expression with hardly any equivalent which can encompass all the nuances of its meanings. Even if we presume that the word 'design' is a transplanted one in the context of India, we should not lose sight of transforming the Indian traditions, culture, aesthetic sensitivity and heritage to create an Indian idiom of design which is distinctive and strong in the world. Some of the well-known designers in India have many insights to offer in this regard and here's how they spontaneously explain design and the gamut of areas design envisages:

> Design intervention exercises in India go beyond making pretty products in attractive colours. It is rooted in value creation. In India, the perceived value of a product far outweighs aesthetic appeal. In India, 'Style follows Substance'. – S. Balasubramaniam

> (Good) Design is the ultimate evolution of man, and a focus of all his energies. It pushes the envelope of experience to make man feel more human – to feel more tender or powerful, to sense grace and be gracious. – Shirsendu Ghosh

> To create any real impact, we will need to take a good hard look within, to seek that which will have an inherent Indian consciousness with high value, which the rest of the world can look upto and be inspired. We should be able to break away from the process

> of being subservient, apeing and embarking on a journey of only making immediate profits. Take cognisance of the fact that we as a design community are a very small part of the system, but which as a vocal one, can be leveraged into taking on a critical role in shaping our futures ... Much as we might like to deny, the focus on India right now is only because of a perception that there are huge profits to be made. But at whose cost? We need to look at what India really needs? Why are we so urban centric? Are we creating sustainable systems for a secure future?
>
> – Rajeev Manikoth

These and many more explanations, aspirations and questions need to make us ponder over the real role and substance of design and how it can add value to every sphere of life. Adding value is not only in terms of its commercial sense but design should necessarily add 'values' to a product or service in order to make them stand out in a crowd – values that reflect the character, philosophy and the world view of a brand and the product itself. In a fragile scenario such as today's with the planet being devastated by global warming – lakes, rivers and water polluted to their entrails by stilt and effluents, green cover laid bare by mindless deforestation and urbanization, animals and birds threatened by poachers and other predators – design has a significant responsibility when it comes to values which each element finally represents. Design should obviously find new solutions to existing problems and build scenarios to 'create' new contexts to visualize and realize creative answers. The designers have to straddle several worlds – industry and society, the present and future, visceral and virtual, individual and community, aesthetics and economy, market realities and sustainability – and all at the same time.

Indus, electric three wheeler designed by NID product design student Piyush Sharma for Electrotherm (I) Ltd.

culture crafts and design

a wealth of traditions

A display of ceramic and glass design concepts at NID during 2007 convocation.

Indian crafts form the core foundation of design culture in India as they use a wide range of inherent skills and technologies in various forms. Indian designs would do well to leverage this immense wealth of traditional knowledge to gain a leading edge in the modern industrial and communication design scenario through truly orbit shifting innovations.

It needs to be reiterated, given the context, that Indian culture has a long history of 'aesthetic sensitivity' and design exploration, although they are known under various other heads. Indian civilization, which has a history of over 5,000 years, has developed its own language of colour, structure and form which can be seen in myriad rituals, objects, art forms, and performances. In the post-independent phase, India looked at design as all-encompassing – from making a better safety pin to planning a new highway system in tandem with the onset of a new 'industrial age'. However, all that has changed dramatically today as the country is marching towards a developed economy on a technology and creativity-led growth curve.

The way we understand traditional crafts today is obviously not the way it was perceived at the time it took root. Traditional crafts are innovations of yesterday; they defined not only the cultural moorings but also the search for economic sustenance. As many studies clearly establish, most craftsmen derived their inspiration, innate wisdom and skills not from recorded material but what was easily and authentically available – nature. Crafts reflect the immense creativity of ordinary people and their quest for self-expression and fulfillment. Just as human evolution, crafts also evolve over time by mixing and churning influences and events. The Indian way of life, for example, is replete with products made with the help of simple, indigenous tools by craftspeople who belong within a strong fabric of tradition, aesthetics and artistry. The range of Indian handicrafts is as diverse as the country's multi-cultural and linguistic palette.

Although in Asia, India is the closest competitor to China in producing handicrafts, it enjoys only about

Handmade in India, an indepth study initiated by the Development Commissioner of Handlooms (DCH) office at the NID, is based on extensive field work and research, and maps out the regional craft clusters across the country on the basis of prevailing craft-work patterns. It is closely woven with images to reveal the array of diverse crafts in India. Some of these are renowned, like the *pinjrakari* and *khatumband* wood work of Kashmir, blue pottery of Jaipur, *chikankari* embroidery of Lucknow, the *kannadi* or metal mirrors from Aranmula, *chappals* from Kolhapur, and the bamboo craft of Assam. Other lesser known crafts like the *Paabu* or stitched boots from Ladakh, *jadupatua* paintings from Jharkhand, the making of Kathakali and *Theyyam* headgear, khadi or tinsel printing in Ahmedabad have also been described in detail. This study makes it possible to discern subtle, sometimes unusual differences in the same craft practised by distinct regions or communities – like tie-resist-dyeing which is called *bandhani* in Gujarat and Madhya Pradesh, and *bandhej* in Rajasthan.

A lady weaver in rural India.

'Anjar' knives created by an NID exchange programme student.

2 per cent of the world market share as compared to China's 17 per cent. Within India, handicrafts accounts for about 15-20 per cent of the manufacturing workforce, which is rather encouraging, but only on the face of it as rural artisans are still dependent on their local markets. Barriers of entry to other markets include tedious government regulations, tax policies, transportation and handling costs, absence of marketing infrastructure, brand building and marketing strategies. Such constraints result in extreme dependencies of rural artisans on the intermediaries – a story that is oft-repeated but remains unchanged since time immemorial.

From the buyer's perspective also, there are high rejections, as the products generally fail to maintain consistencies in terms of volume of work and standards of quality. There are no quality interfaces between the manufacturers, artisans and the ultimate buyers. Therefore, with increasing competition, the pressing need is to strengthen this sector and to focus on product quality, contemporary design issues and both professional management and marketing strategies.

In India the *patola* saris from Patan, Gujarat, or the *Pochampally* from Andhra Pradesh, padlocks from Aligarh, or knives from Anjar in Gujarat are excellent examples of craft with distinct uniqueness or traditional reputation based on specific characteristics of respective geographical locations. The urgent need of the hour is to ensure IPR protection under Geographical Indications or GI, for all the significant crafts and craftspersons for the sector to sustain and grow in the long run. There is no reason why 'Anjar' cannot stand for knives and Kutch in Gujarat for embroideries as also lacquer and pottery work and so on! When a student designer from Germany, Tobias, under a student exchange programme in 2005, created a series of contemporary knives with a common graphic identity of camel silhouettes for 'Anjar' knives, over seventy families involved in production were happy to accept the same. There is little doubt that many craft clusters have the potential of linking the product range from a Geographical Indication to a branding perspective with better chances of success under the World Trade Organization or WTO regime. In a globalizing and increasingly digital world, which is searching for emotional and cultural connections, crafts can bring forth harmony and form the foundations of a long term competitive advantage.

However, in several instances somehow the traditional uniqueness is slowly but surely eroding and getting homogenized under the pretext of new 'innovations' or cluster development approach keeping in view the lowest common denominator. For instance, a block printed fabric from Bagh in Indore after couple of years would have almost similar motifs or techniques of block printing, like say that of Machlipattanam in Andhra Pradesh. This could jeopardize the distinctiveness of crafts produced across Indian villages and in turn impact their unique differential positioning.

A solution lies perhaps in direct linkages with hundreds of specific niche markets of high value to connect such products through a process of contemporary design immersion to the marketplace. KAARU in Delhi, a design consultancy and product development organization, led by an architect and designer team, which undertakes breakthrough interpretations to inlay technologies like the Pattachitra painting, is an inspiring example of this approach. For wider reach of handicrafts a networking model of collaborative distribution and design creation would be desirable, even with the support of TV and direct marketing options. This system needs to be supported by the existing and numerous outlets of Khadi Gram Udyog, handlooms, handicrafts and even private sector retail sales outfits spread across the country as delivery touch points. Some well-known aggressive retailers (Shoppers Stop, Big Bazaar, Reliance Mart) can also be part of the new network for such 'One village, One Product' movement. The need is to collectively brand handicrafts and handlooms to be supported by a consortium of relevant ministries or organizations in a global marketing campaign.

There is no escaping the fact that over time, even as Indian economy becomes more globalized and societies get affected by the permeating influences and cultures along with an array of global products and services, the role of crafts will inevitably become even more significant as they singularly represent a nation's culture and traditions. In this context it is necessary for like-minded institutions to come together in providing strategic direction and action plans to evolve systems, procedures and norms related to design, market, technology, innovation and quality of life so that they become an integral part of the craft upgradation and repositioning process. Most importantly, crafts have to become a fountainhead for both industrial and communication design, for deriving the differential advantage of Indian design in the global marketplace. The Titan Heritage Collection encapsulating the essential architectural heritage of India designed by Abhijit Bhansod, an NID alumni is a good example. The collection beautifully combines iconic architectural motifs, folklores and tales, the Puranas and other epics in a contemporary context. Abhijit Bhansod recollects the experience as follows:

TITAN HERITAGE:

Confluences of culture and time

As designers, we often ponder the questions – what is Indian design, and when will it make tall inroads into global culture? Even as the world so often swoons over an increasingly cool India, will the Indian design aesthetic stand up to be counted, alongside Bollywood, hot curry and Salman Rushdie?

Truth is, the soul of Indian design lies deep within India – our infinite history, our rich heritage, and our fascinating culture. The Heritage Collection from Titan engages deeply with the ancient and medieval traditions of Indian architecture, yet interprets this heritage with modern sophistication.

These are watches which stand at the confluences of the old and the new, the many faiths and styles, the flowing centuries and grand monuments which define India. An ancient India, unchanging like mother earth herself. Yet a resurgent India which stands proud and tall at the crossroads of tomorrow's world.

Titan Heritage Collection emerges from these beautiful stories silently told by grand ancient monuments of our great country. Blending a timeless muse with contemporary workmanship, drawing on the essence of each inspired monument, and interpreting it in today's design vocabulary and evolving what could be the beginnings of a true Indian design aesthetic.

Heritage Collection of Titan watches, a journey through the streams of Indian architecture, its various history and myriad influences, designed by Abhijit Bansod for Titan Industries.

THE DESIGN STORY

The Heritage Collection is a journey through the streams of Indian architecture, its varied history and myriad influences.

Beginning with the *mandala*, the fundamental building block of Hindu temples. Spiritually and mathematically enhanced grids of squares, translated into the source of water and community living – the stepwells. The Mandala line is designed from these subtle levels of square forms, and the crisscross of light and shadow they create is etched on the dial.

The Stambha line, second in the series, recreates the stone textures of the cosmic pillars, the *stambhas*, which are said to join heaven and earth. A requisite feature of all Hindu temples, the *stambhas* come to vibrant life on the dials and straps of these watches.

The magnificent Sun Temple in Orissa is the inspiration for the Konarka line. Featuring the colossal chariot of the Sun God, Surya, led by seven horses, as it moves through the heavens. The wheel of this chariot is etched delicately onto the dial of the watch. A brilliant sunray finish ensures that the watch remains true to its inspiration, the sun.

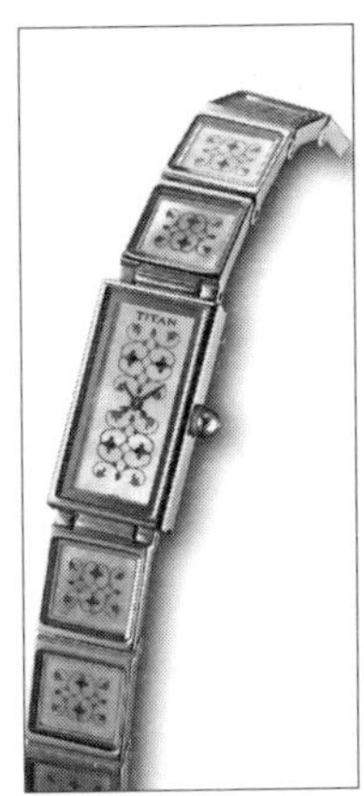

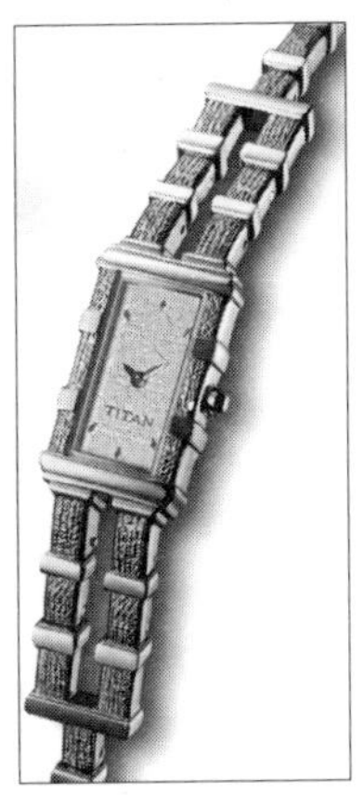

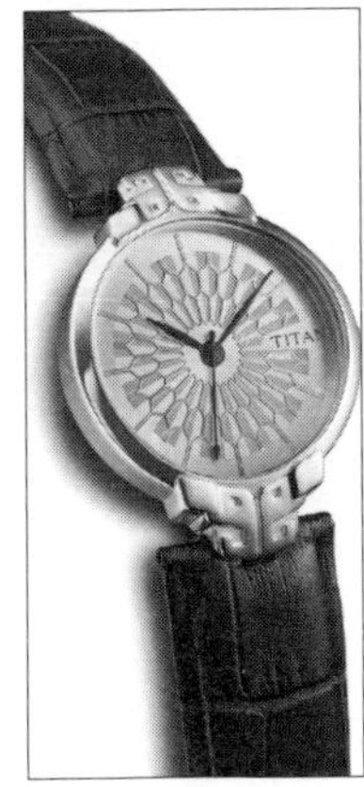

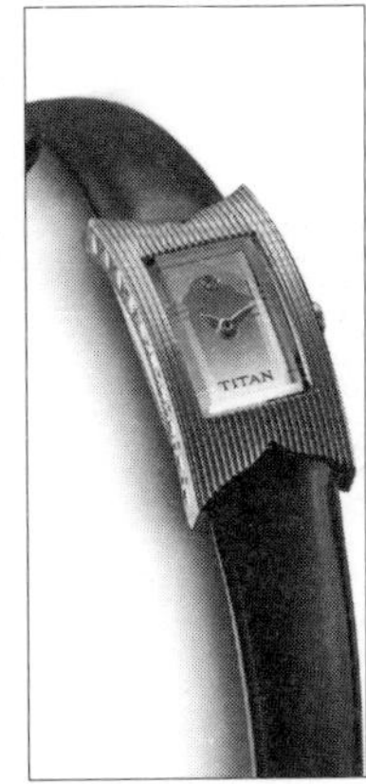

The Heritage Collection also includes unusual watches that pay tribute to the rich tapestry of Indian myths and stories, which have been a source of inspiration for Indian architecture over the ages. The Kurukshetra watch is inspired by the site of the legendary war fought between the Pandavas and Kauravas, in the Mahabharata. Legends and tales of valour from the war were inscribed as motifs in temples, and these are translated onto the watches in exact miniature.

Similarly, the Ajanta line is inspired by the painted narratives of the Jataka tales which cover the walls and pillars of the monolithic Ajanta and Ellora caves. This watch explores the unique colour, light and stone textures of the paintings, in a setting which is at once timeless yet contemporary.

A stunning example of the fusion of a geometry, discipline, refinement and new skills from Asia Minor and Persia is exemplified in the combination of Mughal and Rajput architecture in the jharokas which lined the façade of royal palaces and buildings. The mystique and romance of these windows to the world is captured by the frosted glass cover of the Neemrana line. The detailing of the niches in the frame of the window is carried onto the side of the watch, as are the fine lines of the design, creating an enchanting play of light and textures.

Of course, the best known example of the confluence of cultures in Indian heritage is the Taj Mahal in Agra. One of the seven wonders of the world, the Taj has inspired generations. It combines Persian, Islamic, Indian and Turkish architectural traditions to create poetry in marble. The Taj line is directly inspired by this monument, and carefully constructed out of mother of pearl. The watches resemble and highlight the purity of marble, even as they celebrate the exquisite inlay craftsmanship which decorates the Taj. The unmistakable silhouette of the dome is captured on the crown of the watch.

And coming full circle to the magic of the mandala is the watch which pays tribute to the architecture of time, symbolized by the Jantar Mantar. The line is drawn from the extraordinary structure built in the 1700s by Sawai Jai Singh, Maharaja of Jaipur. Combining the inherent logic and beauty of the mandalas with scientific principles, these buildings became observatories of the skies and the stars. The Jantar Mantar watches are inspired by this observatory and the mysterious infinite cosmos that it was designed to study and hence, the watches are embellished with fine lines and three-dimensional cyclic motifs which are indeed patterns of infinity.

crafts as foundation of design innovations..............

The Northeast of India is a great crucible of creativity with its fascinating tribal and folkloric culture, art, craft and music.

Designs inspired by crafts often succeed in humanizing technology and developing user-centric approaches. The new generation of designers have an opportunity to strengthen India's design edge by decoding the tacit knowledge embedded in the crafts. The reason: design in an innovation economy is more of a strategic tool for finding a creative solution to a problem, defining a new phenomenon or problem and creating solutions through appropriate design processes. Innovations most often require to focus on the problems afresh in a new perspective. Since design is not defined by the boundaries of any one knowledge domain and is eclectic, it is open to many diverse sources and influences. Crafts are a significant source and foundation of innovations in modern design especially for deeper insights into humanization of technologies, and for connecting culture to emotions.

If craft is one river which flows into design thus bringing in culture and emotions, technology is another which enables swift realization. Both need to flow into design continously for aesthetic appeal and functionality. There was a time when crafts were at a crossroads as the country's agrarian society was transiting to industrial. We are now gradually moving on from industrial society to one which is driven by innovation and services. In the innovation-led economy, affected as it is by the market forces of globalization and technological forces of convergence, crafts can play a key role in bringing 'harmony' and delight. A period of rediscovery of crafts and traditional knowledge is, therefore visible across the world and needs to be accelerated in India as well. In a country such as ours it is all the more important to place crafts at the core of India's design edge so that Indian products and services retain their cultural and emotional identity while being global at the same time. For instance, the north-eastern region of India is a great crucible of creativity with its good-looking people, majestic mountains, waterfalls, rare orchids, enthralling birds and butterflies, serene monasteries, fascinating tribal and folkloric culture, arts, crafts, music, bamboo forests, and the luxurious Eri and Muga silks.

It is a great idea to combine the inherent creative spirit of the Northeast with the immense skills and competencies available in the rich crafts sector to promote Indian design in Southeast Asian countries as a window to other oriental cultures. Unfortunately, this has only remained an idea and not happened yet. I strongly believe that Indian crafts need to be perceived not only as part of our cherished heritage, but as foundations of innovations for tomorrow. Some of the reasons are as simple as follows:

- Crafts form the core of a culture and also its best argument for sustainability.

- 'Pickled crafts' for the benefit of visitors to India is not a lasting solution. Evolving crafts should become part of the essential life skill of Indians, so that we have a generation of 'Hands On, Minds On' people.
- Crafts provide a differential advantage to design through 'sense and sensitivity' of encoded tacit values and aesthetics.
- They provide a connection to the 'heart' unlike any other expression.
- Crafts create a sense of continuity in a rapidly dematerializing world thus bridging the 'visecral' with the 'virtual'.

Crafts at one level are utility driven but the utility nevertheless is layered with experience and craftsmanship. They represent in a way the antithesis to individualism and clearly focus on communities. The twentieth century preoccupation of providing designs only for individual delight, which continues even today, can only be countered through crafts which addresses the collective aspirations of the people. At another level, crafts represent only the 'very best' in creativity – be it the 'haute couture' status in the fashion industry or the 'shilp guru' status at the other spectrum. Even when we are swept, or rather influenced by newer technologies and modern management concepts like TQM and Six Sigma, it is important to recognize that the best expressions of quality can be understood from crafts which are supremely human-centric.

As Mahatma Gandhi had once said, though in a different context, the heart of India continues to beat in its rural landscape, where crafts and festivals create a continuous celebration of life. However, as mentioned earlier, it is time to rediscover Indian crafts in the contemporary context of India's emergence as an economic power house of Asia. Like Abhijit Bhansod, some of the other modern designers in India like Neelam Chibber, who has been working on natural fibres has had significant success converting Indian craft traditions to contemporary products in a global context, and the following brief case study provides interesting insights.

evolving crafts: industree's success story

IndusTree Crafts Private Limited was started by two industrial designers in 1994 and is today one of the best examples of the power of 'design thinking' and 'design solutions'. It reached its present enviable position in an extremely difficult area of hard goods, and was much more complex in comparison to the fashion and clothing sector. This perhaps was singularly possible only due to unusual creative thinking and solution-based approaches. The lead designer of IndusTree, Neelam Chibber, had to play multiple roles of an entrepreneur, a business manager, an accountant, a sales person, a CEO and that meant designing saleable products, capturing the market share, and competing with aggressive Southeast Asian countries in global markets. The efforts were gradually centred around the creation of an artisan-owned company, to focus and forge partnerships between the private, public and NGO sectors, and to meet the huge market demands, in order to ensure that finally the artisans, the custodians of Indian cultural industries, benefit from their trades. IndusTree also focuses on developing partnerships and collaboration across stakeholders, to create a new organizational model, which has the best of social and market based economies, which thrive simultaneously in India.

Indian crafts has an enormous potential for exports in the home furnishings market and one of the reasons for this are the artisans across the country who cater hugely to this sector. IndusTree, for instance, supplies natural fibre home furnishings to IKEA, as also Pier Europe and other leading buyers in Europe. There are indeed immense opportunities here. Sample this: currently IKEA buys sixty million euro worth of natural fibre furniture from Vietnam, and is looking towards procuring the same from India. With an overall economic boom and particularly in the domestic markets, only to increase in years to come, the demand across all handicraft sectors will definitely get a fillip, be it stone, wood, metal, glass or ceramic. And IndusTree endeavours to bridge the gap and ensure maximum benefits to individual artisans and not just middle men or traders in realizing this dream.

IndusTree today boasts of a turnover of a million dollars and is targeting towards a 100 million and currently provides employment to over 3,000 women. The company, set up almost a decade and a half ago, has five home furnishing stores in India till date apart from brand 'IndusTree' available at some of the largest retail stores. Like all good businesses, the company is driven by a mission and that is to elevate the artisanal sector from the production of knick-knacks, souveneirs, artifacts and accessories into more mainstream and market-driven, utilitarian home sectors such as furniture and home furnishings. Its purpose is to feed large markets initially, and the more exclusive markets in the next phase of its growth, and that seems possible as there is a huge supply of artisans available, who need to be employed.

It has been witnessed time and again that any production base is best owned by artisans, as it is the ideal self-empowerment tool, eventually ensuring that they move up the value chain, towards higher wages, with the onus of maintaining the crucial issues of quality and productivity. IndusTree's production base is spread across four southern and two eastern states of India and touches over 5,000 producers, some through direct orders and others through intensive training.

KAARU is yet another inspiring story of how crafts can lead the way in innovation for contemporary markets. Perhaps one of the most surreal experiences of the twenty-first century is that sitting in one place, we can access information about diverse cultures from various locations on earth within an unimaginably short period of time, only to find very soon that there is nothing actually diverse about them anymore. Today few global organizations decide what to cultivate, eat and wear for the rest of the world. They have access to local human and natural resources from any part of the globe, the ability to process them into global goods and services, and then selling them to the world. All made possible by the power of 'modern-technology'.

Most intriguingly, this 'global' phenomenon seems to be perpetually emerging from the West and re-surfacing in other parts of the world as a pasted copy. People, especially in the countries which are fast aligning their model of growth with the West, are getting accustomed to living in a singular way without even asking, 'Do we really have to?'; 'Is this the only "modern" way to live?'; or 'the only "valid" way to live in every part of the world?'

One just has to visit various parts of India to see the vast tracts of rising sameness everywhere. It is common knowledge now that this very sameness in the developed world has scientifically been proven as environmentally non-sustainable and disastrous. People in these countries have already been taking steps to reverse the process and guard their residual bio-cultural diversities and resources.

Against this backdrop, for India, its 'soul' identity which is deeply rooted in its arts, crafts, architecture and a certain spiritual consciousness becomes an extremely valuable reference point more than ever. This is especially so if contemporary innovative ideas, which are original and home grown, were to emerge for the future. The enormous challenge for the country is not just in being able to think original, but to stick to what it genuinely believes in.

In spite of India's humongous efforts and contrary to what is made visible everywhere through the media, I believe that there exists a large void in India's recent history and that has to do with the C word –'credibility'. India hardly figures in the list of countries that have created a brand for themselves in terms of progressive ideas and truly path-breaking concepts of excellence in modern times. Even to this day we depend hugely on designers, architects, and consultants from other countries to think and build for us.

It is, therefore, time that we begin to reinterpret innovation seriously all over again. The value addition that is possible through design will be feasible only if creative expressions have certain originality and the feeling – 'It is not just made in India, it is Indian'– is reflected in some of our finest crafts. Imagine if this was applicable in creating cities, industries, educational institutes and all other areas? The world would indeed be a better place to live! Let's not forget that for a long time India has supported developing nations with two extremely important resources for growth – intellect and manpower. It is time we employ these two to accelerate growth within the country.

In order to do that we face a choice. On one side is the choice of huge amount of hard work, working against red tapeism, corruption, dust and heat but with an incredible resource of ideas, work force and natural wealth. It will obviously be a challenging and slow process and coupled with an awareness that either parts of the world have already achieved it or are in the process of achieving it.

The other option, easy and oft repeated, is to channelize all our energies towards cloning ourselves on the pattern set by the West. Whether its innovation, invention, research or development, the western countries have successfully created a distinct language for themselves and that is now up for sale to other lesser developed nations. Can we honestly say that a parallel language exists such as 'Contemporary Indian' in comparison to this? Does India have a genuine brand of its own which stands for original contemporary thinking? From path-breaking financial services, the idea of computing, measurements of growth in GDP or even malarial vaccine, everything is a brand today but has not originated from India.

So at this point of history what do we want to choose as a nation of one billion and as one individual out of that one billion? What is it that we can do with that choice? Here, I can only think of quoting what KAARU resolved to do ten years ago.

Painted bamboos lining a venue wall by KAARU.

Kutch bandhani (tie & dye) mirror work with Kantha embroidery work by KAARU.

shaping an indian brand identity

THE KAARU INNOVATION TOOL KIT

A drop in the ocean perhaps, but KAARU over the years has developed a unique tool kit and is continuously innovating and improving upon it. A kit that essentially maintains a delicate balance between myths, legends, beliefs, time-honoured skills and sensibilities of the master artisans of India. KAARU believes that these are extremely valuable references, decisive in shaping a new language of art, design and architecture in India, which will take its own time and evolve layer by layer.

Elaborating on this, Sanjib Chatterjee and Anjalee of KAARU say:

> We believe that our country has the magic of people. It has their hands and their innate cultural sense of beauty and functionality. It is a consciousness that is unique and which has its roots in this land. This has to be finely and cautiously balanced with industrial production processes and understanding intelligently the phenomenon of global consumption patterns. If it is necessary to produce in large numbers and lower prices then let us involve as many people as possible. Let us take the drudgery away from their hands with machines but not their livelihoods. Or better still produce less at optimum prices that sustain the dignity and wealth of the makers as well as the consumption of resources.
>
> We can be a part of the global world and cater to international market demands offering very high standard of original designs and quality and create a demand at the deserved price.

KAARU's design philosophy challenges the creativity of its own team constantly. It's a family of traditional masters, and a completely committed group of architects, designers, finance and management people. Its way of working consistently prevents the team from opting for conventional solutions or following trends and styles. KAARU is very clear on one thing and that is its undivided attention and solid investment in time. No wonder its process of innovation has been slow but the organization focusses intensely on finance and R&D as long term strategic tools.

At KAARU, architecture and art overlap with a way of living. Designs, with both beauty and a story, are created whether for display or use. In this, KAARU blurs the lines between art and craft and design to bring out the outcomes as one entity as the centre of people's lives.

Integral to the work is a high level of consciousness towards preservation, be it metal, wood, glass or stone. Wastage is kept to the minimum. Conventionally regarded flaws in natural materials are not rejected, but integrated and enhanced as a feature of design. Every design is customized according to the space and the context of its location, always carrying a story within.

All this could be made possible only through our own large in-house production setup and a team dedicated to coordination with each artisan. All projects are done turnkey and we see to it that the client's trust is returned with quality and a space that gives them value for money and makes them happy.

It has taken time to create awareness, organize a unique group of people, and create designs that are highly contemporary but completely based on the spirit of the land. Today KAARU has a very conscious clientele both in India and abroad who have made it possible to create our tools to suit global needs but keep our idiom intact. Thus, in a way helping us to preserve the diversities which still exist in India through very high level of design. These are people who have given the team hope that one can slow down in one's consumption patterns and be extremely tolerant and sensitive towards the way we use our land, people and resources.

The team at present builds shelters, makes furniture and accessories, shapes inner spaces of buildings, and green tiny parts of the earth with flora and our own installations. With our 'Art For Everyday' lines of furniture and products under the brand name KAARU, we are retailing from our own studios in Tokyo and London and the best part is that clients are drawn to the design because of all that we believe in, speaks quietly!

Working with hundreds of craftspeople, KAARU is trying to present an alternative to the general tendency towards mass production and homogeneity. KAARU thus celebrates the diversity, which we seem to be losing and which is essential to life itself.

The KAARU team builds shelters, makes furniture and accessories, shapes inner spaces of buildings: ceiling installation at Hotel Ashok, New Delhi; workstations and other spaces for Petro IT office, Gurgaon, and The Lily Bowl – stone inlay of lily leaves in stainless steel bowl for Jindal steel exhibition.

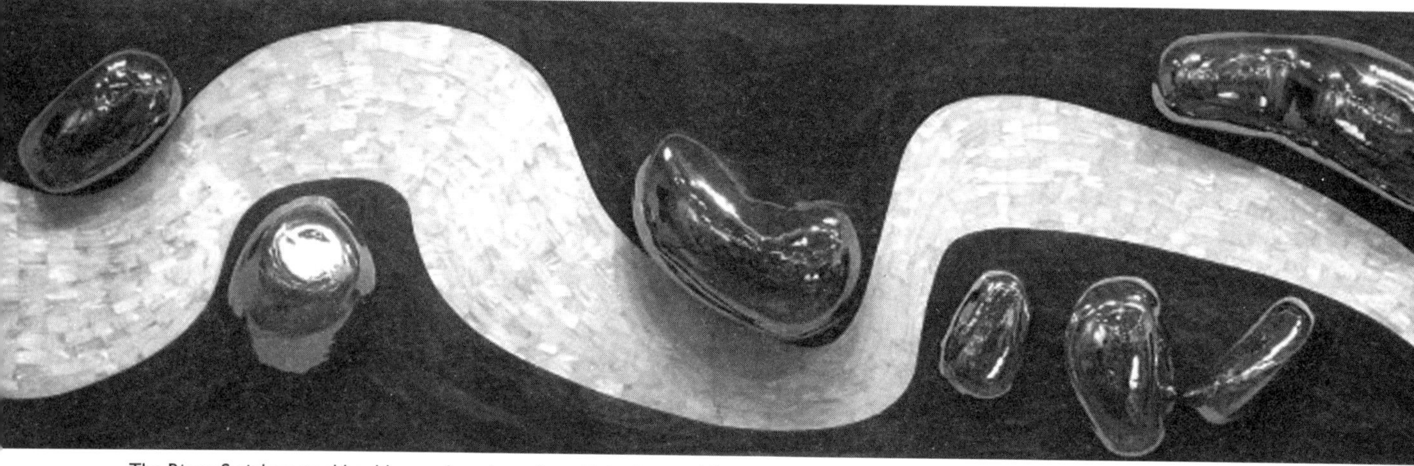

The River: Stainless steel boulders and mother of pearl inlay in wood for Jindal steel exhibition

Below: 'Lizard', a wooden CD rack

Above: Product Design: Coffee table in stone and steel

Below: Painted chest of drawers

Below: Sofa in beaten stainless steel, inlaid wood and silk for Jindal steel exhibition

Right: Painted floor lamp

from village *melas* to shopping malls

As crafts continue to be the foundation for modern Indian designs, it is imperative that they graduate from village *melas* to shopping malls and perhaps as a natural progression, from local to global and 'glocal' markets. Currently the market linkages for rural artisans are mostly limited to their local markets because participation in national and international markets is very expensive for not only the independent small entrepreneurs but even for cooperative societies. The story remains the same so far as barriers of entry to other markets is concerned: archaic government regulations, skewed tax policies, high transportation and handling costs. Such constraints naturally result in extreme dependencies of rural artisans on intermediaries. This results in unfair wages and limited orders – for the number of reflections by the consumers rise as the product does not meet the parameters. The truth is that there are no quality interfaces between the manufacturers, artisans and the ultimate buyers. Even when markets have been found or created, the same has not resulted either in increase of wages or in providing round-the-year employment. Therefore, with increasing competition, the pressing need is to strengthen this sector by focusing attention on product quality and design issues. Proper designs are required not only for products but also for all integral aspects of production processes – tools, small machines, reducing drudgery, improving the quality of work environment and improved productivity of artisans.

If we take a look at the marketability of Indian handlooms and handicrafts, the income generation potential at village level, and the diversity of Indian craft and heritage proved not only unique but advantageous in many ways. As a comparison, we have seen earlier, how China is projected as the next big economic giant in the world and this is not without any reason. If we focus on specifics – first, the Chinese textile industry development has been on the lines of 'one village one product' philosophy. The garment industry in the country is also located in very specific areas and specializes in different products as per the location. Second, for any country to surge forward, it requires a consistent and earnest attempt at putting processes and systems in place. For example, the Chinese Textile Policy for the tenth Five Year Plan (2001-05) stated that of the total fabric production in the country, the proportion of clothing textiles, decorative (home textiles and industrial textiles) is 64, 21 and 15 per cent, respectively. It would be ambitious to expect such information anywhere in the entire volume of textile policy developed by the Government of India! Also, the Chinese textile policy goes to the extent of directing the industry to reduce the energy consumption per metre fabric by 15 per cent in 2005 compared to year 2000 and to also reduce the water consumption per metre of fabric from 3.6 ton to 3.0 ton in dyeing and printing industry.

Indian crafts move from village *melas* to shopping malls and as a natural progression, from local to global markets: a shopping mall and flower vendors in Ahmedabad.

That is how much China invests in getting ahead of other nations in Asia!

Coming back to the Indian model, it is desirable to evolve a 'village' in India that identifies with 'one particular craft' and a traditional technique for focusing on manufacturing, infrastructure and marketing including branding. The IndusTree case study provides insights into the whole process of identifying niche products, transforming products, processes and people to win at the marketplace. In order to help the consumer, one needs to look at detailed resources and technical skill mapping of the potential craft and handloom producing villages across India. We also need to inform ourselves about the traditional crafts communities who may be economically displaced from their traditional activities and are no longer in the trade. Can they also be brought back into this fold? After the crafts and skills mapping, if 10,000 villages are identified with each having one diverse and distinct craft, this can be a good starting point to scale up. One also needs to understand the additional work force in surrounding villages and the consumption capacity of the market if further scaling-up is done. The other important aspects that need constant monitoring are: focus on marketing and or branding and positioning in the context of new retail trends; careful evaluation of structural model of corporations, apex societies, primary co-operative societies, self-help groups, micro enterprises and new delivery systems for possible synergies and impact.

Lack of commercial and market orientation has always been a major hindrance and that not only makes the craftsmen non-competitive in the open market but leads to complacency and the eventual marginalization of crafts. If we need to make the difference and impact both at the 'village' and aggregated market level on an ongoing basis, there is a need to ensure quality interface between buyers and producers. Further, direct linkages with hundreds of specific niche markets, who are willing to buy products of high value, will reduce the bottlenecks in the issues of 'supply' and lower the rejections at final stages due to direct market feedback.

A serious concern is that the young generation of craft-based households have no interest in continuing with traditional crafts. It is perhaps time to set up national crafts universities in select states on the lines of agricultural universities, which probably should have been done fifty years ago, to provide education to craftsmen. A base paper presented to the Ministry of Textiles had the same suggestions with the intent of respecting both the crafts and craftsmen in society and for the former to evolve in modern contemporary contexts.

However, what we cannot lose sight of is the fact that it is most difficult to grasp the massive expanse of Indian crafts. There are more than thirty million craftsmen engaged in different craft sectors in the country and it is estimated that there are over 360 such craft clusters in India. Crafts and culture have to be vibrant not just in terms of colour and texture but also in terms of continuous visibility and impact in a marketplace. Stagnant crafts are bound to languish and die, but evolving crafts will always survive and may even grow. Design can revitalize and contemporarize crafts. The wheel, so to speak, has to be constantly reinvented and perhaps overhauled. Unlike other fields which may totally discard the past, the constant search for an Indian idiom in design has often led to marrying yesterday's innovations with today's and the crafts have been an endearing bridge between the two.

designs for grass roots innovations

Innovations can happen anywhere. But even the most innovative idea seldom gets realized into workable products if it happens at the grass-roots level, because of the inaccessibility of technological and design support for such spontaneous spurt of creativity. The Gujarat Grass-roots Innovation Augmentation Network (GIAN), a technology business model focused on grass-roots innovations, was set up in 1997 under the leadership of Prof. Anil Gupta (IIM, Ahmedabad) to commercialize such innovations.

GIAN has since then done commendable work in this area and aims at sustaining the spirit of innovation, encouraging experimentation, nurturing creativity, and providing wider markets at grass-roots level to people who are knowledge-rich but economically poor. Most of the innovations address a demand gap that exists at the grass-roots level which is not being currently met by products and services offered by the formal sectors of the industry. For a developing country like India, the grass roots or the rural sector is predominant, comprising more than 60 per cent of our population and with agriculture as the primary occupation. The grass-roots innovations, therefore, have a potentially large market and commercialization of these innovations, through the means of building an appropriate value chain, makes sound business sense. According to GIAN, partnering with the industry and by tapping the commercial potential of these innovations, new avenues of targeting the hitherto unknown rural consumer markets can be unveiled.

In 2001, the Grass-roots Innovation Design Studio (GRIDS) was jointly established by NID and GIAN at the NID campus. The rationale behind setting up such a studio within an educational campus was to provide the design expertise of NID to such grass-roots innovations, and to encourage young designers to explore creativity in a holistic manner by developing an aptitude to appreciate creativity at the bottom of the pyramid across the country. The joint venture, financially supported by GIAN, also focused on how original innovations can best reach relevant markets. To put it very simply, GRIDS provides the flesh and blood to the skeleton of an idea of an innovator albeit in an unobtrusive manner. Sometimes an innovation may be functional demanding further design interventions from the point of view of ergonomics, safety, optimum use of materials, ease of manufacture, ease of storage and above all aesthetic forms, colour and graphics. The big gap between the rather unrefined grass-roots innovation and acceptable product for the marketplace is huge and requires considerable investment and support.

The two products which stood out for their excellence, as a result of the confluence of GIAN and NID, were Shanti – a bullet-driven, multipurpose farming machine, and Vanraj – a small tractor, based on jeep components – which were later put on display at an international auto fair, the Auto Expo 2002 at New Delhi and evinced great interest from visiting foreign delegates. One of the best results from such intervention of design and designers into grass-roots innovations and innovators was the camaraderie which developed between young designers and grass-roots innovators. One of the greatest qualities of the human mind, to overcome adversities to produce significant innovations, came out significantly in the two major national workshops conducted with grass-roots innovators, designers and technologists working on different ideas during 2001 and 2003. The suggestions made by young designers were often not necessarily acceptable to the innovators, but there was always a great sense of empathy and open-mindedness. In retrospect, the problem in scaling up the model to commercialize many more grass-roots innovations has been because of an absence of a 'relay race' kind of mechanism within the design education system at NID to keep iterating, prototype testing and fine tuning of ideas on a continuous basis and also availability of adequate risk capital for the same. Often the design workshops stopped short of complete intervention, thus failing to deliver the desired commercial results and outcomes.

Shanti and Vanraj were both undoubtedly very good results of innovations created by grass-roots innovators. But in retrospect, the distance between the prototype and the marketplace was proving unviable from the point of view of the gap between the product and market expectations and the quantum of funding required as well as the payback period for entrepreneurs.

Apart from the need for design community to work closely with grass-roots innovation, a system needs to be put in place where the faculty and student teams continue to work on the innovations and the prospective market or distribution company which holds the exclusive or non-exclusive rights or IPR to financially support the complete cycle of the developmental work associated with such products. The example of the cotton stripper developed as a student project at the NID by Alexander Bošnjak of Germany in 1997-98 and later commercialized by a manufacturer is a case in point where a small innovation could create a major impact from both points of view: commercial viability and quality of life. The grass-roots innovations can effectively help both and the fusion of grass-roots innovators and professionally trained young designers need to be actively promoted and most importantly, financially supported.

Shanti: A bullet driven, multi-purpose farming equipment designed by Product Design students of NID.

designing change

change for design

A historical monument at NID's Heritage Campus – one of the most important landmarks of NID, this tomb provides a historic backdrop to the convocation ceremonies.

Well-known American business consultant, Jim Collins, author of *Good To Great* said, 'They got the right people on the bus, the wrong people off the bus, and the right people in the right seats – and then they figured out where to drive it. The old adage "people are your most important asset" turns out to be wrong. People are not your most important assets. The *right* people are.'

Like it is universally accepted, change is constant, and some are in degrees and some in kind. Change is often necessitated as the environment transforms, technology leapfrogs and there are corresponding expectations as a result of all these. Although it is often seen but still deserves mention, in certain groups or organizations, over a period of time the internal dynamics remain the same – mainly the people and their processes. The result: a hiatus which grows unimaginably wider. Such organizations often run the risk of becoming completely irrelevant and obsolete. It is important that the people involved understand the need for change and accept change as a necessary trigger for growth and transformation. In fact, change is the very essence of design and surprisingly NID over the years has become more or less impervious to change and the stirrings of any are viewed with great cynicism. But then, as the noted American writer Ken Kesey said, 'There are going to be times when we can't wait for somebody. Now, you are either on the bus or off the bus ...' The people who purposefully block change bring great harm to any organization as logical and consistent change plays a significant role in moulding people and their futures. Jim Collins in his book, *Built to Last* says: 'When you have disciplined people, you don't need hierarchy; when you have disciplined thought, you don't need bureaucracy; when you have disciplined action you don't need excessive controls. When you combine a culture of discipline with an ethic of entrepreneurship you get a magic of alchemy of great performance.' This was certainly missing at NID by the turn of the century, when I took over as its director and there was a great need to design a growth strategy and change in almost everything became an overarching theme.

Indira J. Parikh wrote in an article about transformation of organizations elucidating that there are three types of energies in any organization and the interplay of energies give shape to its identity, viz. captive energy, frozen energy and free energy. The first, says Parikh, is captive energy which was available to the organization in the past. This at a time when the organization was alive, movement oriented, viable, directional and vibrant. Over a period of time, the level of energy gets diminished, and the performance becomes mechanical. Frozen energy is that which reflects the present where new relationships and new meanings do not get generated. Finally, free energy is that which broadens horizons and pushes forward new frontiers. This energy is reflected in the creativity of people, their dreams, hopes, aspirations and initiatives. This is the energy, which pushes an organization to climb and touch new heights. At this juncture, an organization bursts open in new directions and uses the energy for its own benefit. As always, the quality of leadership, according to Parikh, is a very critical ingredient in this situation. This, I feel, is one the most accurate analyses of organizational transformation.

In the twenty-first century, many Indian organizations are in the throes of change mainly on account of the rapid changes of market forces and the need is to positively channelize the interplay of energies, as identified by Indira Parikh, so that creativity and innovation can blossom. This will require considerable unlearning and relearning with an outlook which is distinctly global, coupled with an ability to connect with the traditions, crafts, technology and different disciplines and domains in a broad-brush stroke through design.

Watertight compartments and boundaries are fast disappearing and more holistic design approaches like 'experiential design', and 'integral design' are emerging. There seems to be a clear shift from cosmetic expressions of design to a strategic level for improving the quality of life. Technology and design have to co-exist and designers who fail to encompass such a 'dematerialized' approach find it hard to break new grounds. As of now, NID's heritage campus at Ahmedababd focuses more on 'skill', 'individual', 'materials', and 'learning by doing' whereas obvious change necessitates a new approach of 'knowledge, team and dematerialization along with more conceptual learning' and this, I am happy to say, is the focus of the new campuses. The struggle between tradition and modernity is palpable but nevertheless unavoidable but the way forward is obviously to combine both in a strategic manner.

It is very clear that winds of change are blowing not only in India but also elsewhere in different institutions and organizations across the spectrum. The future of design will be decided by its ability to adapt and synergize with technology to define new problems and find creative solutions. It won't be wrong to say that in a way, a designer's profession depends largely on tackling change. If the need for change is not recognized then design automatically becomes redundant. However, I have seen that often designers tend to develop a cocoon around them and then they can be the most difficult people to deal with!

Apart from what is termed as mood swings, difficult temperaments, and egotistic arguments which are attributed to many in the creative field, and which I think is normal, my experience says that designers often refuse to comprehend, respond and or stay ahead of change. Let's face facts – designers who tend to be team players, with a flexible outlook and an open mindedness are better suited to produce results in today's world where 'change is the new normal'. Like I have said earlier and would do once again, the days of 'star performer' and the 'demi-God' days are long over and done with. One of the best ways of defining 'designer' would be – essentially an 'ideator' and at best an orchestrator amongst a group of brand managers, technologists, scientists and others who believe in the final product in the consumer space.

When I became the director of NID, I found that often it was the mindset of the early generation of the design faculty which proved to be a major impediment in initiating any change or going forward. Even the infinitesimal changes or introduction of a new technology created an uproar from both internal members and external onlookers. Change is the raison d'etre of design profession. Indian design and design professionals cannot remain as islands where time stands still while the world gallops forward and there is a real need to connect with the changing global design directions while searching for a distinct Indian idiom amidst the din of noises from around the world. Although many a times the 'argumentative Indian' has been lauded, I feel that incessant and mindless arguments kill a thought before it takes root is also perhaps one of the worst traits of our people. Edward de Bono, thinker and eminent author, was recently quoted in the *Economic Times* in an article titled – 'How creative are Indians?'

> From the limited interactions I've had, I find Indians very argumentative. Argument is a primitive way of discussion – not constructive at all. Americans are creative and have a "go getter' attitude. The Chinese are not much creative. The Japanese, on the other hand, are moving from logic based thinking to more creative thinking. French think they are the most creative. But in fact, they are not!

Although such analyses may sound like sweeping generalizations, I am sure my experience in running the NID is a good enough parameter for assessing a 'progressive' designer from a 'retrogressive' one and example abound both among faculty members and professional designers.

NID Heritage Campus at Paldi, Ahmedabad.

R&D Campus at Bengaluru.

people and processes by design

The challenge for today's design leaders is to manage the future from the present and more than in any other field as they have to constantly learn the art of designing for the future while remaining relevant for the present. The ability to create futuristic designs becomes very crucial especially in the commercial context for taking decisions in what is deemed as the next big thing – new retail formats, which are being planned in a humongous way across the country and likewise for novel 'services' and 'digital' products. The short time horizons of decisions regarding operations to manage today's concerns and the time horizons and mindset required to create a blue sky vision or leapfrogging ideas are vastly different and can create considerable complexities within a system. Managing organizational growth is a tough call as often the vision-to--action gaps along with widening communication hiatus bring in its trail enormous problems of people and process management.

Left to Right: A high chair/stool designed by NID furniture student – Yusuf Mannan.

Ladies Sports Watch "]:[" is a pull on bangle-type wrist watch.

Iris – Fashion Glasses for the blind.

In the twenty-first century, with an increasing focus on the knowledge work force and rapid movement of 'knowledge assets' – almost like flights of capital, managing knowledge-intensive organizations has become more challenging and exciting at the same time.

The American writer Henry Miller's statement: 'One's destination is never a place, but rather a new way of looking at things,' is a good perspective to understand the processes better. Most often the destination is seen by people as something final – as a promotion in the professional sphere or a personal achievement of sorts. What is interesting is that often destination is a state of mind and perhaps a new way of appreciating and looking at things. If institutions have to make strategic fitment plans they would have to develop the ability to recognize the right competencies which include the right kind of people, right mindsets, and skill sets as well. However, it is not as if existing people in an organization cannot adapt to change but it takes a lot of effort to instill the 'can do', 'will do' attitude within a large cross-section of people and quite surprisingly even in creative organizations like the NID.

In huge conglomerates, it is often difficult to align the organization's visions with individual stakeholder's vision and this again involves major processes of dialogue and

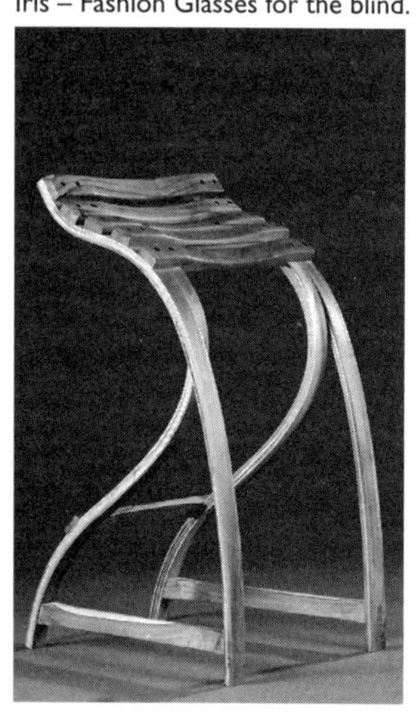

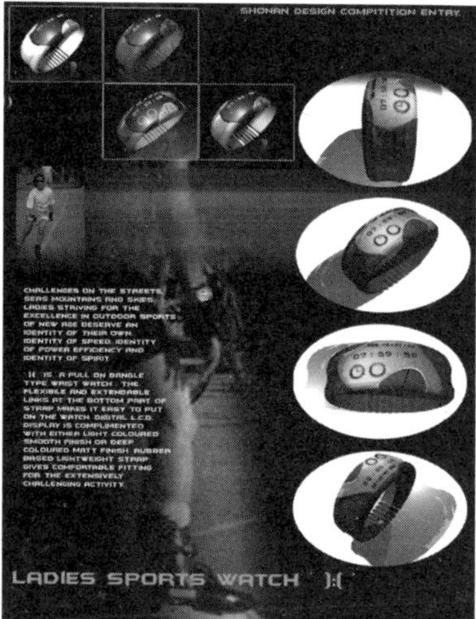

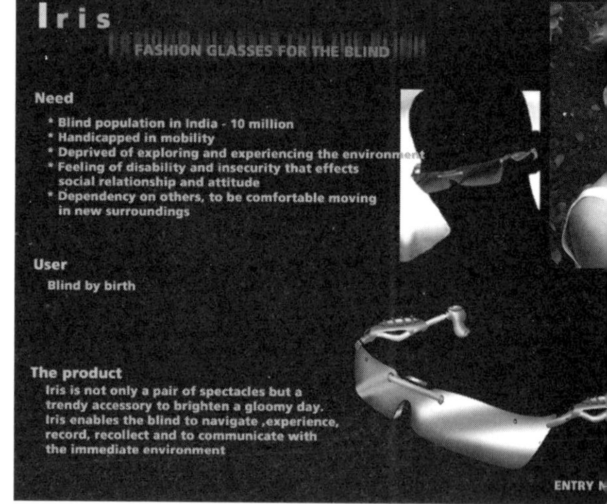

exchange. At the outset, any organization can be viewed as one which is beset with a constant struggle between progressive and regressive forces. If progressive ideas and forces have to succeed, then communication at all levels has to be robust with enthusiastic support from different stakeholders. However, if regressive forces have to be kept under check, then a lot would depend on an organization's internal dynamics – the time, events and people. It is at this juncture that any leader-manager needs to be resolute and above all show courage to rise above the collective tide of resistance and obscurantism. Here nothing could be more apt than what one of the ex-presidents of US, Theodore Roosevelt once said: 'It is not the critic who counts, nor the man who points how the strong man stumbled or where the doer of deeds could have done them better. The credit belongs to the man who is actually in the arena; whose face is marred by dust and sweat and blood; who strives valiantly ... who knows the great enthusiasms, the great devotions, and spends himself in a worthy cause; who at best, knows the triumph of high achievement; and who, at the worst, if he fails, at least fails while daring greatly, so that his place shall never be with those cold and timid souls who know neither victory nor defeat.'

It is important that while managing growth, lateral and horizontal communication among target groups is achieved to enhance the success of vision and the resultant plans. One has to certainly remember that the decisions taken by any leader need to add value, upgrade reputation, increase the inherent self-image of people and above all achieve what brings 'general good' to most. 'Without Vision, People Perish' is a mantra to be learnt by rote since a vision for the future and making people see the future is the biggest challenge in the institution-building processes especially in creative economy wherein people with 'differential creating' ability are in high demand.

The process of change initiated at NID since the turn of the century, is a case study in bringing about a massive change which has been both transformational and strategic. In 2000, NID was beset with a chequered history, dilapidated infrastructure, obsolete labs and equipments, pulls and pushes of cliques, adverse age profiles, precarious finances, a history of violent conflicts, penchant for arguments without action, and a complete lack of alignment of vision with action. To turnaround and transform the organization under the constraints of a governmental system logistically and above all to rid it of a 'legacy mindset' proved to be one of the biggest challenges for me. Gradually as NID emerged through the agonizing process of change over an eight-year journey (2000-08), it feels rather strange to see that the Heritage Campus in Paldi, Ahmedabad, looks just the same from the outside and that is a great reminder that design is essentially the process of a change within to bring about the change without!

designing success for SMEs

In India, the manufacturing competitiveness of industries, particularly the SMEs is facing a major challenge in terms of change ushered in by globalization. The challenge involves a major shift from traditional methodologies to an innovation-led product development process in order to sustain and grow in businesses with a competitive advantage. So, to put it simply, it's once again about adapting to change in time. Therefore, there is a critical need for design interventions based on a 'user-centric' approach to create new opportunities. In the race to finish first in the ever changing market place, the SMEs have to develop new products on a continuous basis which meet the demographic, psychographic and psychological needs of the 'new age consumers' in India and elsewhere. In India the markets are today more and more defined by a constituency which seems to be establishing all patterns of growth – the youth. Further, in the context of such a fluid domestic market, there is even a greater demand for product differentiation through research and discovering new values for products and services.

For the SME sector, intense competition and the moving targets of customer predilections have made the very survival extremely difficult. The domestic market has shifted from a sellers' to a buyers'/consumers' market where a consumer looks for novelty and several choices. The products therefore have to 'stand out', attract and persuade the customer to make the purchase. The challenge, therefore, before the Indian SMEs is to grasp the customer's needs and aspirations and develop a winning edge through continuous value addition for which design innovation is the key.

Until recently SMEs were quite successful in selling their products in a protected market place without feeling the need to pursue R&D or design research for staying in tune with the rapidly changing market requirements. However, today these SMEs are encountering serious difficulties in withstanding the tough competition in the open market scenario with surging imports and rising expectations of quality. There are also other issues, for instance of auxiliary units associated with certain industries which are facing major market forces of change like that of the component or accessory makers for scooters as the market has shifted dramatically to motorcycles.

When a customer has to choose from competing products which are more or less based on the same technology, his or her decision to choose one from the other depends mainly on the 'eye appeal' of the product triggered by aesthetics, colour, form, graphics etc. Taking cognizance of the changed business and industry dynamics, which pose serious challenges to the SMEs, there is an urgency for developing alternative strategies and appropriate design-technology interventions.

If we take a look at some of the successful international parallels, the furniture sector in Italy has greatly benefited from an intelligent use of design. For example, there are about 38,000 furniture companies in Italy which makes it the second largest producer in the world after the US. Forty-six per cent of the furniture is exported from Italy giving it a 17 per cent market share in the world. It is also interesting to note that Italian manufacturers of furniture in recent times have come together to set up an umbrella marketing organization. For instance, I-style, a consortium of ten such small and medium sized furniture manufacturers, that is, Concept, International Office, Coro, FEG, Giellesse, Lema, MisuraEmm, Mobileffe, Salvarani, Turri and Zanaboni have got together to project their synergistic capabilities for undertaking large projects. This is a good example for the Indian small scale sector to emulate in order to join forces and scale up their operational capabilities witht better 'brand' recognition.

One of the most successful models for SME sectors in Italy where the 'academia-industry interface' has been effective is in the transformation brought about in the Lombardy region. The Design for District Approach experimented in this region has resulted in creating several design-led companies and the design workshops were coordinated by Politecnico di Milano (a 144-year-old university in Milan) involving over twenty organizations spread over a decade. This kind of sustained intervention can make a major difference in our growth centres and India can draw upon this experience with the help of the Italians for improving the value chain of industries in clusters for automotive components, toys, appliances, knitwear, and several such products. A premier design institute like NID which has diverse design disciplines under one roof can contribute a great deal by working year after year through student projects in select small scale industrial clusters, like Peenya Industrial Estate in Karnataka, which specialize broadly in one or few product categories.

In the UK, for instance, the Design Council recently started a new initiative called 'Designing Demand' (which makes designers deliver lasting and successful solutions for businesses) mainly aimed at SMEs with multi-disciplinary teams and regional development agencies involved in the process. One of the recent beneficiaries of the UK Design Council has been quoted as saying: 'Designing Demand left us with new skills and a fresh outlook that will help us stay strong in the future.' Lee Mowle an entrepreneur from UK says of 'Designing Demand': 'Designing Demand gave us a way to make sure the new ideas, we come up with, match customers' needs, get to market faster and have maximum commercial impact. In a competitive sector like ours, that's really valuable.'

The above examples bring forth this one fact: design plays a major role in making a product stand out from among the sea of products and also helps in conveying its worth and value to the customer thus building their enduring confidence in a company and its products.

It provides the essential inputs in terms of features – its form and colour, ease of its use, safety parameters, new affordances and above all distinctive positioning in the market. Understanding customer needs, aspirations and developing products based on such deep insights or what is called as 'user-centric design approach' can greatly increase the rate of success when a product is launched in the market. Systematic and methodical process of product development followed by a designer's inputs will immensely benefit the SME sector as it will result in new products brought out at a much faster rate and with more compatibility with fast changing customer requirements.

designing success through design clinics

Design Clinic is a typical mechanism wherein clinical solutions are made available for problems related to design. The idea is to bring industry and design education on to a common platform, to evaluate the efficacy of the latter in proffering expert advice and solutions. Design clinics are modeled after medical clinics to provide substantial value-added and quick remedial solutions to any design ailment!

As a concept, the Design Clinic model applies to needy segments of industries, like the small scale manufacturing, where conventional models of design consultancy and training may neither be feasible nor affordable. In this model the SME sector and design expertise are brought onto a common platform providing expert advice and solutions on real time. As said earlier, this would result in continuous improvement, however incremental, for existing products. It can also lead to developing creative solutions for sustainable competitive advantage to the SMEs.

Design Clinic is a time-tested intervention model, where a solution to an existing 'problem' is diagnosed and remedial steps suggested by a multi-disciplinary team of designers, technologists and marketing experts. In this approach, the value additions to an idea or a concept is initiated through interactions at an affordable price to a specific cluster of industry or sector. This model brings design exposure to the doorstep of industry clusters for evaluation, analysis, incremental improvement and in certain cases long term strategic design initiatives.

The Design Clinic model can be easily replicated on a national scale, as this alongwith 'brand clinics' have the potential to unleash the immense power of the small scale sector to transform the economic landscape and most significantly leverage India's strength of small batch production, and a high level of creativity as in the case of handlooms, handicrafts and a number of non-traditional products.

Ideally in this model, three to five consultants including designers with different domain expertise could be attached to the SME industry clusters for a defined period to provide need-based design solutions. At the first stage, a team of experts could undertake a feasibility study to understand the critical and pre-competitive design issues of the selected SME cluster. This would help the design team to identify appropriate design intervention methodologies which are mostly generic in nature.

At a later stage, the consultants and designers could operate through regular design clinics over a specified period of time to provide need-based solutions. Also regular training programmes could be organized for capacity building for a longer period of time. Here the intervention could also include areas of aesthetics, branding, and packaging.

The National Manufacturing Competitiveness Council or NMCC, set up by the Government of India in October 2004 incorporated the Design Clinic model developed by NID in their manufacturing strategy in order to catalyze a value-added approach among SME enterprises.

In the final analysis, Design Clinic is an effective diagnostic tool which will hugely benefit the SMEs to withstand competition and expand markets while equipping them with tools to overcome the onslaught of globalization and the fierce games based on scale and reach.

technology-design – fusion for success

The International Council of Societies of Industrial Design defines industrial design as 'a creative activity whose aim is to establish the multi-faceted qualities of objects, processes, services and their systems in whole life cycles. Therefore, design is the central factor of innovative humanization of technologies and the crucial factor of cultural and economic exchange.'

I believe that proliferation and application of technology alone can never satisfy people. Technology is only a means to an end, and finally technology has to metamorphosize into innumerable consumer-friendly marketable products and services. Despite having the right technology, right design, and abundant local raw materials, there have been innumerable examples in the country where the industrial sector has been adversely affected. The discerning consumer of today demands acceptable quality, novelty and competitive prices perhaps more as a right than an option. It is time for technologists, designers, business leaders and entrepreneurs to find real solutions especially, an affordable design, for the masses. The Nano, or the wondrous one lakh rupee car conceived by the Tata Group is one such example. I can say here that it was during his visit to the NID in January 2003 when Ratan Tata, chairman of the Tata Group, for the first time ever made the plan of launching the one lakh rupee car (now Nano) public! Apart from inspiring India and the world by achieving what his critics said was a distant dream, the Tata Group also inspired NID in finally starting a 'Transportation and Automobile Programme' in 2005, a real example of technology-design fusion.

The shifting paradigms of today's knowledge economy have placed demands on every profession emphasizing on constant innovation and nowhere is this more evident than in design. As the systems and artifacts we generate become increasingly complex by combining many features and customizable options, present-day designers are engaged in visualizing new scenarios and contexts and defining new problems and solutions, at the shortest possible time. The rapid 'mind to market' travel of ideas is quite characteristic of the innovation driven knowledge economy and the new technologies based on 'virtual prototyping' facilitate this. In the near future, robotics, nanotechnology, geo-visualization, are likely to expand their spheres of influence stirring many more pathbreaking innovations and design perforce will have to play a more proactive role.

Although technology alone does not fulfil need-gaps, there's no gainsaying that to a large extent it has made immense contributions to the rapid economic growth of India. During the year 2006-07, India's GDP grew at 9.2 per cent. The contribution of the agriculture sector was 18.5 per cent, industry 26.4 per cent and services a whopping 55.1 per cent. It is also evident that the crucial difference between developing countries and those that are developed is not only because of a disparity in resources but also due to the hiatus in technology and applied knowledge.

Just as in a newly-independent India led to new aspirations which included self-reliance in food grains, milk and basic commodities in the early post-independence period, the vision of a developed India needs to inspire a developed design environment in India. What is at once both interesting and disconcerting is that for many the designer's preoccupation with physical products and tangible designs in some form or the other perhaps has led to a condition which almost neglected the silent service revolution. The coming together of media, communication and information technology in an 'unstoppable innovation tide', is redefining many products as we knew them earlier and in the process rendering many of them redundant. The mobile phones, for instance, have rendered the watch, alarm clock, calendar, video, camera, voice recorder, and even an ordinary torch redundant for many consumers.

So far as economic growth is concerned, India is now looking at 9-10 per cent annual growth with a hundred per cent literacy rate and a high technology base coupled with self-reliance in critical sectors. According to Dr APJ Abdul Kalam and A. Shivathanu Pillai in the book, *Envisioning an Empowered Nation*: 'Technology is a non-linear tool that can effect the most fundamental change in the ground rules of economic development.' What the quote perhaps overtly does not specify but clearly indicates is that the authors consider 'design' as a part of the broad technology umbrella and stress unequivocally on its significance as something which adds value to a product. Design adds over 60 per cent value to any product!

It is very significant, as technology and design have so far remained far removed from each other without breaking common grounds. It is ironical that the technology policies over the years have never provided any role for design. There was a complete disconnect between the two and the fields of science and technology and engineering unfortunately saw nothing significant in design and dismissed it almost as a necessary evil. It was in 2002-03, that the then secretary of Department of Science and Technology finally agreed to meet the team from the NID and we made a presentation to bring technology and design closer. In that meeting it was conceded that there was a need for a 'window to design' in all technology schemes and a technology-design fusion group was set up to formulate necessary schemes and initiatives. The National Design Business Incubator, or NDBI, was set up in NID in 2003 as a result of this initiative.

Dr Kalam and Pillai in their book, also unveil the new and amazing technologies for the next fifty years: 'Micro satellites, hypersonic vehicles, edible vaccines, next green revolution, micro motors, micro gears, nano-gears, nano-tubes, and space colonies.' The trajectories of technology and design point to the fact that service and experience design are likely to capture the imagination of the people and the industry in the coming years. A major paradigm shift, therefore, is on the anvil.

A symbiotic relationship between design and technology is a natural corollary to economic progress if the quality of life has to change for the better. For instance, technologies for health or well-being related products including a simple inexpensive water purifier for drinking water would be in the realm of symbiotic design development between technology and design. Similarly services are becoming increasingly technology enabled and hence need to be designed just like products by a team of designers and technologists. Earlier, design was only seen from the point of view of humanizing technologies but now design has to be seen coupled with appropriate technologies to become a product, service or brand through its visualization and realization.

The example of fusion of technology with design can be better understood from the example of some fantastic work done by an NID student, R.S. Rajasekaran who utilized nano-plasma technologies for creating a series of new products like nano masks, gloves for scooter riders in cities and protective clothing for soldiers in high altitudes. The technology for this was developed under the guidance of Prof P.B. Jhala, the John Bissell Research Chair at the NID since 2005.

lessons from an innovation economy

If there's one country which has had a chequered past and faced turmoil almost around the same time as India, it is Israel. Its interesting to see how nations which are torn apart by internal and external strife tide over numerous problems and create benchmarks. Israel's forays in the field of science, cutting-edge technologies and creating well-heeled entrepreneurs has generated immense respect for the country in global markets and there are important lessons to be learnt here especially in such diverse areas as communication, IT, software security, hi-tech applications in materials like plastics, stem cell research and cardiovascular applications. One of the reasons for such progress can be attributed to the well-developed and professional support infrastructure which encourages hi-tech innovations and venture capital funding for the same through various stages. As I have personally seen, the office of the chief scientist, State of Israel & Trade and Labour are all well networked in this process. The various support schemes like that of MATIMOP (the Israeli Centre for R&D), the TNUFA programme (which encourages and supports technological entrepreneurship and innovation at pre-competitive stage) and the Magnaton programme (promoting technology transfer from academic institutions to industry) are excellent schemes.

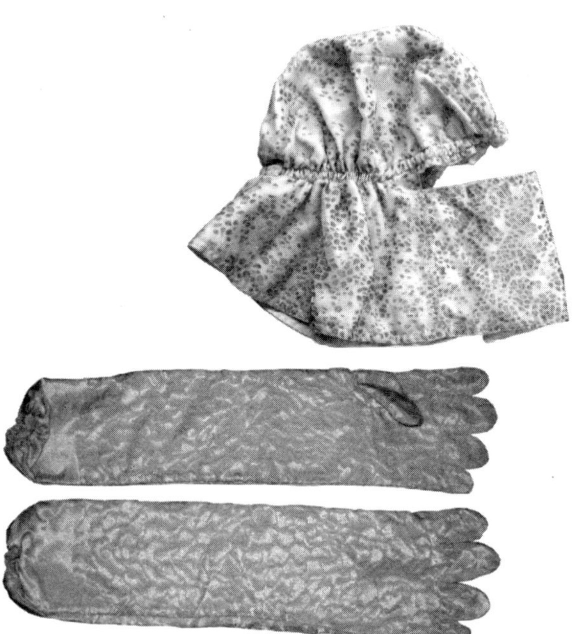

NID student R.S. Rajasekaran utilized nano-plasma technology for creating a series of new products like nano mask, gloves for scooter riders. The technology for this was developed under the guidance of Prof. P.B. Jhala, the John Bissell Research Chair at NID since 2005-08.

If we make a comparison between India and Israel then the national expenditure on R&D in India is hovering around a meager 0.7 to 0.8 per cent of the GNP whereas in Israel it is estimated at around 4 per cent. In Israel, companies are focused on hi-tech inventions mostly as part of a multinational innovation project or as being part of a hi-tech venture. In short, Israel is perceived as 'long' on R&D but 'short' on marketing, branding and design; it scores on innovations but user-centric developments and applications are often carried out by collaborators in the US or elsewhere. If we take the example of Zoran, a successful chip manufacturing company in Israel, which supplies chips to mobiles, imaging devices, digital TV, digital camera, then it could be best described as a company which leads in technology, and which makes sense in today's times. However, they have not been able to make a mass impact, like say Intel as there has been no direct consumer interface at Zoran. Similarly Celletra, yet another prominent Israeli company, which supplies networking solutions to cellular players like Reliance in India or to companies in Mexico also have no desire to get into the front end of business as a vertically integrated player. In these cases, the technologies are somewhat 'commodity' like, though with a cutting edge, as the prices are driven by the ultimate service marketer based on scale and scope. Hypothetically, if Reliance Infocom purchases telecom equipments from Israel and if it is meant for large-scale implementation across Indian metros and cities, the price could be driven down through negotiations which is actually the case on ground. Mass production is not viable in Israel owing to rising labour costs and the size of the market which is rather small with just 6.5 million people and therefore for developing most of the technology, Israel has to depend on other countries for market sustenance.

It is worth reiterating that the model of close collaboration between research institutions, office of the chief scientist and the industry is extremely robust in Israel. This innovation ecosystem is missing in India and the onus perhaps lies in the new National Design Policy and the proposed India Design Council to pay special attention in this area. Institutions of higher learning like the IITs, IIMs and even large technological universities have to play a role in this regard like many of the American universities like MIT, Stanford, have in the previous century. Modelled after the American system, research in Israeli universities like Technion, Ben Gurion, Hebrew, Haifa, Tel Aviv and Weizman have a very close working relationship with hi-tech industries and entrepreneurs at different levels. There are also specialized bodies and programmes for giving support to entrepreneurs undertaking technological innovations. The bias is of course towards hi-tech and knowledge intensive ventures (and less labour intensive), which can fetch good returns in a three to five year time frame. This can be broadly compared to the programmes offered by the Science & Technology Department in India through Technology Development Board (TDB) and Technology Information Forecasting & Assessment Council (TIFAC).

However, when compared, the absence of a venture capital-culture in India is in sharp contrast with that of Israel where it is considered as a pool of money invested in an evolving industry. In a span of a decade, that is, from 1991-2000, Israel's VC funding grew from a mere 58 million dollars to 4,557 million dollars! From the point of view of supporting technology incubators for catalyzing new developments, both Israel and India are more or less on even footing with Israel having thirty-four incubators of which thirteen are privatized and in India, about eighty incubators are in public sector and thirteen in private.

Another area, which is well developed in Israel is the collaborative hi-tech ventures through bi-national funding as in the case of Bi-national Industrial Research & Development or BIRD, which was set up almost thirty years ago to stimulate and promote industrial R&D for mutual benefit of both the US and Israel. Going by the experience of the BIRD foundation, the success rate is estimated at around 33 per cent or so while in most cases of general VC funding, a 10 per cent success rate is considered normal. In India, this kind of approach is yet to take off.

It is clear that Israel has a well-developed hi-tech culture but lack in good design and marketing initiatives. As said earlier, this is mainly because Israel has a limited domestic market of 6.5 million people, who can neither mass produce competitively nor offer mass consumption. Meanwhile India is at a major advantage here and all it needs to do is to actively promote an innovation ecosystem through innovation hubs, symbiotic academic-industry nexus and a liberal venture capital regime. It is heartening that the Planning Commission and the Department of Industrial Policy and Promotion have responded favourably to set up a 'Rolling Venture Capital Fund' to support designpreneurs during the eleventh Five Year Plan. Global investors already see India as the third preferred destination for global R&D and there is scope for major forays in hi-tech with a design approach and formulation of 'collaborative strategies' for long-term sustainable advantage.

designing a new design ethos

Similar to the unique ability in human beings, the power to 'create' is the most important strength of design. Design harnesses this power by borrowing from several fields and by creating a bridge between different levels through the undefined labyrinths of options and solutions. How does a designer find his or her way through current ideas, concepts, products, systems, services, environment, technologies, aspirations and expectations to create a 'new design' in order to satisfy a new want or to create a new want or to add value to the existing needs of consumers? Sometimes it may seem as if too much is expected from design and designers. Can design be a panacea to all the problems in a growing organization, economy, or even a country? Unfortunately not and there in hangs a little tale! Although let me once again say that design, unlike any other process or force, has this 'uniquability' to imagine, visualize, and create.

Nowadays more than 'design' as a noun, 'design' as a verb, or as a process, is more in vogue. The verb 'design' as a process can flow through many layers and create new contexts, frames and paradigms. Even a well-planned design process need not necessarily lead to good design. Good design is finally an act of faith, conviction and creativity to redefine what is known, rewrite existing rules and link the unrelated. Design is more a result of synthesis, than analysis. It follows a designer's ability to 'create', which is a function of the quality of mind supported by highly honed and developed skills. There has to be a constant process of not only challenging oneself, but also existing ideas and exploring the 'whys' and 'why nots' that ultimately makes for a good designer. A fine blend of liberal arts, ability to connect technology with design, understanding user needs as also gauge expectations about the form, function and fashion (timeliness and aesthetics) of a product makes a designer successful.

When we look at the attributes of a potential designer, then the key components are: aptitude, attitude, functional skills, communication, general awareness and a world view. In a budding designer, the clusters around each of these components are identified and further developed in a professional design programme. The new design ethos calls for original knowledge through indepth research, scenario building and team-based innovations and often collaborative work carried out by many from different locations. However, there is no gainsaying that each product after design has to emerge successful and the designer, as a vital team player with the rest, has to be well-equipped to transcend the 'mind to market' distance in the stipulated time frame. Each link in this entire process adds value and probably design adds more value than the rest as it answers the 'why use me?' or 'how am I different?' questions very emphatically. There is definitely a separate linkage established by design culturally and emotionally

Multi-sensory spiritual jewellery inscribed with Gayatri Mantra designed by NID student Amaresh Panigrahi.

Clockwise from far left:
A porcelain tea set designed by NID student Abhimatha Kala.

Standard 'Bombay Screw' for the Ganjam Line of earrings designed by NID student Jasleen Bindra.

A writing aid designed by NID for arthritic patients.

A still from a twenty-minute crossover genre animation film *2 Fish in 3 Parts*.

with a customer which goes beyond the functional use of a product or service. Design thinking has to reflect the cutting edge and this manifests in a designer's ability to push the envelope and anticipate the future.

Whatever may be the level of design intervention, if the designer fails to deliver value through a multi-disciplinary and often trans-disciplinary approach, the cause of design suffers. Designers have to act locally but connect globally. Gone are the days when a designer could afford to be insular; as a community, they need to network with other designers and professionals constantly. Apart from keeping their creative urge alive, designers also have to be on top of the several 'economic' and 'ecological' criteria and the short, medium and long term goals. The choices are undoubtedly hard to make. However, the boundaries, size, scale and proportion in a designer's language are best defined by the individuals themselves despite external pressures.

I reiterate, the most significant part of any design culture across the world – design outcomes are much more effective and are likely to be more far reaching when they are created in a multi-disciplinary and trans-disciplinary manner. The Samsung design team, for instance, spread across the world, is a good example of a variety of designers and creative people with nearly a 500-strong team to create new scenarios and story boards to work on new products and systems.

Back home in India, Infosys, Bengaluru, has a 140-member strong design team and, is in fact, headed by an apparel designer, which proves how there's a need for more lateral thinkers to head design teams in a nation which is growing from strength to strength.

discovering the design edge

individual creativity to societal innovation

Below: A still from an animation film *Boond* by NID student Kavita Singh which won the Silver Conch at MIFF 2006, Mumbai and IPDA Award for Excellence in 2005.

Facing page: A still from an animation film *Swoosh* directed by Ranveer Singh Sahmbi, winner of the Silver Conch at MIFF 2006, Mumbai.

Mahatma Gandhi once famously said: 'I do not want my house to be walled in on all sides and my windows to be closed; instead I want cultures of all lands to be blown about my house as freely as possible. But I refuse to be blown off my feet by any.' This in my opinion is the most appropriate design philosophy for a country which is being swept by winds of globalization.

Whether directly in the context of design or even otherwise, one often correlates creativity to a particular person or a group with some specific skills – some god gifted and the others honed over the years. I strongly feel that the word creativity cannot be just limited to those who carry tags of being directly connected with it – artists, writers, sculptors or designers – but includes others who have lateral and 'out of the box' thinking capability. It is very interesting to note that at an individual level a majority of the people in most democratic societies are very creative. It is also true of us – be it an auto-rickshaw driver, a vegetable vendor or a housewife in whom most often we can, if we want to, discern sparks of creativity. If eyebrows are raised at such a statement then it is perhaps because of this – as a vastly populated nation with an immense human resource, we have failed to transform the individual creativity of each or many to a collective societal innovation. And why, some may ask, is this required? As I have repeatedly said, design in the ultimate analysis is about bettering the quality of lives and this could be one of the best ways to do it.

The celebrated services of the *dabbawallas* (or mobile lunch deliverers) in Mumbai or the online auction of airline tickets by several new airlines in India or the new 'Street Car' service in the UK are all illustrative examples of services making an impact on the lives of the common people. The system of electronically monitored numbered sequence of devotees' queues at Tirupati Tirumala Devasthanam in Andhra Pradesh is yet another example. The shift is more than visible now, from individual-centric designs and designers to a renewed thrust on communities. The concept of true design democracy thus is here to stay and let us not forget how difficult it was a few years ago for the 'vernacular' to become 'global' or the 'local' to reach every nook and corner of the world. In the case of cuisines and clothes, this has already happened whether it is the *idlis*, *chole-bhature* or the *salwar- kameez*!

In a knowledge economy, which is also virtual in many respects, the possibility of 'long-tailed distribution' which becomes very profitable over a period of time, ensures that there will be many avenues for people from ethnic and vernacular backgrounds to access specific products and services. Here, as every one has a chance to exercise their preferences and customize what they aspire with the help of ICT (Information, Communication Technologies), it will be useful to recognize the role of strategic design in enveloping these approaches so that they can be driven horizontally across segments of industries, commerce and development. The individual is of course important but the concerns of society, community, and humanity at large need to be recognized in this framework. Design education needs to cultivate the

necessary values as design encodes the tacit culture and values and the user decodes continuously through emotional and 'heart-led' connections. Therefore, the significant role of design education in catalyzing individual innovation to societal innovation cannot be understated. Societal innovation comes to fruition through a proactive entrepreneurial approach enabled by technology. Tradition of course plays a key role in providing the connectivity to community, society and humanity at large.

Issues like poverty, illiteracy, shortage of drinking water, shelter, productive employment, access to information, care for the disadvantaged, challenged, and the socially deprived, occurrences of natural disasters, child mortality and infanticides, infectious diseases and epidemics all cry for attention in the least developed and developing economies and design interventions addressing these issues are often categorized as 'Design for Societal Development'. Good and affordable designs for many products and services and strategic designs in order to develop systems for mitigating difficulties and disparities would go a long way in spreading design democracy, in the truest sense of the word. Democracy is a way of life – and nowhere can this be more true than in India – and for design it should be no different. It is clear that vernacular designs available to the masses and some of the design classics indicate the need to remain closer to the ground if design has to succeed in a complex, layered country like India.

The vernacular designs are ethnic in origin and deeply rooted in the daily lives of the common people. Though short on aesthetics, the functionality and utility are very high in such products and they still continue to be used in several parts of interior India. The Indian classics generally represent the quest of the earlier generations of designers to go beyond ethnic designs, to interpret and satisfy 'Indian' needs that is, a string chair, wet grinder, and Symphony dessert cooler, whereas some others represent the use of new materials as in a plastic *lota*, citrus squeezer, while certain ethnic designs like Kolhapuri *chappals* have become design classics transcending time and place.

The vernacular designs are ethnic in origin and deeply rooted in the daily lives of the common people. These classics of Indian design generally represent the quest of the earlier generation of designers to go beyond ethnic designs to interpret and satisfy Indian needs, that is, a vegetable vendor, an Indian *thali* decorated with various food items in it, a chef preparing *tandoori roti*, an Indian style of *belan* (rolling pin), *chakla* (rolling top) for making *chapattis*, a variety of hand grinders to crush crops like wheat, rice, jowar, bajra to turn into the flour, an Indian style bettle-nut cracker, Symphony dessert air cooler, Vishala Utensils Museum, Ahmedabad. The three pots, one above the other, made up of brass have become a design classic transcending time and place.

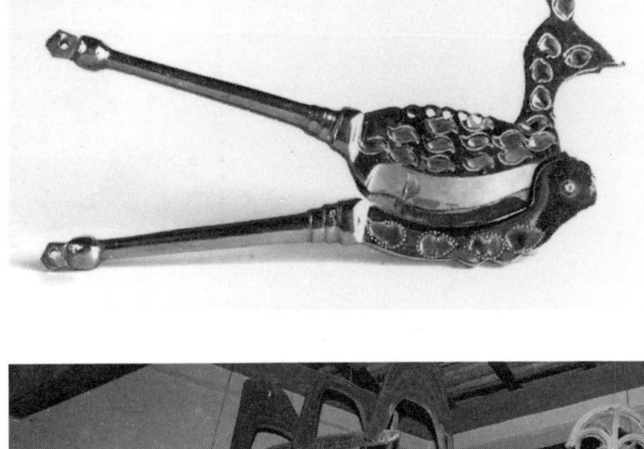

Traditional *kaavad*: Storytelling box is a good example of the fusion of folk art and technology inspired by the *kaavad* of Rajasthan.

towards an indian idiom in design

In retrospect, if the twentieth century had its 'firsts' and a great character, the twenty-first is also distinct in its texture – knowledge creation through innovation has become the key differentiator. If the twentieth century belonged to seeking creative solutions to problems, the twenty-first focuses on defining problems and creating new opportunities; the earlier century concentrated on customer satisfaction through products and services; this century lends credence to the value of 'experience'. Boundaries are blurring for products and services and experience is soon becoming a comprehensive value definition in the new age. Designers are sought for their imaginative and ideating capabilities and are expected to act as 'imagineer' and 'synthesizer'.

In the twentieth century, design was at best seen as a tool for gaining competitive advantage in the marketplace and designers were seen as esoteric people with magic wands who made products look more appealing, and often expensive. Real breakthroughs from designers were few and far between, though many notable exceptions, do exist. Sooner rather than later, technology overtook and enveloped design to acquire a more prominent profile and path-breaking technological advancements gradually sidestepped designers.

The new-age designers have the chance of their life time in the twenty-first century to leave a lasting foot print what with the attention gradually shifting to the more fundamental issues of sustainability, global warming and quality of life. As mentioned earlier, the designers have to often go beyond the given brief to humanize technologies and envision new products, systems and services. Successful designs need to be in sync with culture and traditions to

e-kaavad developed at NID.

improve the quality of life. When the list of people, who may have influenced the world in an impactful and positive manner in myriad fields is routinely drawn up, designers unfortunately hardly find any mention. This has to change and change fast.

From post-independence to almost till the early nineties, Indian design was trapped in the confines of a protected economy. It is said very aptly, 'If you think good design is expensive, look how much bad design costs.' In India this is precisely what happened and faulty design took a heavy toll on human life whether it was unsafe roads, lack of concern for the elderly and children or products which flouted all safety standards and proved to be health hazards.

The statement of the legendary American philanthropist, Richard H. Driehaus 'Good design doesn't cost, but it pays,' should perhaps be played and replayed for manufacturers, policy makers, and urban planners in India. For starters, there has been no organized effort to make design promotion a corollary to design education. There is a pressing need for designers to reinvent their role if design has to exist as a profession in the twenty-first century. And this is indeed a challenge! But thankfully not insurmountable because in a creative economy it is possible for designers to realize new ideas faster and leverage intangibles imaginatively to make the tangibles relevant and meaningful. Individual designers have to realize that the time has come for working on big ideas and within a team.

If India becomes a developed nation by AD 2020, as some political visionaries of our times say, and an economic superpower by AD 2050, how do then designers anticipate and shape the future? With the multiplier effect of communication through internet and mobile telephony taking over India and with a dominant and growing young populace especially those who were born in the 1980s and 1990s, what is the new role and strategy adapted by industrial and communication designers to become leaders? The new designer has to respect the global design directions while remaining sensitive to local needs and spur design breakthroughs. Today's innovations need to be inspired by an exciting future while being relevant to the present.

A major churning process is on, not only in the design scene in India but also globally. One stream of thought that has emerged in the world is: the very definition of industrial product has changed and, therefore, design activity has become a system or specifically a design system. Another emerging paradigm is that the age of the storyteller has dawned; the story comes first and then the design, because design is 'storytelling' for products both in physical representation and communication about the product or brand. Yet another plea is the search for a distinctive quality of each culture and representation of the vernacular by the designer in a world fast becoming one networked village with global brands and identities dominating the consumption patterns. Culture and design values, therefore, now assume an ominous foreboding for designers as the search for identity by consumers gains momentum. As cultures get affected by the discontinuous and swift technological changes, the designers have to act as interpreters of culture and emotions to reduce the conflicts and the growing hiatus between technologies and end-users to achieve harmony.

Indian companies are now seriously discussing the need for connecting culture and emotion through design and the new products hitting the Indian marketplace frequently indicate this trend. It is argued that in the coming years an important mission of design will be to harmonize the polemic positions such as, East-West-North-South; of past, present and the future, and such numerous often-opposing concepts and issues. Though the post-industrial realities of the developed world may not apply in the same manner to India, the emergence of a tech-savvy, 'mobile lifestyle' and an information-rich society are very much part of the new Indian reality.

Unfortunately, there is time for an encore yet as there seems to be only a partial understanding in India about the role, purpose and scope of design. Design is on the threshold of moving from the tactical to the strategic; the methodology and process of design and its capabilities to transform the economic landscape are almost missed; more often than not, aesthetics have dominated the perception of design and the strategic role of design has been eclipsed. As we have discussed in an earlier chapter, unlike India, several developed countries like the UK, Singapore, Korea, Japan, and China have taken bold and imaginative leaps by using design as a powerful tool for economic transformation. If we refer to some successful examples elsewhere in the world, the UK Design Council is one which was set up as far back as 1949 and in the last few years has restructured its role and become a powerful interface with industry and the government. The DoT (or Design of The Times) 77 programme in North-East England brings out the diverse sustainable design interventions shaping the lives of the people of the region. John Thackara who led the project believes that such projects are the harbingers of a designer's new role amidst societies and communities.

Indian design has to go through such an accelerated phase of transformation which will then hopefully result in creating an Indian design idiom. The following case study of designing a new series of coins within India indicates that Indian designers, in this case Anil Sinha, a senior member of the NID faculty, are more than just capable:

> To design Indian coins in the 25 Paise, 1 Rupee, 2 Rupee, 5 Rupee, 10 Rupees denominations the following parameters needed to be considered:
> For the highest denomination, the weight should not exceed 8 gms and the size should not exceed 26mm x 2mm.
> Rs10 and Rs 5 coins may be bimetallic while the lower denomination coins may be of one metal or an alloy.
> Intrinsic value of the coin may not be more than its face value.
> It should be acceptable to vending machines.
> There should be maximum utilization of existing equipment and technology and minimum requirement of new equipment.
> Design should ensure portability and acceptability by the general public.

RECAST DESIGN BRIEF

While designing the coin series the following design constraints shall apply:

The largest coin shall not measure more than 26mm x 2mm.

The heaviest coin shall not weigh more than 8 gms.

The designs shall be acceptable to vending machines.

Intrinsic value of the coin shall not be more than the face value of the coin.

The coins shall be user friendly even for special groups such as the visually handicapped and the unlettered.

The design shall draw upon the rich Indian culture yet represent a contemporary and forward looking India.

Size, thickness and weight would be used as distinguishing criteria between denominations.

RESEARCH PHASE

The research phase was carried out primarily to get a feel of the issues involved in coin design and to find a way to deal with each critical issue. Research consisted of studies in four different areas:

Coin usability

Pertaining to Human Factor (HF) issues and the use of coins in payphones and Automated Vending Machines (AVMs). HF issues addressed the storage, identification and handling of coins, and the problems encountered thereof. Special attention was given to understanding AVM technology.

Production Methods

The production cycle at IGM was studied in detail to identify various processes that go into it as well as to understand the various bottlenecks and their effect on productivity.

Materials and processes

An independent investigation into modern coinage materials and processes such as cladding of coins and manufacture of bimetallic coins were studied to better understand production constraints.

Graphics

A detailed study of form and graphics of ancient coins, pre- and post-independence Indian coins and some contemporary global coinage was also carried out to identify visual and formal clues used worldwide in the design of coins.

The insights gained from the research phase allowed us to remodel the initial brief.

The graphic fonts have been selected keeping in mind the following points:

Readability and legibility

Clean reduction to small point size

Visual elegance

New series of coins for Rs 1 and 2, designed by NID graphic design faculty Anil Sinha.

PROPOSAL FOR EDGE TREATMENT

Edge treatment may be imparted to a coin at different stages of the minting cycle.

It may be done during blanking by cutting a non-circular shape which imparts to the coin a distinct edge, easily differentiable by touch. It may be done during the striking process by incorporating a design on to the collar which imprints upon the coin when it is struck at high pressure.

Finally, it may also be incorporated in pre-production using milling techniques. Using a milling machine it is possible to engrave horizontal and vertical grooves, intermittent grooves etc.

A fourth option in the form of edge lettering also exists, where the text may be inscribed on to the edge of the coin. This is similar to milling and may occur at any stage of production.

SHORTLISTED CONCEPTS

In addition, cultural, scientific and technological achievements and progress of our nation were used as starting points to generate new themes.

Some new design stories/concepts that were considered for the coin development were:

Growth/Prosperity
Unity in Diversity
Networking/Connectivity
Indian Classical Dances
Progress in Aviation and Aeronautics
Progress in Defense Research and Development
Progress in Space and Satellite Technology

CONCEPTS ELABORATION (ILLUSTRATIVE)

Mudra: One of India's most famous classical dance forms, Bharatanatyam, is represented here by way of *mudras*, the hand gestures that typify the dance form. Similar representative elements from other dance forms may be used to generate a homogenous series of coins.

The five *mudras*, keeping with the number of coins, represent the inherent fluidity and grace of the dance form and also serve as visual codes to help in quick and clear identification of the denomination.

The visuals appear on the reverse side along with the denomination in Roman numerals. The obverse side carried all the other information along with the Lion Emblem.

Such work, as above, truly signifies a search for an Indian idiom in design by encoding many layers of meanings. The cultural and tactile aspects provide holistic solutions keeping the masses in mind while surprising them with the beauty and elegance of the coins while giving them a new value through design.

decoding design identity

The designers' ability to stand out in a crowd using distinctive expressions in various products, services and systems through design is well recognized. 'Dream', 'vision', 'imagine', 'innovate' are all nowadays being interchangeably used by authors, speakers, thinkers, policy makers and image gurus alike. While dream has no confines, vision definitely sets a clear path far into the future. Designers are called upon for 'innovations in design' to imagine that which does not exist and therefore their visualization capabilities need to be at its best. Innovation is at a higher level than design and creativity embraces all these expressions in its wider ambit. For making the designs successful and unique, designers have to necessarily assimilate the spirit of 'creativity' of various cultures that the products and services represent.

The creativity of a culture is best manifested through design, crafts, art forms, performances, folklores and other such forms of expressions. Cultural expression helps designers to make distinctive products and services which connects the consumers or users emotionally and culturally. This in turn creates brand loyalty leading to competitive advantage for companies at a micro level and countries and economies at a macro level. Design is thus becoming a strategic tool for creating long-term competitive advantages. As we have seen earlier, many Indian companies are now beginning to realize the value of design for their very survival, growth and above all distinctive identity and brand positioning. Design identity creation travels through many stages of unravelling the clients' philosophy, product, and most importantly the end-users', before arriving at the final visual expression. Some of the most memorable logos created by the NID perhaps represent all the philosophies of design most succinctly: the logo for Indian Railway's 150th anniversary, beautifully encoding a peacock; the symbol for the Election Commission of India, excellent for its sheer simplicity; the

Logos designed by NID.

symbol for the Agricultural and Processed Food Products Export Development Authority or APEDA, capturing the essence of our cultivated products; and scores of others including that of the National Human Rights Commission or NHRC, the brand new ones like that of IIM, Shillong, and Janmarg in Ahmedabad, and the very effective Handloom Mark promoted by the Ministry of Textiles and many such exemplify brilliant visual resolutions which encompass many intangibles rooted both in tradition and modernity.

Yet another Indian classic identity creation is the one for Hindustan Petroleum by Sudarshan Dheer, the famed graphic designer. This actually is a study which reveals the struggles and pain that a designer has to undergo in creating such unique identities. The logo, with both a Hindi (Devanagari) and English script, are reproduced here to elucidate the conflicts which often arise between a designer and the client. In a letter written by Sudarshan Dheer to the then chairman and managing director of HP, dated as early as 15 July 1994, asking HP to drop the Hindi script, explains the agonizing story of the iconic HP logo creation rather well. This is what Sudarshan Dheer's letter said:

> The design was conceived such that the verbal identity of "HP" in letter form should complement and strengthen the visual identity – i.e. the spouting of oil. By replacing English letters with Hindi text arbitrarily without interacting with the original designer of the logo, the entire concept has been destroyed and the purpose of the logo defeated. Thanks to the complementary nature of the verbal and visual identity, the original HP logo is quite memorable. In fact, several petrol stations act as landmarks for the public. It's so easy to say. "I am next to the HP station" or "Meet me at Colaba's HP station." Here "HP" is important and much easier to say than the full form of Hindustan Petroleum in Hindi.

India has gained tremendous respect in the

international community with its recent liberalization. Indian companies are going global to meet the challenges of international competition. A lengthy Hindi logo will make Hindustan Petroleum look regressive. While everyone is going international we are taking a step backward. This will not only affect the commercial interests of the company but is also not in sync with national policy.

The HP logo has an inherent advantage which even Bharat Petroleum doesn't enjoy. The original HP logo is integrated with the symbol, where it has to live and grow. The laboured replacement of "HP" with Hindi is incompatible with the symbol and appears contrived. In fact it destroys the image and the visual impact of the symbol too.

In this highly competitive market we cannot afford to get carried away by emotions. We must remember that HP is a national organization with nationwide outlets. Not everybody in this country can read Devnagri script and instead of hurting regional sentiments, retaining English alphabets would be most appropriate as everybody can identify and read it.

The designer finally succeeded in making the point and HP reverted to the original. I have often observed that in general people do not attribute much importance to brand identity creation or the commercial value it creates. Let's not forget that graphic identities represent many encoded intangibles and each logo has a story behind it and often represents a quest for an Indian idiom in design.

Various logos designed by NID for IIM, Shillong; Janmarg Limited; IIM, Indore; 'Handloom Mark' for Ministry of Textiles; HP; and Indian Railways 150th anniversary.

competing on design edge

Design has to walk the talk and repeatedly so. Its is rather unfortunate but true that design is understood only by a few even now when the country is surging past and registering unprecedented economic growth rates. Most of our communication efforts are still directed at the 'choir' that is, the ones who are 'already converted'. The constituencies for design have to be strengthened and catchments of users expanded and this can only happen through consistent work by a group of designers and allied professionals over a period of time as ad hoc design interventions sometimes do more harm than good. Several industries typically approach design only when the chips are down, and design is then seen as the 'energy pill' to deliver some punch in the marketplace. It obviously cannot work this way! Design needs to be continuously embraced by the industry with a hunger for innovation to produce substantial results. It needs to be a long term strategy rather than a short time horizon-bound tactic.

The shift from national to global markets has also created consciousness for technological innovations to become more humane. Close relationship between design and business strategy no longer needs any emphasis. In the same way, designers also need to be consciously working in a specific sector for a reasonable length of time to generate visible impact. They have to invest in thorough user research and modern technology tools to convert ideas and concepts into viable products and services. A survey done by NID in 2004 highlighted how almost 50 per cent of practising designers were either not aware of or not using modern tools for product development and innovation. So far as the industry is concerned, several who are beginning to invest in design are mostly enamoured by its glamour value and eye appeal rather than design as a strategic force. Design touches the consumer directly and often intimately. It stirs emotion, unleashes delight and above all, delivers many intangibles which the consumer

The Bajaj-Pulsar.

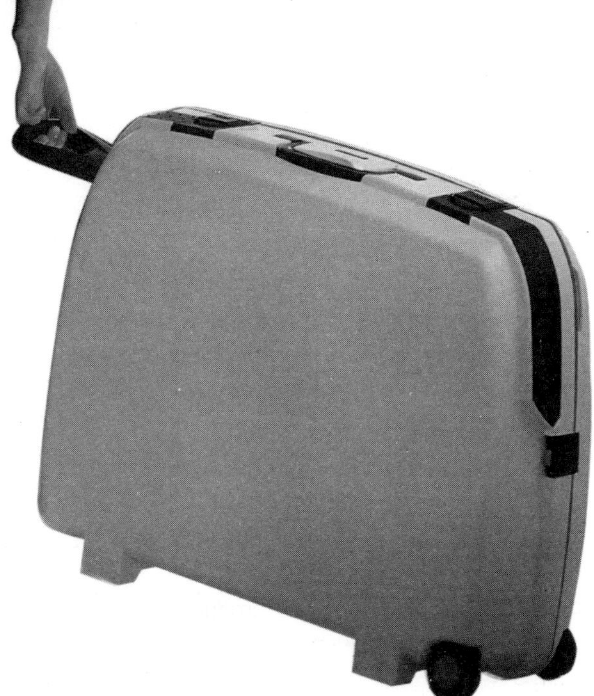

The VIP Elanza.

holds close to heart. In this case, it is not the head which rules the decision but the heart.

The power of design has to be demonstrated continuously and systematically to Indian industry, whether large, medium or small to compete on the design edge. In the case of large industries, it has been observed that several enterprises often resort to import of technology and design. In certain cases some adaptations are carried out in the in-house R&D facilities and as the co-founder of MIT Media Lab, Nicholas Negroponte once said 'Incrementalism is the enemy of innovation' and it is proven correct by such half-hearted adaptations. In such instances, the chances of real breakthroughs become minimal and the customers have to in several cases 'cut the head to fit the hat' so to speak. In the case of SMEs, design can and should play a significant role in creating competitive advantage in the market place, as illustrated earlier. A majority of SMEs fight shy of creating original designs as either their brand building capabilities are insufficient or they have a very high level of risk perception. Whether the unit is small, medium, or large, there is a general lack of understanding of the need for design philosophy and there are huge gaps in comprehending the methodology, processes and flows of design.

In recent years, there have been some great examples of the impact that industrial design has created in several product categories. The Hawkins' Futura, Ventura, Contura pressure cookers and the new product range of Prestige 'Double Decker' gas stoves represent unique innovative approaches. The VIP Elanza range, the Titan Thin Edge line, and Bajaj or TVS' two-wheelers, indicate the arrival of design edge in the Indian market. The Bajaj Pulsar in the two-wheeler category is a good example to elucidate.

Before the introduction of the Pulsar, the Indian motorcycle market trend was towards fuel efficient, small capacity motorcycles (that formed the 80-125 cc class). Bigger machines with higher capacity virtually did not exist (except for Enfield Bullet). The launch and success of other motorcycle manufacturing companies in 1999 showed that there was demand for performance bikes. Bajaj took the cue from there on and launched the Pulsar twins in India on 24 November 2001. The Pulsar excited the Indian youth, mainly due to its muscular shape and stylish designs as well as the powerful engine (in the Indian context) at reasonable fuel efficiency and affordable cost.

In retrospect, the Pulsar actually succeeded in redefining the market trends because since then, the Indian youth began expecting high power and other features from affordable motorcycles. It became the symbol of the sports bike in India which started a new trend and culture amongst bikers in the country.

Talking of automobiles, the indigenous cars made for India, though helped by Italian designs, 'Indica' and 'Indigo' and the Nano from the Tata stable and the proactive use of considerable Indian design in the Sports Utility Vehicles or SUVs like Scorpio and Bolero augur well for India's march towards design-led market leadership. The fact that Nano made it to the cover of *Newsweek* indicates the paradigm shift in so far as innovative design is concerned.

NIDUS, the design shop at NID, conceived and branded by Darlie Koshy with a team of design faculty led by Shimul Mehta, Neelima Hasija and Jitendra Arora.

strategic design

design edge in the creative economy

Originality in creativity is often debated unless it belongs to the bygone eras. In India, for instance, original designs truly existed only in the traditional sectors, which spanned several centuries, like handlooms and handicrafts. As a result, a majority of design interventions during the immediate post-independent period till the economic liberalization of the early 1990s were directed mostly at those sectors. Therefore, in the protected Indian economy, design largely languished as an 'also ran'. Indian companies of the time were at best copying or undertaking reverse engineering for most of the products available in the country.

Economic liberalization initially introduced an atmosphere of fear amongst Indian industry constituents. There were calls for a 'level playing field' from some quarters. The opening up of markets and rule-based world trade regime made it necessary for Indian industry to either 'shape up' or 'ship out'. The manufacturing sector underwent rapid transformation led by sectors like automobiles, two wheelers, light engineering and became lean and robust. A hunger for innovation began to surface in products such as watches, appliances, lifestyle goods, as also in automobiles, two wheelers and a host of others. FMCGs riding on an emergent retail boom also began to look for the design edge. Along with sweeping and rapid technological developments, 'form' began to overtake content in India and design arrived with colours, shapes and new affordances. Even the humble refill pen like Lexi, the ubiquitous Anchor switches and stainless steel products like Art d'nox by Jindal Stainless began to invest in design. An example of this trend, given in the case study below, involving a low unit value product like Lexi pen may throw some light on the early stirrings of design in a number of such products in India. The design project for Lexi was initiated by an NID alumni, Manoj Kothari who runs a leading design and branding studio called Onio Design Pvt Ltd.

THE MARKET

• Fast growing: the number of people buying pens is proportional to the growing rate of literacy
• Fast growth also means cut-throat competition, who have graduated from mould-makers or traders into branded players
• Mass-market means tight price control

DESIGN CHALLENGES

• Design uniqueness
• Visibility of the pen on the shelf
• Trouble-free writing
• The price challenge
• Rapid design cycle

SENSING AND STRATEGIZING FOR THE INDIAN MARKET

• Incremental innovation: continuity of experience, no sudden shocks in product experience
• Utility factors: importance of the clip (identity of pen)
• Auditory feedback as value: the ubiquitous 'click'
• Visual overcoding: needs more saturated colours and bolder fonts
• Packaging: bold but clean (European clean but bold 'Indian')

Paradigm Shift in Economy

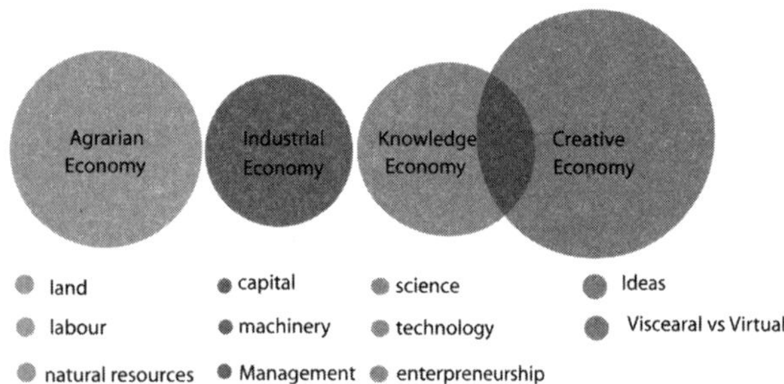

Indian lifestyles have undergone dramatic changes with the onset of 'mobile telephony' and a vibrant electronic media. Connectivity through mobile phones and internet, fast and cheaper air travel, all have begun to impact the daily lives of even the common folks. The economic boom, accelerated by improved infrastructure and an increased pace of urbanization brought in a heightened demand for novelties, better looking products and convenient services at the click of a mouse. The increase in a young working population, considered to be one of the major strengths, along with women as a major work force, transformed both the demographic and psychographic profile of the Indian consumer who now demanded well-designed products. Terms which were unheard of till a decade ago have now become part of popular economic lexicon – 'Double Income No Kids' or DINK families and 'Full Nest Families' who have very high disposable incomes and live either in the fast expanding metropolises or in satellite cities fuelled by the IT culture or outsourcing like Pune, Hyderabad, Gurgoan, Cochin, and Chandigarh. In a way, the demand for designed products has been a result of these trends.

For the layman, the word and concept of design was and is still limited to the fashion industry. Some writers would still argue that the Indian fashion industry is at a nascent stage and taking baby steps but it is today a major force to reckon with as a result of some exceptional work done by designers, educationists and the media in the last decade and a half. The latest trends and fashion began to synchronize with the aspirations and 'feel good-look good' tendencies of the first and second wave of new value consumers of India. Soon, thanks to extensive Page 3 and electronic media coverage, fashion designers became household names and fashion crept into small towns, mofussils and took a big sweep in metropolises. The ordinary shirt and trousers became prêt-a-porter or 'ready to wear' and were then 'morphed' to become formal suits as climate controlled offices and automobiles became easily accessible to Generation X. Young women in smaller towns also became fashion conscious and that showed in the salwar-kameezes, bags or jewellery that they wore to work and for social dos. Therefore, in very simple terms, design to most people in India meant fashion.

Industrial and communication design began to be noticed in this country, only in less than a decade with sustained efforts by leading institutions like NID as also for fashion by the National Institute of Fashion Technology or NIFT, in the late 80s and early 90s. The media has played a key role in the spread of fashion not only in the hip metros but even in the interiors of India. The retail boom began to surface from solo stores to specialty stores and chains, department stores, factory outlets, discount stores, destination shops and malls in the last few years. The organized retail fuelled the need for more branded products and services with consistent standards, quality and design. This led to vitrified tiles being imported from China, Fast Track eyewear coming from Taiwan and Hong Kong to Samsung and LG penetrating deep in white goods and electronic goods from Korea and automobile majors from the West joining the new economy bandwagon in India. Mobile sets unleashed competition between several players like Motorola, Nokia, Sony Ericsson and mobile services ushered in a new 'design democracy' with Vodafone challenging Airtel through value-added mobile telephony. The improved and interesting visual display on screens of computers, mobiles, and hand-held devices have become part of everyday life of a large middle- and upper-middle-class population of India. The teenagers became avid 'screenagers' switching between 'iPods' and 'mobile phone' screens.

'Design Edge' was seen earlier as purely tactical and as a variety and choice creating activity. It was mostly understood at a peripheral level and not as a connection between designs and brands, design and businesses, design and consumer, design and emotions and culture. It is important to understand that design is truly inter-disciplinary and multi-disciplinary. Unlike management and technology which are based on 'analysis', design is about 'synthesis'. The competencies need to be both 'hands on and minds on'.

Some of the recent examples indicate that from the peripheral levels, of colour and form, design is moving through the higher echelons of business strategy. The fields of management and technology have appropriated the word 'innovation' to define the response to an idea driven world. It is very clear that twentieth century was an 'asset-based' era and twenty-first is 'idea-based'. Design is the practical application of creativity in the process of innovation. Creative economy is different from knowledge economy, as the former places premium on ideas and the ability of organizations to bring ideas as products and services to the marketplace at the shortest possible time to create value, wealth and quality of life. However, by and large Indian companies have been generally focussed on 'business strengths' and have been investing heavily only in this area; design strengths have been very weak with hardly any investments in design research to understand cultures, emotions, sensibilities and feelings and, therefore, original Indian designs have also failed to hit the marketplace in adequate numbers.

There is no doubt that technology has indeed been the dominant force in the last part of the twentieth century. But the twenty-first century has proved through the iconic 'iPod of Apple' that contexts are going to redefine products through design and companies advocating design strengths are going to outwit those with only business strengths. 'iPods and iphones' have become the new symbol of strategic design elevating design from a purely skill and competency level to one which has lasting economic value with an equal impact on the emotional retina. Swift by Maruti in India is a good example of how a user-centric approach to design in cars could create a sensational success. The Swift instinctively read the aspirations of the consumers by giving the vehicle a sporty look and married technology and ergonomics efficiently.

As design is contextual, synergizing various aspects which lend a final product excellent quality and shape, it is imperative that designers get global exposure while having strong empathy and insight of local realities. Above all, they should learn to marry business strengths with design to help companies produce successful brands in the marketplace. Titan's foray into design twenty years ago and the quest for original design creation is a good example of a company trying to combine business and design strengths as the following case study on launching ultra-slim watches titled, EDGE initiated by Michael Foley, Tata's former chief creative associate, illustrates:

> When Titan launched a line of ultra-slim watches, a new landmark was created in the watch-making industry. For the first time a company had designed, developed and marketed a range of wrist watches that defied conventional norms of mass manufacture – raising benchmarks for times to come.
>
> This line was appropriately named "EDGE", for its record-breaking slimness. This is a story of great collaborative spirit that challenged the watch making world. An Indian company had created the slimmest watch, on a "mass scale". What was even more striking – this watch could be worn like any other, without hesitating about its water resilience, corrosion or durability! Since its launch, EDGE has stood its ground and has now become synonymous with being a world-class designed product from India.
>
> As a watch designer I had the privilege of being involved in the creation of this unique product line. A product of such magnitude would not have come to life without a very dedicated and 'innovative' research and development team.
>
> Titan has had the good fortune of having the most brilliant minds in the Indian horological industry behind it. It took close to four years to commercialize EDGE through a series of iterative developments each establishing the viability of the whole 'slimming' down process. Every step of the manufacturing process was challenged and trials done to establish the design. The movement (the mechanism that drives a watch) was slimmed down to 1.19 millimetres, a huge breakthrough for the R&D team. The slim movement was then tested for durability and refined until it could be manufactured on a large scale. This created a platform to create a watch that could potentially measure less than 3 millimetres. At this point a call was taken to create a line of very slim watches "without" compromising the product's "water resistance". Water resistance was seen as a very strong functional feature from a user's perspective. The project saw several new benchmarks being created in the course of time: the precision "cold forming" of such a slim watch bezel, grinding of the sapphire crystal, slim yet durable bands, achieving 30-metre water resistance, development of a slim battery, to name a few.
>
> As a product designer it was imperative to articulate the "essence" of slimness from a consumer's perspective. A design language had to be created to bring out the beauty of the slim movement within. Several routes were explored before taking on the final direction incorporating a wedge-like treatment to accentuate the slim silhouette of the product. Each design route was developed as working prototypes to establish viability. "Detail" was the essence of such a line. The beauty of EDGE was in its sensitive treatment of form, functionality and workmanship. EDGE was launched when the 'trend' in the industry was leaning towards bold, heavy sporty products, yet it did successfully primarily due to the intrinsic innovation in the product line. EDGE transcended beyond being a style statement, to a product that instantly gratified consumers with its almost "weightless" experience and timeless design.
>
> The overall design experience in EDGE led to the notion of creating a unified design language for the line. All products designed in the EDGE collection

carry a common "DNA". The design effort extended homogenously beyond the product to the packaging design and store display; thereby building a 'larger than life' experience to the consumer. Today EDGE is a substantial contributor to Titan's top-line, and synonymous to the very best achieved by Titan.

Great design can ultimately achieve a sublime status when consumers recognize the intrinsic value of its innovation. Success for EDGE also came from the great sense of pride it created, of being "Made in India". EDGE has been a great attempt in making an "iconic Indian product".

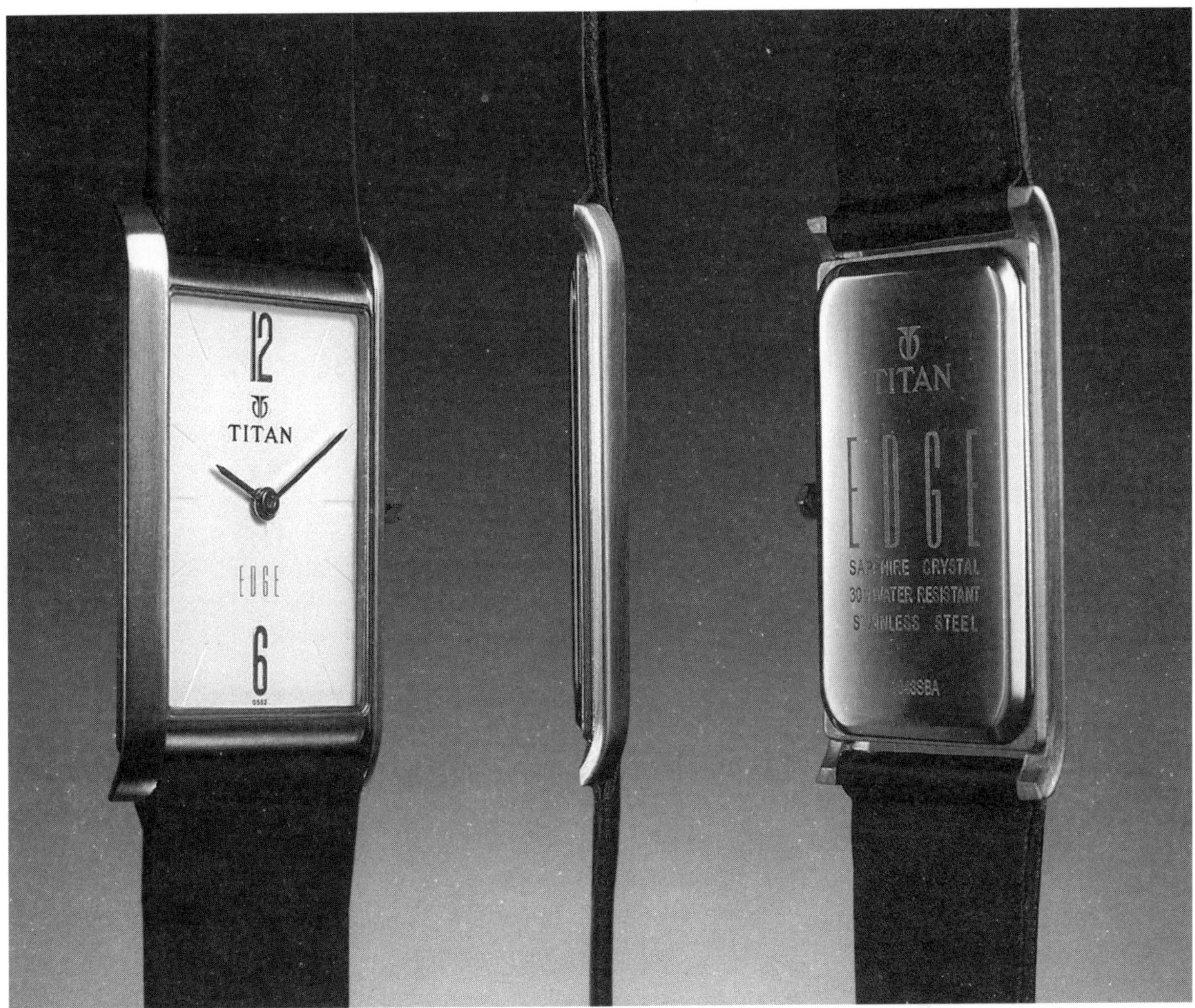

Titan's ultra-slim watches appropriately named 'EDGE' for its record-breaking slimness designed by NID alumnus, Michael Foley for Titan Industries.

design as strategic force

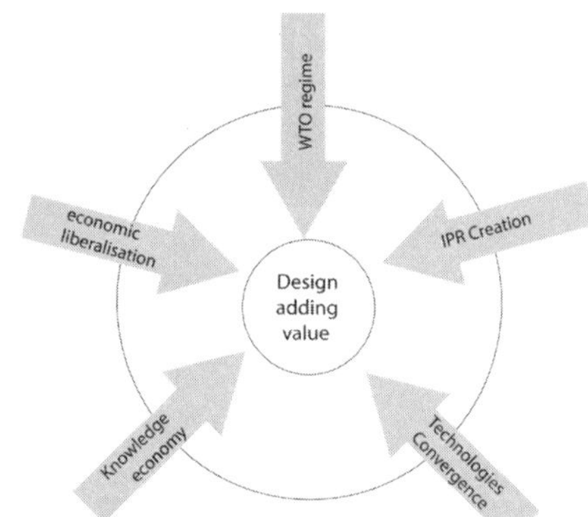

Design in the emerging innovation economy is a 'strategic force'. Strategic design has now gone beyond the narrow definitions to an all-encompassing phenomenon creating waves across consumer landscapes. Design now clearly defines contexts, new problems, conjures up fresh scenarios and through technology and material provides delight and experiences to people.

Yet another critical factor in this entire spectrum is time. The reason: today product obsolescence gets inbuilt at the conception level itself. Knowledge needs to be converted to tangible products or intangible services or else it has little or no use. The mind to market journey has to be fast paced. In China, for instance, a car from mind to market gets ready in just a few months! Afterall, the lifecycles of digital products, mobiles and hand-held devices now border on the 'perishables'. Design has to be conceived quickly and brought to the market at a greater speed. As Narayana Murthy, one of the founders of Infosys, once said: 'Survival and success depends on speed and imagination.'

In the above context, the following diagram illustrates the change in focus.

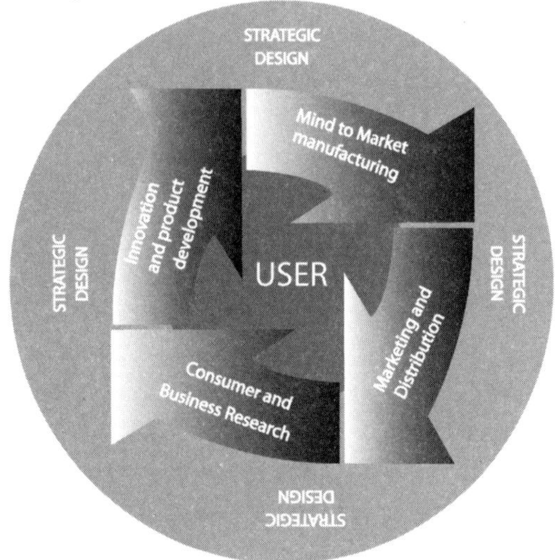

However, various design institutions, design councils and design promotion organizations have different perspectives of design. For instance, institutions across the world, which have tried to combine art and design under one umbrella, have a somewhat different interpretation of design; design is understood in technology oriented departments of design like that of IDC in IIT from an engineering perspective. Yet another approach is a more recent one where design makes an integral connection with innovation as in D-School (Hasso Plattner Design School) in Stanford University, California, USA. The NID is quite different in this regard and has been so right from its inception. The institute has followed the approach to design from a multidisciplinary perspective. The ecosystem which developed around universities like Stanford resulted in the emergence of excellent design consultancies like IDEO and most significantly exerted positive influences on the educational priorities at the university. This is something our educational institutions like the IITs, IIMs, or NID have not adequately addressed or succeeded in so far.

From 1991 when the liberalization process started in India, there has been a blurring of distinctions between tiny, small, medium, large, private and public enterprises with the emergence of either 'competitive', 'non-competitive' or rather 'good' or 'bad' sectors in India. And design is proving to be one of critical factors in showing the way to gain a differential sustainable competitive advantage.

businesses and brands by design

How do you build a brand through design? Well, actually brand and design are almost the same side of a coin. You tell a story via products to consumers and that is how you build the brand through design language. The story, however, is the critical link between brand and design.

Design should ideally help in developing brand personality. When you combine design with communication, you take the story forward and build a strong brand.

Businesses get into consumers' mind-space and live only when they transform themselves to brands. Brands communicate on a continuous basis to customers and those which succeed in staying lead to gaining market share and dominance, and eventually become market leaders. In India, building of brands has not been given adequate attention. This has probably something to do with the fact that technology, management and design could never see eye to eye. Building brands in the short run is not only an expensive proposition but the returns are uncertain as well. But in the long run only brands stay and make sense and wealth.

Design led leadership

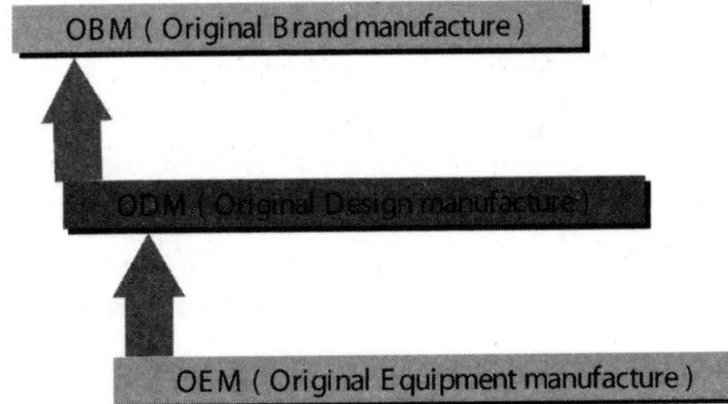

The markets in India, till very recently, were a sellers' market and for most products demand outstripped supply. The 'have money will buy' or rather the consumers seeking variety are the result of the nascent economic boom witnessed in the last decade and there's yet another more evolved set of customers who seek more than just variety but want experience for all the senses.

Design has become the answer for multi-sensory experiences, whether in a luxury retail outlet, entertainment filled domestic air travel or fully stretchable seats in multiplexes or Tata Sky movies delivered at home. Traditional management schools meanwhile have been teaching 'diffusion of innovation', 'product development', 'product lifecycles', 'brand lifecycles' and the STP concepts – segmenting, targeting and positioning – and presume that these would be enough to create successful brand managers. The way the brands, even in the case of multinationals in India, have been managed by some MBAs betray the reality of disconnect between brands and design in India. Consumers' emotions, culture, usability, emotional connections and feelings have not been converted into 'brands' whispers through design by most brands in India and the overwhelming feeling conveyed has been probably just short of 'consumer is a moron' statement. There are of course a select few exceptions. Lack of design consciousness and knowledge are key reasons for the lackadaisical and an artificially hyped up performance of Indian brands. Compared to Italy, Korea, Sweden and Switzerland which have produced outstanding global brands even from SMEs, the record of Indian SMEs and even large companies has been rather dismal.

The Italian luxury and fashion brands which have 27 per cent of the world's market were all started as small enterprises, using the last names of entrepreneurs, and today are global brands. Some examples include Gianfranco Ferré, Guccio Gucci, La Perla, Missoni, Salvatore Ferragamo, Valentino, Versace, Zegna, Bvlgari, and Ferrari. Fulvia Visconti Ferragamo, daughter of the legendary twentieth century Italian footwear designer, Salvatore Ferragamo, in her speech in June 2006 in Milan provides interesting insights into development of brands with the core of the brand being design:

> The story of my father, Salvatore Ferragamo, has already been told by himself in an autobiographical work – *Shoemaker of Dreams* and reads like the story-line of a film, in which the hero embodies a world of values and ideals through which his dream of a lifetime comes true ...
>
> ... My father left us an immense heritage of values and ideals.
>
> In the sphere of the intangible: courage, the value of family relationships, the capacity to act with self-assurance and coherence, passion for work, pride in belonging to the world of Ferragamo, the desire to communicate a lifestyle through our products and services, sensibility and respect for individuals and their needs.
>
> In the sphere of tangible elements: quality, creativity, and innovation.
>
> Over time, the Salvatore Ferragamo brand has jealously guarded and strengthened these values – the values that have achieved such success in the world: the quality of the materials and craftsmanship, imagination and design, by which we mean both creative development and the application of skills handed down with our artisan traditions. Values that people identify with 'Made in Italy', values that made 'Made in Italy' world famous.
>
> Today, the Salvatore Ferragamo Group is a world leader in designing, making and distributing footwear, leather goods, perfumes, accessories and clothing of the finest quality. The group operates in 55 countries and has approximately 2,000 people working for it. Salvatore Ferragamo products are on sale throughout the world in over 450 branded points of sale, of which 221 are directly operated, all located in prestige metropolitan and tourist venues.
>
> The success of Salvatore Ferragamo today is the fruit of integration – between product development and communication designed to consolidate our brand values. Salvatore Ferragamo continues to renew formal codes of elegance by talking directly to consumers. International consumers, not only Italian but American, Japanese, Indian – consumers who appreciate the sober, contemporary elegance of our collections.
>
> All our collections, and especially iconic products like the wedge, the Audrey shoe, the Marisa bag, the jungle foulard, the patchwork prints, are delivered at the same time to over 221 stores in the 55 countries where we operate. The rather glamorously exotic store opening event in Grand Hyatt, Mumbai, sprang from an encounter between the symbols of our brand and those of local culture – coloured silhouettes of animals produced by floral mosaics. A "special guest" at the opening was an elephant painted in the colours of the Fiera line.
>
> Today, India is experiencing a period of very exciting economic and cultural development. India is a market we are focusing strongly on.

Leather sandal with multi-coloured beads. Made by Ferragamo for Maharani Indira Devi of Cooch Behar, 1938.

International brands like Nokia, SAAB, Volvo (Sweden), Samsung and LG (Korea), coming out of rather smaller countries and with much less creative talent and histories as compared to India have made worldwide impact. If you take the example of Korea which is into its third edition of Design Policy, it can be seen that even in a hierarchical and regimented society like theirs, there has been a serious attempt in connecting designs to brands for seeking the new value customers. This is evident in brands like 'Mando climate control', market leaders in Kimchi fridges, which became successful only when refrigerating Kimchi (a Korean traditional delicacy) was given a focus thus connecting culture with design. Other brands soon followed suit and went on to notch up successes. Samsung has nearly 500 designers around the world pushing the envelope of design and technology of their product families and brands. They even have an Art and Design School–SADI to hunt for and develop top-class talent.

In India, on the other hand, businesses seldom seek out talent or support breakthrough research even in top design schools like the NID which is listed as number thirteen, according to *Businessweek*, USA (2006) among the top twenty-five design schools in Asia and Europe. Design is often relegated to be dealt by junior level managers and lower down functionaries. In this context I recall what I said in 2005 at the CII-NID Design Summit in Mumbai, 'When they (the Indian industry) have time, there is no money for design, when they (the Indian industry) have money they have no time for design.' Therefore, engagement with design needs to be continuous and committed over time to produce visible results. This view, of course, is changing in many forward looking organizations. When I scan the Indian market, I find that most of the products, even those labelled Indian, have been designed by overseas designers or design companies. It is obviously not the lack of Indian designers' talent which is necessarily driving Indian companies to seek out design houses elsewhere but it has to do more with how design companies overseas carry out design operations by aligning strategy, brand and design often with the aid of technology. Even a company like IDEO which was carrying out only design projects in the early years had to change gears under Paul Bennett, its head of Consumer Experience Design, to bring strategy and brand into their design process. Most of these companies are able to go just beyond being a creative hot shop to giving breakthrough ideas, to evolve as 'full service' providers which includes ideation, visualization, prototyping, fine-tuning, market testing and branding, The Indian design agencies with the exception of a very few have so far been under the impression that designing one product or a service is limited to form, colour and appearance, and thus do not make serious efforts to link technology and design or management and design by working closely with technologists, engineers and board room decision makers.

The core of a brand is design. The communication of the brand which is the external skin is, of course, what people see as manifestation but even the core, namely the design philosophy, drives the brand whether it is 'Star-Bucks' as a retailer or Alfa Romeo or Lancia, under the FIAT group which have distinct design philosophies and a clear 'design DNA' to drive their brands. Such companies continue to invest heavily in design.

The world over contexts are changing brands and therefore designs. It is not a need or a want which is any longer powerful in the marketing pot-pourri. Contexts have become the key driver of designs and brands. Apple is one company which has understood the context and intrinsic relationship of design and brands very well and realized that although people buy products they view them as experiences. Similarly, their product range though are the results of great technology, the fusion of design aesthetics and technology have created new usability dimensions which drives Apple's design and therefore the brand. The power of design has helped Apple to emerge as a leader in music and entertainment industry. Design has a major challenge, as it has been shown through the examples of Apple's incredible holistic 'designing process' to strive to combine the product and an ecosystem around the products including retail systems to create a great leap forward in designing experiences for the users. This has been a paradigm shift and a 'strategic success by design.'

Despite India's prolific record in generating ideas and thought, it has not been successful in creating a substantial number of brands that capture popular imagination. In addition to a very limited understanding of the process of branding and the lack of design applications in the context of brands and consumers, the problems are more acute now as we have moved from asset-based physical approaches and products to one of virtual or digital realms. For instance, Google has become the new power brand along with Wikipedia and YouTube in the world. Designing has, therefore, shifted from the visceral to virtual and digital. Here also a paradigm shift is taking place and it is not just an accident that Google has replaced Apple from the top slot. It is because Google has not only designed new experiences and more customized options for different users but has also become the symbol of participatory and dynamic branding. If Indian businesses have to discover new markets and growth horizons, the commitment to create brands which represent the aspirations of the consumers has to be firm. If this has to become central to the company as corporate or marketing strategy, they need to learn to use design as a fundamental tool in the process. No wonder some design-friendly management gurus have realized this and Christopher Lorenz, author of *The Design Dimension* was quoted by Tom Peters, world renowned management expert in his book, *The Circle of Innovation*, 'The old weapons for achieving real differentiation have become inadequate. No longer can comparative advantage be sustained for long through lower costs or higher technologies ... The design dimension is no longer an optional part of marketing and corporate strategy but should be at their very core.' Tom Peters elsewhere also said: 'Design is a huge deal not because it makes things beautiful and garners awards, but because in our rapidly changing, customization oriented, service added, software added intangibles-oriented business environment, design is a critical focus for knowing what a product is, what a customer is, and what an organization is.' Seeing the company, products, and services through the 'design viewfinder' is a new approach the Indian business have to learn and if Indian brands have to make an impact globally as 'Designed in India, Made for the World'. A whole new mindset and approach needs to be instilled in the new generation managers and designers who are called upon to guide and navigate businesses and brands.

designing experience

Design is essentially meant to realize a better 'today' and 'tomorrow' for the people. The core of design is the 'user'. If a design succeeds in touching the lives of 'the user – the people' positively, we call it good design. To touch lives, designers and design have to straddle people in three different time horizons at the same time: past, present and future. Since the designers have to respond to the environment and variables around us, design has to remain relevant for today; neither far behind nor far ahead of time. Still, the designer has to traverse the boundaries of time with a crystal ball gaze and bring the future to the current context. Designers necessarily have to depend a great deal on their ability to 'dream' which we call 'visualization'. Their ability to connect different dots and realize their vision into a product, service or experience is the other side of the same coin. The focus is on the process of 'designing', and 'defining a new problem' and seeking a 'creative solution'. There is need to perceive and understand 'designing as a series of iterative processes which sees a tantalizing blurred vision at the end of the tunnel, which the designer pursues with dogged persistence.'

As we have seen earlier a fact that is well-known but still exceedingly fascinating, is India's various art forms

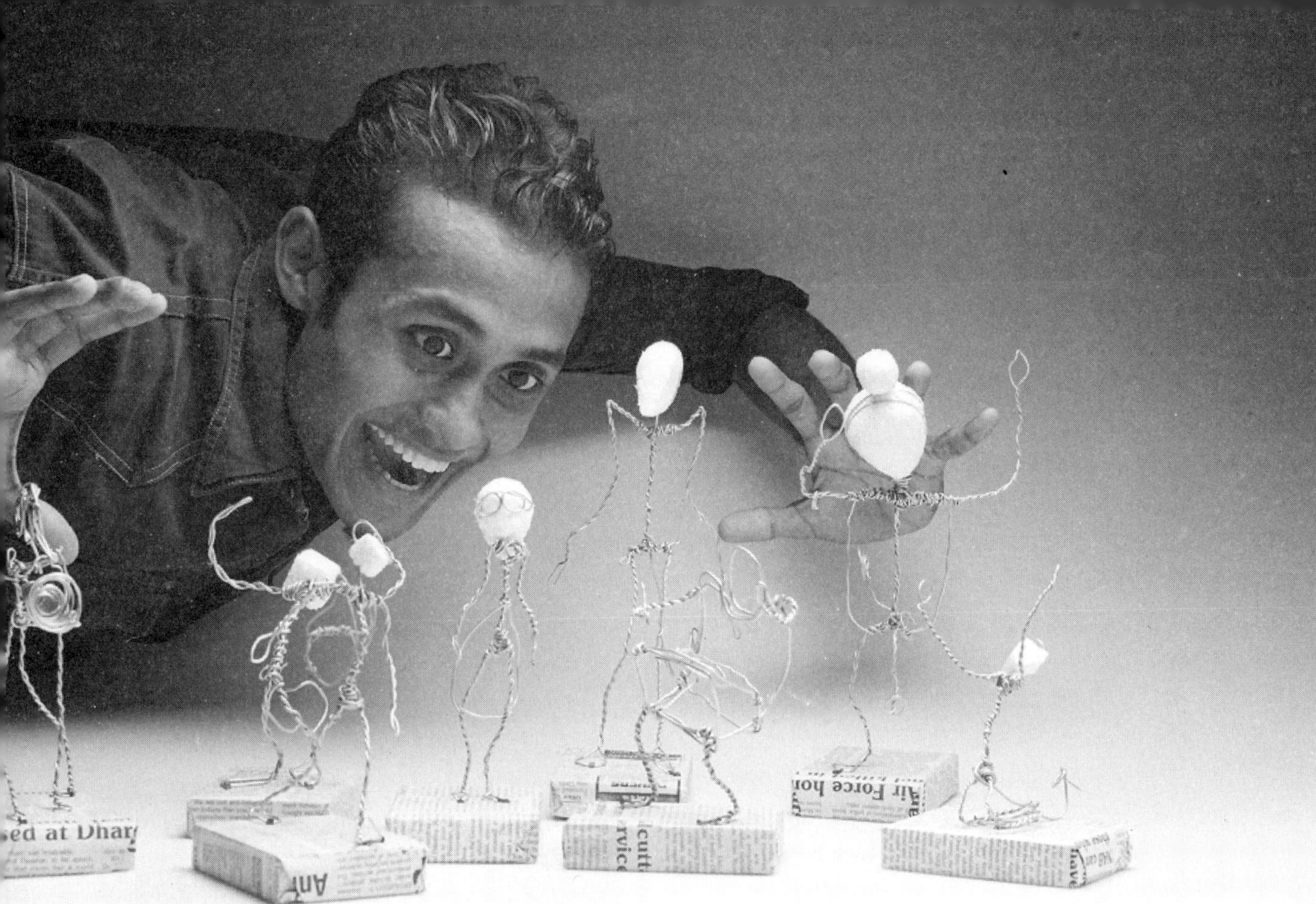

Fascinating world of animation: Vivekananda Roy Ghatak, animating the story.

which have sustained only through several oral traditions prevalent – tales, poems, songs, music and folklore. However, today this capability of 'storytelling' seems to have considerably eroded and has percolated to designers as well, since telling a story about their own designs seems to be hard on them. If Indian designs have to make the desired level of impact nationally and internationally, this ability has to be rediscovered by the Indian design fraternity.

The emergence of 'experience design', combining products and services with experience, is a result of the rapidly changing expectations of the new value customers, whether in India or overseas. For instance, bathing can purely be to remove dirt or bathing can be completely transformed as an activity to an experience through jacuzzi, bubble bath, aromatic foam and large number of shower variations into a complete sensual experience appealing to several senses at the same time. (Luxury hotels make a bathroom part of the bedroom by glassware fittings where one can watch TV while taking a shower.) It is, therefore, necessary to re-discover the 'senses and sensitivity' in greater depth by designers. This will determine the extent to which a designer succeeds in conveying the tangibles and intangibles of his or her designs to the target group.

Do sound management principles and well-researched strategies translate into sound businesses? Yes

A real example of folk art: *Phad* paintings are used for narration and storytelling.

Top left: *Ganjifa* cards are round playing cards of 2-2.5″ diametre with pictures of kings and nobles or icons associated with mythology. *Ganjifa* is derived from the word *ganj* which means money or treasure.

and no. Let us take some examples such as Tupperware, Philips, Nokia, Apple, Toyota, Google and some home companies like Tata Motors, Titan, Mahindra, TVS, and Hero Honda. All these are success stories but not only because of corporate management theories but also because of design strengths which lie mainly in senses, emotions, values, culture, and feelings.

In a vibrant and volatile marketplace, where consumer is the king, manufacturers are shifting the responsibility of design directions to the users directly and are focusing more on engineering and logistics. The consumers in turn are seeking out designers for customization of their aspirations and expressions. This is indeed a key challenge before the new age designers. Participatory and user-centric design increasingly calls for a higher level of interactive visualization and realization on a real time basis with 'real' and 'virtual' people in the loop. Thus a new 'design democracy' is seen to be emerging where the designer not only has to change the rules of designing but has to necessarily wait for the verdict each time. There is a distinct possibility that for a large number of products and services, the designer perhaps will have to chase after both the manufacturers and consumers simultaneously. But as 'nature' and 'culture' both sit in judgement over the designer's actions and outcomes apart from manufacturers and consumers, the future of design and designers get inextricably linked to protecting both. The following case study of Infosys shows how the leading software company of India has developed a proprietary creative problem solving approach:

> When technology and business become commoditized, experience design becomes a key differentiator.
>
> A US-based photo-sharing and print ordering direct-to-consumer website was losing its sheen amidst stiff competition. The site helped people upload photos, store, share, order prints and collect them in a few hours from the nearest store. There are global giants operating in this space and the competition was hot!
>
> The company hired Infosys to address this concern. The team from Infosys' Communication Design Group (CDG) entered the fray and conducted a usability study on the client's photo site and this is what they did.
>
> We benchmarked the photo site with four leading solution providers in this space. Then we ran a heuristic evaluation to understand usability issues. The evaluation was based on current trends, industry standards and best practices. We also conducted an eye tracking study in our labs.
>
> The results were predictable. The photo site fared poorly on all usability indices against competition. Its user satisfaction index was 33.7 per cent lower than the competition. It required 18.8 per cent more clicks, took 72.6 per cent more time to complete simple tasks, and led to 30 times more errors.
>
> Armed with these collective insights drawn from a quick but rigorous evaluation, we set out on the redesign journey. The designers worked closely with the users and the customer teams to nail down usability issues upfront and set priorities. The next four weeks were an action packed thriller ride. Valuable inputs were derived from onsite end-user study and contextual enquiry. Through an iterative design process and multi-disciplinary approach involving users, business teams and technologists, both onsite and offshore, we came out with a fresh design.
>
> The new design, mapped with the users' mental model, looked cool and impressive. But does it fit the bill?
>
> We ran another series of user tests and reviews on the new design. We were all waiting for the results with bated breath and clenched fists. Voila! The results were upbeat. The usability of the new design increased 44 per cent post design. User errors were reduced by 558 per cent. Users were 12 per cent faster and 15 per cent more successful in completing the tasks.
>
> Yet another successful design journey and a delighted customer! We have helped our customer teams take important design decisions based on the data.
>
> For over a decade, the Communication Design Group (CDG) at Infosys is involved in delivering thousands of user experience solutions for large global clients in retail, banking, healthcare, energy, hi-tech, transportation and many other industry verticals. Today, the usability maturity levels among the clients, users, designers, and technologists are rising, setting the bar higher and driving increased sophistication and quality in experience design delivery.

Sridhar Marri, Vice President and Head – Communication Design Group, Infosys elaborated further the design process:

With our user experience design process fully integrated into Infosys' software development lifecycle process, we are able to consistently provide this differentiator advantage to our clients. At a high level, we follow a three-pronged approach. Combined with Infosys' proven Global Delivery Model, this approach helps us converge business, technology and user experience strategies for our clients.

Collective Insights	Iterative Design Process	Multi-disciplinary Approach
Drawing collective insights into user behavior from expert reviews, user testing, user study and contextual enquiry	Achieving consensus among diverse business, technology and user groups with a series of rapid prototypes	Deploying diverse teams of UI designers, content strategists, technical analysts, architects, and project managers to design solutions

With this simple yet effective approach, we are now increasingly focusing on defining user experience strategy for new business opportunities. To illustrate a few, we have helped a global semiconductor giant achieve 1400 per cent ROI for one of their applications.

We have delivered user experiences ranging from field force automation and collaborative web 2.0 portals to information visualization.

We have gained newer insights into handheld experience design through our benchmark study of handheld devices from a Japanese conglomerate and a computer and consumer electronics giant.

We have touched and connected a global community of 80,000 employees through our intranet experience. Nielsen Norman Group (NN/g), pioneers in the field of usability, named it among the 'top ten intranets in the world' in 2007.

Our Communication Design Group has been ranked highest in internal customer satisfaction surveys for four years in a row.

protecting industrial designs

Robert Hayes, the Philip Caldwell Professor of Business Administration at Harvard Business School wrote at the beginning of this century: 'Fifteen years ago, companies competed on price, today it is quality, tomorrow it will be design.' One of the critical aspects of modern trade and commerce under the World Trade Organization framework is that it is driven by Intellectual Property Rights or IPR based global competition. The integrated product development process has become part of design and innovation-driven twenty-first century economy. Minimizing the mind to market time for delivery of the final product has made it necessary for harvesting the benefits of design-related IPR rights.

The entire activity surrounding consumer research, integrated product development, mind to market travel of the product and marketing and distribution is now being assessed and seen from a user-centric perspective through strategic design. The uninspiring number of design registrations from India is a wake-up call, not only to register designs more aggressively but also to derive commercial benefits through more imaginative market development.

A dip-stick study carried out by the NID on the status of IPR protection among design firms showed very clearly that designers find this very cumbersome and the rather unfriendly rules do not help either.

The share-led market dominance is slowly but surely giving way to IPR-led marketing warfares and India needs to be prepared for the slugfest. The following graphic released by the World Intellectual Property Rights or WIPO in April 2006 reveals the trend and China is way

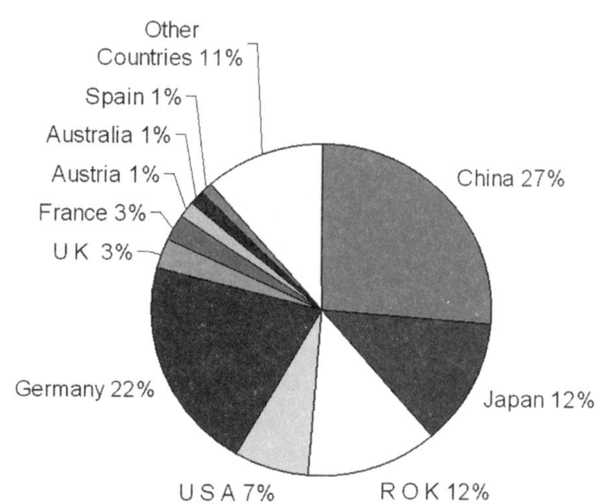

Inferences on Intellectual Property Considerations by Selected Design Practices in India								
Design Hub	Nature of work/ products	How many IP registrations	Facilitating IP protection to client	Handling of IP portfolio at level of firm	Experience of infringement	Difficulties faced	Awareness and of understanding of IP regime affecting designers and suggestions for improvement	Remarks
Ticket Design	Consumer Appliances Lifestyle Accessories Business Models	None on own tie up with clients	Working on royalty model directly with clients. Fixed (5% of Retail Sell) was given in one case	Lump sum project-based arrangements preferred	None	Lack of transparency; delivery time shorter than registration	Overseas client work hampers due to IP anomalies. A simple fast track method like online registration is required. Need to create role models and success stories	Difficult to sell design rights; IP discipline required for young design professionals
Elephant Design	Branding, Communication Design	None so far	Sending reminder to register the work with consent	Don't know how!	Big corporates took away concepts and didn't turn back	IPR being attached to legal profession; Not enough awareness	Focus should be on how to make it work for SME's rather than what is IPR & how to protect. Small case studies need to be generated and documented	IPR field is neglected so far in practice
Quetzel	Furniture Design	None but many NDA's have 250 products in pipeline	Suggest and facilitate wherever required. Some of the customized designs are not required to be registered	Design manager takes care of IP issues. Product line divided in groups for easy classification	Past employee copied designs. Polo chair design has been copied by many	End up spending a lot of time and money	Make IP laws more enforceable. new products and making old ones obsolete	Have more awareness through workshops/ seminars/ newsletters etc

ahead in the game with 27 per cent followed by Germany, Korea and Japan.

The significance of IPR is well illustrated by the case study of Ravi Sawhney, a designer with almost two decades of international experience. Sawhney who lives and works in the US decided to protect his intellectual property under various heads such as:

- Utility Patent
- Inventions/Innovations
- Design Patents
- Copyright/Trade Marks obtained
- Non-Disclosures signed in both directions

Ravi Sawhney at the CII-NID Design Summit and said how he uses all possible forms of IPR to get maximum protection and employs a 'bunch of grapes' approach to register many design variations of the same design as protection against possible violations by competitors.

Industrial design is one of the categories of IPR where the design system focuses on the aesthetic feature of an article derived from its visual appearance. Relevant aspects are the shape, configuration, surface pattern, colour, line or a combination thereof as applied to an article which produces an aesthetic impression on the sense of sight.

- It is heartening that the definition of "design" under the Designs Act 2000 has been widened, thus offering more coverage and traction.
- Under the previous law, design registration was granted only for the visual appearance of an article which included shape, configuration pattern and ornamentation whether in two or three dimensions.
- Under the revised Designs Act 2000, a design registration can now be obtained for new or original features of shape, configuration pattern, ornamentation or composition of lines or colours as applied to an article, whether in two or three dimensions or both.
- A concept of "absolute novelty" has been introduced whereby a "novelty" would now be judged based on prior publication of an article not only in India but also in other countries.

Under the previous law, the position was ambiguous. Key manufacturers like Titan, Apple USA and Herman Miller are clearly using strategic design in their approach and for them to develop a system for design registration becomes critical for survival and growth in the competitive global economy.

Obviously design is much more complex than what the law states, but one key aspect of design is that it enables a product to differentiate.

Symphony is one Indian company which is creating competitive advantage through design protection and the statistics below reveal how the company uses design trademark, patent and copyright as a composite approach in managing the intellectual property.

Here, the approach is to use all the pillars of IPR for driving the competitive advantage.

IPR filed for	Total applications
Design	38
Trade Mark	93
Patent	18
Copyright	01
Total	**150**

The case study of renowned textile and fashion designer, Ritu Kumar throws some light on the struggle a designer has to undergo to protect her designs and the fact that even after it is granted how difficult it is to get the benefits given the poor deterrence and rather indifferent law enforcement systems.

However, the case clearly indicates that designers need to engage in proactive protection of their designs for a culture of protecting IPR in the country. Design institutes have even a greater problem on hand and NID was one of the first institutes to initiate a detailed policy guideline on IPR issues and laid down a methodology in dealing with them in a community of faculty members, students, IPR creators and users.

In the case of the research chairs and collaborative work with other institutes as in the case of Institute of Plasma Research where the IPR is held jointly. Similarly 'spin-off' products which are part of a research process but when taken up for commercial application like in the case of furniture products of Jindal Stainless Steel Research Chair taken up by Art d'nox and high altitude clothing under the John Bissell Chair taken up by S. Kumars' or the garment hangers taken up by Foley Designs call for royalty agreements and non-exclusive IPR rights to the marketing or distribution channels. While this is the experience of a premier design institute like the NID which engages in many emerging issues in IPR portfolio management, there is even a greater difficulty for commercializing the IPR.

From cars to consumer electronics, the design, shape

RITU KUMAR: Fashion Designer

For the first time in India, the fashion industry has used the design protection tools to safeguard their interests related to new designs. Renowned fashion designer Ritu Kumar has filed a suit against firms in Calcutta for reproducing, printing, publishing and distributing her fabric designs with a commercial motive. This is for the first time that a designer has enforced existing laws.

Ritu's designs are probably the most copied, in fabric, cut and embroidery. Says the designer, 'Going to the court was probably an aggressive step to take, but I am glad I did it. Probably this is the only way to stop easy forgeries.'

Ritu Kumar adds, 'The individual or company which copies, picks up the best of a designer's end-results, they have no expenses for designing and take advantage of the market response to the designer by pirating the design. This is extremely disturbing and one of the reasons why a number of very talented designers do not show their work in India. Today, in India, copyright laws exist and are being looked at with great sensitivity to the issue. We hope to see a similar situation soon that exists in the Western countries in India too.'

Symphony

CAUTION NOTICE UNDER THE DESIGN ACT 2000

h!COOL

Under the instructions from our clients SYMPHONY COMFORT SYSTEMS LTD., A Company incorporated under the Companies Act 1956 having its Registered Office at 'Sanskrut', Old High Court Road, Navrangpura, Ahmedabad 380 009, the Exclusive licensee of the Registered Design No. 194305 in Class 23-04 in respect of 'AIR COOLER', the front view of which is reproduced aside hereby caution that :-

The design aside has been originated and created by the proprietor Achal A. Bakeri, which is having novelty in all respect.

Our clients being the exclusive licensee have been manufacturing and marketing AIR COOLERS bearing the registered design under the trade mark '**h!COOL**'.

As a result of the statutory rights conferred upon the registered proprietor by virtue of the aforesaid registration and the exclusive licence granted in favour of our clients, our clients are entitled to manufacture and/or market AIR COOLERS bearing the registered design.

All general public and others concerned are hereby advised to restrain from any unauthorised manufacture and sales of AIR COOLERS identical to AIR COOLER registered under design No.194305.

Our clients hereby warn the public at large and the unauthorised seller/distributors/agents/retailers from manufacturing and marketing the aforesaid AIR COOLER illegally. Our clients shall take deterrent civil as well as criminal legal action if any unauthorised manufacturing and/or marketing of AIR COOLERS, uses identical with or which is an obvious or fraudulent imitation of client's registered design No.194305 under the Design Act.

This notice is given in public interest so that innocent distributors/retailers/agents do not involve themselves in any illegal activity.

Ahmedabad
Date : 20th February 2006
TRADESAFE, Advocates and Attorneys,
9, Shrinagar Society, Near Golden Tirangle,
Opp. Sardar Patel Stadium,
Ahmedabad 380 014 (Gujarat)
Phone No. : 079-26463000

RAJENDRA R. RAVAL
Advocate

and mould of products distinguishes one from the other. With competition hotting up, there is a need to have proactive design protection strategies. However, the number of design applications in India show a healthy trend upwards in recent years due to the modernization of IPR-related systems and infrastructure in the country.

IPR AND DESIGN

As discussed and illustrated so far, Intellectual Property Rights play a critical role in the success of innovative designs in the market place. Although strong IP rights provide competitive advantages, they also present infringement risks when owned by others. Even great designs may fail commercially in the marketplace if IP opportunities and risks are overlooked. Late IP review, for instance, can compromise protection, mandate last-minute design changes, and create unanticipated infringement risks – failures that are painful to accept after developing an otherwise successful design. But what rights do our laws actually provide? Which design features can we protect to

IPR POLICY IN DESIGN EDUCATIONAL INSTITUTES
CASE STUDY OF NID

IPR guidelines at NID support students, faculty and staff in identifying, protecting and administering intellectual property matters.

The Policy Guidelines:

- Define the **rights and responsibilities** of all involved
- Establish **support mechanisms** to facilitate the processes of IP protection
- Provide guidelines as to how **income generated from IP be distributed** between the Institute, creator and owner
- Assist external organisations by providing clear processes for intellectual property exploitation and thus **facilitate collaborative research and knowledge transfer** between the Institute and commercial and other organisations
- Facilitate team and joint efforts
- **Encourage and foster a culture of innovation and creativity**
- **Facilitate and provide clear-cut guidelines** with respect to various IP-related issues.

create valuable competitive advantages in the marketplace? And how can we best secure comprehensive design protection while avoiding the design rights of others? These are questions of critical importance. Uniqueness is often achieved through strong intellectual property protection. The problem that arises with 'innovations by design' or 'concept-based innovations' is that they are very difficult to protect against imitation.

The unsatisfactory state of IPR protection by practising designers and design firms clearly point towards the fact that while promoting designs, we need to learn real fast to protect designs so that the innovator, designer and design-led companies get clear advantages. The government has, of course, taken many steps including the revamping of the Designs Act 1911 with the new Designs Act of 2000 and also introduced Suegneris, a Geographical Indication Registration Act. It has also modernized the Patent, Design, Trade Mark and Geographical Indication registry offices across the country by computerizing their operations through user-friendly systems.

A fact that there is a low level of awareness in India about design protection needs no reiteration. Consider this: in 2006-07, only 5,372 applications were filed with the Controller General of Patents, Designs and Trademark. However, the silver lining is that this is a sharp rise from the 2,874 applications filed in 1999-2000 when the new design act was finalized. These numbers are still very small for a country of India's size.

In the emerging scenario for the Indian industry, new design consultancies and design-led projects, a great deal of attention has to be paid to proactive registration of designs and patents. Conversion of technologies and ideas in the minimum possible time to products and services and then registering patents and designs, to fight the battle in the marketplace has become an imperative strategy. The long time cycles required for market research, search for technologies, developing prototypes, market testing, fine-tuning and then launching the product in the marketplace have all become time and cost intensive in today's world of intense competition. The concurrent activities of product development, market testing, including future proofing have become the order of the day. From 'mind to market' the time cycles have come down drastically. Here, several competing countries are scoring over India apart from the proliferation of protected design innovations into the Indian market. Designers and captains of industry need to ponder over more aggressive strategies in this regard.

IPR registered images and designs of faculty and students at NID. Right: Flick, a novel matchbox created for hotels by NID student Aditya Vikram Sengupta.

Below: LPG stove designed by NID graduate Sushant Jena guided by Gaurang Shah and Pradyumna Vyas.

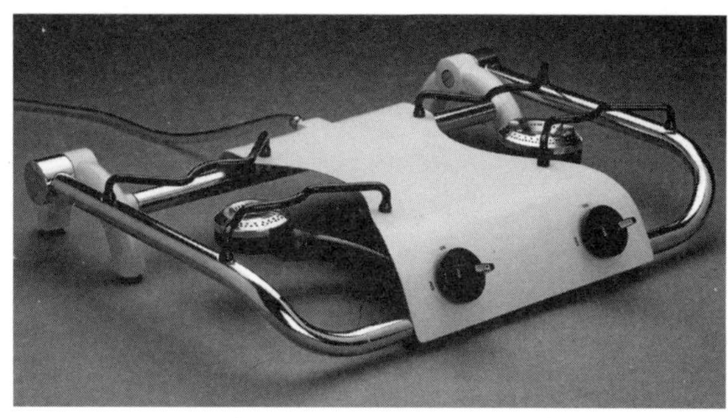

Year	1999-2000	2000-01	2001-02	2002-03	2003-04	2004-05	2005-06	2006-07
Filed	2874	3207	3350	3124	3357	40017	4603	5372
Examined	2067	3207	3480	3124	3228	4017	4400	5179
Registererd	1382	2430	2426	2364	2547	3728	2852	4431

Year	1996-97	1997-98	1998-99	1999-00	2000-01	2001-02	2002-03	2003-04	2004-05	2005-06	2006-07
Patents	907	1844	1800	1881	1318	1591	1379	2469	1911	4320	7359
Designs	1765	1879	2219	1382	2430	2426	2364	2547	3728	2852	4431
Trademark	4686	4120	5300	8010	14202	6204	11190	397662	45015	184325	109361

design and the city

Twentieth century was the age of nations and twenty-first century is seen as the age of cities. Competition has intensified between specific cities of different countries. Richard Florida, in *Rise of Creative Class* has attributed the emergence of creative cities to a combination of talent, tolerance and technology. Many a city in India can lay claim to being a creative city but surprisingly even Bengaluru despite its best chance has not done much to position itself in this respect. India is slated to have 55 per cent of its population living in urban centres by 2050 against 30 per cent as of now. The Mega Cities Association in collaboration with Jawaharlal Nehru Urban Renewal Mission, Government of India has published a very important document *Mega Cities: Poised for Change* which summarizes the leading practices of 2007 indicating that several Indian cities are aspiring to change for the better. However, the projects listed are infrastructure or process oriented rather than of a leapfrogging vision to integrate design and innovation to emerge as a global city.

The leading practices from mega cities in india for instance, lists projects such as development of Sabarmati river front in Ahmedabad, automated parking system in Bengaluru, and solid waste management in Delhi. The Indian cities, even at the current pace of urbanization, are becoming unliveable because of spread of urban slums, traffic jams, serious water/power shortages, pollution, increasing crime, crumbling urban infrastructure et al. Protection of rivers, lakes and water bodies in cities, sanitation and availability of water have become pressing issues in many Indian cities. Several cities have no convention centres, sports, culture or arts hubs which enable 'good' sensitive life in the long run. Our cities are struggling with basic survival issues and developing a larger vision like positioning as a creative or design city has received scant attention. Design is about 'creating a difference that creates a difference' and cities need to do that to achieve a distinct mind space! Time has come for urban planners, architects, artists, designers and conscious citizens to takeup leadership role to positively influence an exciting vision for the future. Let us look at some of the internationally inspiring stories how cities are shaping up in the Innovation Economy of the twenty-first century. The city of Montreal in Canada had put up a tough fight to win the bid for the headquarters of world bodies of industrial and communication design, five years ago, so that design can influence the positioning of the city in the world arena. Today the headquarters of the three world design organizations, ICSID, Icograda and IFI are in Montreal being supported by the city for ten years. Singapore won the bid for holding Design Congress in 2009 and is in the midst of a major makeover with over a dozen iconic architectural projects. Taiwan's bid to hold the Industrial Design Alliance (IDA) Congress in 2010 has succeeded against neck to neck competition with Melbourne. Seoul won the battle for 2010 World Design Capital title against twenty other competing cities. Many Western and even Southeast Asian countries have understood the role of design for shaping and positioning their cities. Torino, the ICSID designated World Design Capital, in Italy for 2008-10 is launching its rollout through a series of events from November 2008. The World Design Capital (WDC) team in Torino has raised over 13 million euros in a short span of time and has planned a series of high profile events and activities. A city like Torino, which was dying after the industrial era signalled its end, has embraced design to turn around its fortunes.

The World Body of Design ICSID has selected Seoul as the next design capital after Torino for 2010-12. Recently, in Seoul, the ground-breaking ceremony for the Dongdaemoon World Design Plaza being designed by Zaha Hadid took place. 'Seoul Metropolitan government is ever more committed to promote the use of design in order for Seoul to be more environment and citizen friendly ... with the aim to bringing in development in many areas of economy and life through the use of design', says the visionary mayor of Seoul. The mayor has launched the first 'Seoul Design Olympiad 2008' with the theme 'Design is Air' indicating the shift from twentieth century which was riveted on 'Earth'. Under the leadership of the current president who was then the mayor of Seoul took a major step in 2003 to rejuvenate a natural stream which was dead and covered up to be used as a housing site, rail and highways during the early 1910s and 20s. The rivulet called, Cheong-gye-cheon, in the heart of Seoul stretching over four kilometers, was opened after restoration to public in 2005. Today it has become the heart and soul of Seoul, being projected as the soul of Asia!

In several other countries many urban development or city projects are changing the faces of cities through major design interventions. Berlin for the last few years, has been rejigging its position by creating new city squares, setting up museums like Judisches Museum (designed by Daniel Libeskind), and has succeeded in attracting artists, designers and other creative people in droves. The striking example of how Guggenheim Museum, deigned by Frank O. Gehry, has changed Bilbao, a decadent industrial city in Spain indicate how cities can be transformed by major design-driven projects. The DOT (Design of the Times).77 project in north-east England now in progress overseen by the UK Design Council, is yet another futuristic example of participatory design. St Etienne, a city in France, has an interesting 'Quality of Life' project as envisioned by Le Corbusier in Firminy thirty years ago brought to life again in recent times by a determined city government. A massive plan is underway for setting up a design centre designed by architect Finn Giepel. The industrial sheds of the erstwhile steel city are being transformed as major galleries. The ESAD, the Design School in St Etienne is playing a crucial role in driving the 'Design City' project which marries culture, architecture and design education into one trajectory.

In India, Ahmedabad the host city of NID, IIM, and CEPT which has been mentioned by Charles Landry as a Creative City; Pune and Bengaluru which are emerging as R&D capitals alongwith Kolkata, Delhi and Mumbai have the potential in different ways of leveraging design to improve the quality of life of its people. The way the Rajiv Chowk gardens have been restored by Delhi Metro and the manner in which the whole project is being implemented is definitely a good example in India. After being inspired by a visit sometime around 2005 to Beijing and the way the students of Beijing Institute of Technology and several design firms have been involved in preparing for the 2008 Olympics, NID had made presentations to the powers that be in Delhi offering people-friendly design interventions for Commonwealth Games 2010. Because of the multitude of agencies involved in decision making, the proposal fell on deaf years. Bengaluru is yet another example of a city which can truly be transformed to become a Creative or Design city but has chosen to remain static without any long term vision and purposive collective action. Development of cities are most often left to multitudes of committees and commissions and it is well said 'a donkey is a horse designed by a committee'. Several projects around us which have become eyesores or visual clutter are speaking examples. Our cities have to wake up to seize the opportunity of using design and innovation to improve quality of life of its people. Unified action is the need of the hour. The earlier, the better. The Indian cities need to 'take people seriously' and stand out as memorable and aesthetically satisfying experiences to find a place in the hall of fame of vibrant cities of the emerging creative economy.

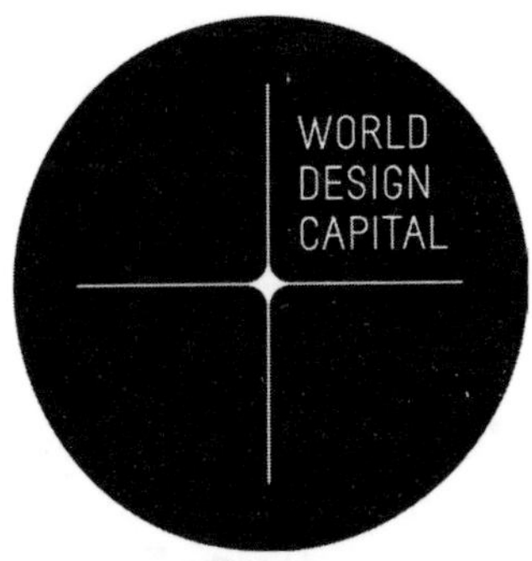

sectoral growth by design

designing growth:
retail, textiles and apparel,
gems and jewellery,
leather, animation and
transportation

India is going through a period of rapid economic growth and the key indicators being the manufacturing and service sectors are both on an upsurge contributing to the overall economic well-being of India. Major segments like retail, textiles and apparel, gems and jewellery, leather, transportation, the new engines of growth are all pushing for original designs and even innovations.

Retail is becoming India's new mantra embracing aspiration of the youth and encompassing new India's way of life. Just a few years ago, there were apprehensions whether India is ready to go full hog into rapid expansion of organized retail. However, organized retailing has already touched 2-3 per cent and is likely to leapfrog to 9-10 per cent by 2015. The consumer finance boom and the changing pattern in rural consumption, have affected retail and the Global Retail Index has given India top ranking in recent years. A joint report by McKinsey and the Confederation of Indian Industry (CII) has pegged the total Indian retail market at 180 billion US dollars which is growing at a steady rate of 11-12 per cent accounting for around 10 per cent of the country's GDP.

Textiles also represent a leading sector of the Indian economy in terms of value of production, exports and employment. This sector has a high potential for growth taking into consideration the availability of raw material, low labour cost and growing markets for textile products. According to a background paper presented by the Ministry of Textiles in 2007, following the elimination of quota restrictions in January 2005, the global textiles and clothing industry which is already touching 480 billion dollars is expected to grow to about 700 billion by the year 2012 just under seven years from the expiry of Multi-

EMERGING ORGANISED RETAILING IN INDIA

INDIA RETAIL: 2006 ***(at current prices)***

Retail Segments	INDIAN RETAIL MARKET 2006*		
	India Retail Value (Rs.Crore)	Organised Retail (Rs.Crore)	%Organised in 2006
Clothing, Textiles & Fashion Accessories	113,500	21,400	18.9%
Jewellery	60,200	1,680	2.8%
Watches	3,950	1,800	45.6%
Footwear	13,750	5,200	37.8%
Health & Beauty Care Services	3,800	400	10.6%
Pharmaceuticals	42,200	1,100	2.6%
Consumer Durables, Home Appliances/equipments	48,100	5,000	10.4%
Mobile handsets. Accessories & Services	21,650	1,740	8.0%
Furnishings, Utensils, Furniture-Home & Office	40,650	3,700	9.1%
Food & Grocery	743,900	5,800	0.8%
Catering Services (F & B)	57,000	3,940	6.9%
Books, Music & Gifts	13,300	1,680	12.6%
Entertainment	38,000	1,560	4.1%
TOTAL	1,200,000	55,000	4.6%
	1200000	54999.6	
	USD 270 Billion	USD 12.4 Billion	

©IMAGES F&R Research

* Quick estimates

Load carrier: Carrying load on head, back and as trolley made of bamboo designed by industrial design faculty, Vikram Panchal.

Fibre Arrangement (MFA). Yet another important aspect is the role of high fashion and apparel from India which are gaining a respectable share of the global fashion space. The tremendous potential in the 'Fibre to Fashion' value chain can be realized by leveraging India's natural advantages of a rich heritage of designs and the creative talent pool which is increasingly facing shortages apart from rising costs. The timely setting up of NIFT in late 80s and ATDC in mid 90s by the Ministry of Textiles, Government of India have certainly helped to mitigate the talent crunch to some extent in this sector as exports have grown manifold in the last twenty years. The textile, apparel and accessory designs can provide us a great source of competitive advantage given the inherent strengths of India. This will help India emerge as the fashion hub of the world, benefitting all constituents of the Indian textile, fashion and lifestyle accessory industries. I have repeatedly argued for the need to become a leader in the global textiles and clothing industry instead of being a generic producer and follower of trends and directions. It is better to be positioned as a creative manufacturer of textiles and apparels than just be a 'production factory' to the world like China. The role of designers could have been much more positive if there were strong linkages between markets and designers instead of fashion designers assuming a 'demigod' position and being only excited about the Page 3 appearances and the hullabaloo surrounding fashion shows.

The gems and jewellery industry has also shown remarkable success as an export-oriented industry in India. The exports of gems and jewellery have shown a buoyant growth rate of 28.6 per cent and the industry is targeting to achieve 65 per cent of the international market by 2010.

An industry which occupies a place of prominence in the Indian economy, in view of its massive potential for employment, growth and export is leather. This sector needs to be repositioned in the emerging context (see case study: Repositioning of Leather Goods by Design). The leather industry with an output of 4 billion US dollars and exports worth 13 billion ranks third after China and Italy. Interestingly, this industry employs approximately 2.5 million people, of which 30 per cent are women. The small-scale sector does a large part (nearly 60-65 per cent) of the production and they are now targeting to grow exports from the present size of 2.4 billion dollars to over 5 billion dollars by 2010.

Another big opportunity is to design and promote luxury and lifestyle products. India as a country has had always a better understanding of luxury from the point of view of hedonism and highly extravagant lifestyles. In many instances, the experience of luxury in the 'Mughal' era went beyond the understanding of ordinary mortals.

Traditional jewellery theme pavilion at IIJS 2006 set up by NID.

However, India needs to discover this sensory and hedonist understanding to emerge as a serious player in luxury and lifestyle products. The case study separately provided throws light on this important area for design play.

As has been argued by several experts time and time again, in the context of an emerging market economy in India it is imperative to strengthen the basic infrastructure facilities in the country. Transportation is one of the most important links towards this end. The Indian automobile industry has grown at an impressive rate of 17 per cent on an average in the last few years and the opportunity landscape for the Indian auto industry would encompass manufacture of vehicles and components for domestic sales and exports. By 2016, India is slated to emerge as the world's seventh largest car producer (as compared to the eleventh largest currently) and retain the fourth position in world truck manufacturing sector. By this year, it is also expected that the automotive sector would double its contribution to the country's GDP from current levels of 5 per cent to 10 per cent. Its contribution to the manufacturing sector would rise to 30-35 per cent from the current level of 17 per cent and the Automotive Mission Plan 2016 as unveiled by the Government of India aims at doubling the contribution of automotive sector in GDP by taking the turnover to 145 billion US dollars in less than a decade. The vision of the Automotive Mission Plan 2000-16 is 'to emerge as the destination of choice in the world of design and manufacturing of automobiles and auto components with output reaching a level of 145 billion US dollars accounting for more than 10 per cent of the GDP and providing additional development to 25 million by 2016.'

These are few of the new growth engines of the surging Indian economy and leapfrogging by each of these segments can have a considerable impact on employment and growth. These segments and more offer great opportunities for design and innovation and the high growth sectors need to leverage sustainable competitive advantage through the design edge.

A CASE STUDY:
Repositioning of Leather Goods by Design

Material resources of a society automatically impacts design evolution and successful designs constantly embrace new materials while updating existing materials. Leather is a very versatile and emotionally vibrant material crying to be repositioned in order to capture the imagination of the youth market which drives fashions.

Creative industries will certainly succeed in the twenty-first century with technology making it possible for realizing the desires through a combination of communication and interactive media technologies. Generally, creative industries thrive in new contexts and lifestyles with boundaries blurring and collapsing all the time. Different natural and humanmade materials like clay, wood, textiles, metal, plastics, leather form the base for creative explorations connecting consumers to crafts and designs.

For instance, if leather is connected to a lifestyle and a certain image like the 'bike and leather jacket' as was in the US, then there is every possibility of leather becoming successful and more in demand than just focusing on the material. If stainless steel signifies cleanliness and hygiene, it sells better not because it is just stainless steel. Design has to connect to culture, emotions and senses. Leather as a material is one of the oldest the humankind has known and hence it is one of the 'skins of culture' itself.

What's beautiful about this material is that it simultaneously connects both to the rural landscape as well as the world of luxury. In the former from the practical point of view of providing employment and livelihood, while in the latter as a critical element whether for automobiles, home interiors or lifestyle accessories. If we glance at the rural areas we find different types of leather products linked both to the economy and socio-cultural milieu:

- The Kolhapuri *chappals* of Maharashtra.
- The *mojdis* of Rajathan; a state also known for its decoration items.

- Bikaner and Jaisalmer produce decorative saddles for horses and camels and also a particular type of leather bottle called *kopi* made of camel hide.
- Rajasthan is also known for beautiful lamps and lampshades made from leather.
- West Bengal especially Shantiniketan since Rabindranath Tagore's times has been famous for decorative leather items.
- Kashmir is known for ornamental leather products.
- Hoshiarpur in Punjab uses leather pieces extensively in appliqué work.
- Madhya Pradesh is famous for embroidered leather items.
- Karnataka has been noted for gold and silver painted leather products.
- Andhra Pradesh is known for leather puppets.

An indepth study of such leather crafts and the related traditions can provide inputs on many techniques and features which can help to make breakthrough innovations leading to IPR. Despite such a vast variety of leather products, what is most glaring is that geographical indications based leather craft products are next to non-existent except 'Kolhapuri' *chappals* from Maharasthra.

Leather crafts can be positioned more aggressively through Geographical Indication based uniqueness, for global marketing and premium value realization particularly when India happens to be the third largest producer of leather in the world after China and Italy. However, what is surprising is that the market share of India in the global leather industry is just around 2.5 per cent. Out of the combined pool of leather products made in India, footwear amounts to 36 per cent, followed by leather accessories at 26 per cent, finished leather at 24 per cent and leather garments which is only about 14 per cent. The unit value realization is also not up to the mark as is expected from a 'creative manufacturer of leather'. The reason: despite world's 10 per cent of raw materials coming from India that also boasts of a number of qualified leather technologists, there is an acute shortage of creative talent especially designers and merchandisers dedicated to this sector.

Left: Kolhapuri *chappals* or handcrafted leather sandals, get their name from the place of their origin, the district of Kolhapur in Maharashtra.

Below: The *mojdis* of Rajasthan, a state known for its decorated leather items. Rajasthan has a long history in leather craft and industry and leather shoes known as *jootis* or *mojdis* are made in Jaipur and Jodhpur.

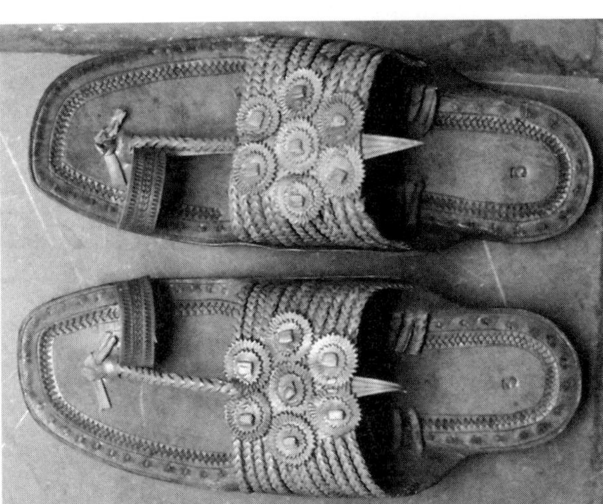

Beautiful leather embroidery and appliqué of Gujarat: The artisans of Bhuj create the most strikingly vibrant leather panels using multicoloured threads, mirrors and cotton cloth.

However, the situation is far from grim. Let us not forget that the leather industry provides over 15 per cent of the total sourcing by leading global brands, including luxury brands in footwear, garments, leather goods and accessories. There are many factories in India meeting the international compliance standards; tanneries are undergoing rapid modernization and integrated leather complexes are coming up. Therefore, there is now a conducive environment for designs and brands to grow and even international brands to enter the market. However as a twist in a happy tale, the right design talent has not been available and those available are not fully exploited.

Like other material resources, leather has to look at contextual and concept based new products and understand the new meaning of 'lifestyles and luxury'. New products of combination materials for affordability need to be looked at for tapping India's huge mass markets, and particularly, for capturing the attention of the youth. There is no doubt that India produces world-class leather goods but customer care for leather is very poor in the country. There needs to be service centres for leather products established as common facilities by the industry if the leather culture has to permeate. As nano, plasma and other new futuristic technologies make their forays to alter the manufacturing scenario, the leather sector needs to brace itself to avoid even wet processing and move into a new orbit. Also devoid of breakthrough innovations, there would not be original intellectual property and in its absence we will remain a copy cat. Innovations like 'creative leather' as in Italy which uses Italian split leather for many products with short fashion lifecycles need to be studied in depth and if required emulated to attract Generation Next.

NID in association with the Central Leather Research Institute (CLRI) and Council for Leather Exports (CLE)

BLUE PRINT FOR LEATHER DESIGN INNOVATION CENTRE

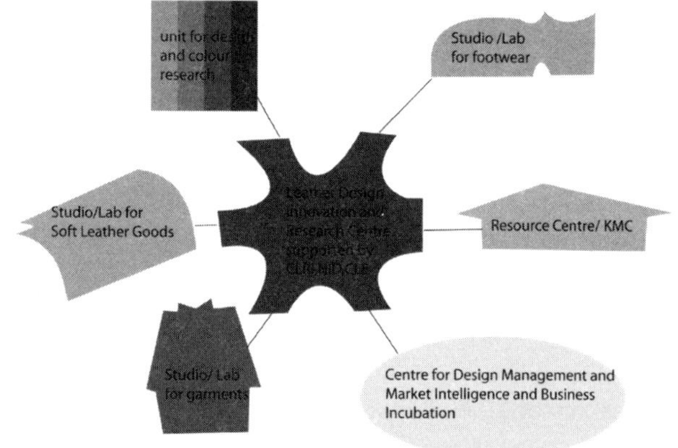

have proposed a Leather Design and Innovation Centre to specifically address value addition, repositioning, branding and design innovation in leather and leather products. The proposed centre's model is illustrated below:

> Such a centre can synergize technology, design and marketing in an impactful manner both in domestic and export markets. The need for converting good technology to good design through the use of research into contemporary lifestyles whether it is for footwear, jewellery, lifestyle garments and accessories cannot but be overemphasized.

A CASE STUDY:

Lifestyle and Luxury Products

Lifestyle encompasses products for different patterns of living, aspirational as well as emerging. 'Lifestyled' marketing focuses on repetitive lifestyle patterns and creating matching products. Multi-sensory retailing and design for lifestyle involves all these layers. Retailing is becoming more and more multi-sensory experience catering to the hedonistic tendencies of consumers. It is almost like a 'Garden of Senses' approach to satisfying every sense and if design succeeds in engaging more senses it is definitely, considered as more successful.

'Luxus', the Latin word for luxury stands for indulgence of the senses, regardless of cost. Luxury is a corollary to this and as Indian consumers become more and more discerning in the liberal economic climate of growth and stability in the recent years, luxury brands begin to capture their imagination and egos. It is important that customers for top-end design products are not discouraged through government policies which may then result in rapid expansion of the grey market for luxury products. Many leading luxury brands have already established a retail presence through franchises in India and a loud demand for opening the doors of FDI in different retail formats is increasing both in frequency and decibel levels. As is evident, the market for luxury watches and luxury cars have also shown a surge in recent times. However, what is interesting, but not sufficiently known is that many years ago India knew the experience of luxury than several other countries. If this DNA can be 'revisited' by Indian designers, the opportunity for design in luxury markets becomes phenomenal.

While estimates of the actual size of fashion, design, and luxury (FDL) markets may vary, according to Marcus, in 2003 the market was valued at 65 billion US dollars and saw a growth of 19 per cent in 2004 and currently according to Simon Brooke, it is worth about 134 billion US dollars globally. Of this, Japan accounts for an estimated 41 per cent of global sales, with US coming in second with 17 per cent. Europe and China meanwhile account for 16 and 12 per cent, respectively. According to well-known columnist Bruce Horowitz of *USA Today*, a big driving force behind this surge for luxury goods is the 'new age woman'. The women, says Horowitz, influence 75 per cent of all purchases. In India, the growing force of working women in all walks of life will, therefore, naturally influence the markets for luxury products even more.

Globally, production of high-end fashion and lifestyle products is highly skill and labour intensive. For example, the world over, a typical high-end suit or exclusive pair of footwear is always handmade and stitched. India thus, has a tremendous advantage in becoming an important hub for production of luxury products. First, India has had a long history of creating handmade designs and second, FDL goods are not new in India, neither are high spends for a wedding dress or an art piece, or a limited edition watch. The best example for this would be the big fat indian weddings! The minimum budget for a wedding ceremony in India is estimated by some experts at 34,000 US dollars, while the upper middle class and the rich classes are known to spend upwards of 2 million US dollars. Compared to this, an average American wedding costs only around 30,000 US dollars! In the context of weddings, let's take a look at the Indian jewellery industry which is again on a rollercoaster. India dominates the world's cut and polished diamonds market and accounts for approximately 55 per cent of the global polished diamond market. In terms of volumes, India accounts for 80-85 per cent of the world's cut-polished diamond (CPD) market and in unit terms 90 per cent of the world market. Traditionally, Indians buy jewellery only from a family jeweller based on a relationship cultivated over generations. But with world-class design innovations coupled with the buying power of women, branded jewellery makers is now replacing the old family jeweller.

Contributing to this change is the rise in the middle- and high-income population and their disposable incomes. This demographic segment, which is widely believed to be a main driver of the global retailing industry, has been rapidly growing at a pace of 10 per cent per annum over the past decade. At the consumer level, traditional customers have fast metamorphosed to a 'New Value Global Customer' and this change is primarily driven by the youth which broadly comprises almost 50 per cent of the population.

The young Indian consumer is well tuned in to the latest trends and aspirations across various countries and societies. Increased access to electronic media, the internet, and frequent travel are some of the factors that have led to this awareness of possible choices and a desire to be 'exclusive'. So this 'new' consumer is not only intrinsically Indian, he/she is very knowledgeable, and most importantly, assertive. Luxury brands are something they aspire to own, as they represent success and many amongst them can actually afford it. The number of Indian millionaires has grown rapidly in the recent past due to the opening up of the economy and corporate and private businesses doing exceedingly well. This has also contributed in creating a buoyant market for luxury goods and premium products.

evolving market for designed products

According to the Ledbury Research Foundation, UK, the number of families in India with more than a crore of annual income is going to exceed a lakh by the end of this decade. Also as per the National Council for Applied Economic Research (NCAER), the middle class have been classified as those who make approximately 4,545 to 23,000 US dollars per annum. NCAER extrapolates that the market for all categories of products, from daily consumables to consumer durables, will double their annual sales by 2010. With the economy expected to maintain a healthy 7-8 per cent annual growth or more, India is widely seen as one of the world's ten largest emerging markets. As a natural progression, the so-called brand fatigue that is experienced in the US and European market will result in luxury brands flocking to India.

The market for luxury products today has the potential to grow further at 50 per cent as opposed to the growth of 20 per cent that it has been cruising along. It is a market waiting for a boom to happen. This is also a market thirsty for innovation, for new ideas and especially for Indian designers who have been staying away from creating high-end, top-end designed products for niche markets. In the recent years, world's top luxury brands have made a beeline for the Indian market and there are reasons for this. Sample this: market for luxury and high-end clothing in India is estimated at Rs1,000 crores and for accessories at another Rs1,000 crores comprising apparel, accessories, cosmetics, jewellery and footwear which have shown a steady growth at 20 per cent.

But in this encouraging scenario, we also need entrepreneurs who put in money in creations which qualify to be global brands. The Design Policy initiatives through the first National Design Policy 2007 focuses on bringing in competitive advantage to Indian industry to equip the various industrial and craft sectors of the country to win markets by using their inherent and traditional strengths of design. The vision behind the exercise is that the traditional sectors and SMEs should become an integral part of wealth creation. The large share of India's unorganized sector in the industries of footwear, textiles and handicrafts need to be empowered to create trademarks of luxury products – 'designed in India'.

Today what differentiates one brand from another is its image. This image has to be relevant to the brand and memorable for the consumers. The way people shop, and the brands they buy, will change dramatically in the future. There will be an even greater drive towards better value, not necessarily driven by lower price. Luxury brands and retail service levels call for new competencies and strategies. Indian companies need to develop proactive strategies and management expertise in the area of corporate identity, branding and design management in good time to seize the opportunities. In this context, two Italian luxury brands need showcasing for their sheer brilliance and ability to create a niche in world markets.

Gianfranco Ferré is the Italian fashion brand which has for thirty years been creating clothes and accessories of high quality dedicated to a clientele that is attentive to the new trends. The brand expresses an elegant style where the sense of sophistication is at once contemporary and timeless. The present and the future of the Gianfranco brand are characterized by some distinctive values that influence every project: creativity, quality, exclusivity, innovation and culture.

The brand encompasses three 'worlds' – Gianfranco Ferré – clothes for men and women; Ferré – accessories for men and women; and GF Ferré – which deals with bags, shoes, leather goods, silk products, umbrellas, eyewear, fragrances, watches and fur collection.

All Gianfranco Ferré collections are the result of the strong synergy with the IT Holding category companies – ITC, Ittierre and ITA – responsible for the production and in some cases also for business management of the various product lines and a well-balanced and articulated licensing network with Italian leading companies.

Jewellery display at the Lifestyle and Accessory Design Concept at NID during 2007 convocation.

The Gianfranco Ferré collections feature gorgeous exclusive/innovative materials and working processes, superlative workmanship and utmost attention to detail. All the while capturing a fashion-forward spirit, anticipating evolution in tastes. The role of the label is to foster and support the brand's mythical allure, sparking a sort of poetic desire. The collections include two complementary parts. In the first one a black label identifies the most exclusive and magical creations. The ivory label in the second one marks the easiest inflections of an unmistakable style.

Ferré on the other hand, captures the brand's sophisticated-contemporary appeal in an easy, immediate, approachable way. These collections are conceived for people who recognize and appreciate the expressions of an unmistakable style and are more sensitive to price and contemporary trends.

The fashion content, cross-cultural spirit, and pricing makes the GF label true and competitive youthful alternative of the Gianfranco Ferré brand. Hi-tech and alternative materials characterize the GF collection along with denim which always plays a major yet not exclusive role. The label aims to show that the brand's sophisticated-contemporary essence can fit in naturally with a more casual way of fashion.

On 17 June 2007, the legendary Gianfranco Ferré passed away quite suddenly. The riveting story of the creation of such a leading luxury brand is summed up by Ferré as:

> Real journeys, imaginary journeys ... They mark the entire course of my professional experience, my path. Traveling, letting mind and heart wander, comes natural to me and is necessary to my creative process. In this dimension, sensations, visions, desires intersect, giving form and substance to my style. Narrating it, enriching it, ceaselessly ...

Let us now look at another world leader among luxury brands to get some perspectives of building brands which are ruled by design. We discover through the narratives that luxury brand experience can transcend cruise boats to boutique hotels and more. It requires great imagination to create luxury experiences.

Leonarda Ferragamo knows first-hand how to market beautiful, top-quality products. He's the son of Salvatore Ferragamo, whose expert craftsmanship in shoes and clothing propelled a Florentine family business into a leading global luxury brand. Forty-nine-year-old Leonardo, who spent his career in his family's businesses, is now successfully applying the Ferragamo touch to another luxury venture, yachts. The new 45-feet Swan took first place in the 50th Giraglia Rolex cup race on 23 June. And Ferragamo drummed up ten prospective orders, many for the company's pricelist sailboats, at this month's Swan Cup regatta in Sardinia.

Ferragamo used his personal fortune to buy money-losing Nautor in 1998 from a state-owned pulp-and-paper company in Finland for an undisclosed sum. That year, sales were 27 million US dollars. Now, a slew of new models and a 12 million US dollar investment in a new high-tech shipyard are propelling growth. While the global downturn has left most luxury-goods makers in the doldrums, privately owned Nautor forecasts a 28 per cent increase in sales, to 84 million US dollars, this year, and a profit of 5.4 million US dollars. 'I had a strong conviction that we could improve many things. There had been no new Swan [models] in ten years,' says Ferragamo, an avid sailor who became smitten with the Finnish boats in 1988 and tried to persuade the Finns to build a 45-foot yacht – a smaller, faster version of the company's traditional sailboats.

Fourteen years later, Nautor Chairman Ferragamo is making that dream a reality. In May, Nautor launched the first 45-foot *Swan*, and it's a winner. Breaking with Nautor tradition, Ferragamo decided to make the *Swan 45* a single design with limited options so production could be standardized, as with expensive cars. Traditionally, Swan boats are semi-custom-built. While a large model can take up to eight months to deliver, Nautor turns out a *Swan 45* in only fourteen days. Nautor, which will make forty of its classic semi-custom yachts this year, has already sold thirty of the $582,000 *Swan 45s* and has ten more on order.

The *Swan 45* isn't the only new ship in the catalogue. Nautor now boasts of nine new models, offering for the first time super-yachts 100 feet or larger. The winner of the first Whitbread around-the-world race in 1974, Nautor enjoys a legendary reputation for quality. Yet its forty-year-old boatyard in Peetersaari, Finland, 400 miles north of Helsinki, has been losing ground to a new class of super-big yachts and rival boats built with new materials. 'The extra big boats filled an important void in our offering,' says Ferragamo, who owns an 82-footer christened *Solleone*. For owners who want lighter, faster boats, *Swan* now offers fiberglass hulls in addition to its traditional all-teak construction.

Ferragamo's real coup may well be the luxury-goods marketing savvy he is injecting into Nautor and the Swan brand. By revitalizing the annual Nautor's Swan Cup and other races for some 1,900 owners, Ferragamo infused Swan with new excitement and cachet. The September regatta in Sardinia drew a fleet of some 120 *Swan* owners to the resort of Porto Cervo, including senior executives from Deutsche Bank, Credit Suisse First Boston, and UBS. 'We are developing a new [racing] class with the 45,' says Ferragamo.

On the Uffizi-side of Florence's Ponte Santa Trinita, at the corner of via dei Tornabuoni, there is a pretty, pink, thirteenth-century palace: Palazzo Spini Feroni, the headquarters of the Ferragamo dynasty. On the ground floor, is the Italian fashion label's flagship store. Up the wide and winding stairs are its offices, and on the top floor is the Museo Salvatore Ferragamo, which few people know exists, where the shoemaker's heritage is displayed in four tiny rooms. Even more unexpected is the fact that the Ferragamos also own hotels. Peer out of a tiny top-floor window of the Palazzo Spini Feroni and you can just about see all five: on the Uffizi-side, the Continentale, the Gallery Hotel Art and Lungarno Suites; on the opposite bank the Hotel Lungarno and Palazzo Capponi. All are within a single block dissected by the River Arno, marked by the Ponte Santa Trinita to the west and Ponte Vecchio to the east. A ten-minute walk will take you past each one.

For the Ferragamos, service matters more than anything else. 'It's the same in fashion: the customer is king,' says Leonardo Ferragamo, Salvatore's second son who is responsible for, among other things, the hotel division which goes under the name of Lungarno Alberghi S.p.A. Recently, there has been a flurry of fashion houses getting in on the boutique-hotel boom. Versace was among the first, followed by Bvlgari and most recently Cerruti. For the most part, these are 'fashion hotels' that rely heavily on well-known brand names to get them noticed. The Ferragamo family has taken a different approach.

'You will never see the Ferragamo name in a room,' says Leonardo. 'For us, it's far more important to work on substance rather than brand positioning.' When we first got into hotels in 1995, we deliberately didn't put out the Ferragamo name,' says Leonardo. 'We didn't want to take advantage of a label that had become famous for other reasons. It's the same with the boat company we now own, Nautor, which produces *Swan* sailing yachts. Why? Because the Ferragamo name wouldn't mean much to the people who care about the most beautiful luxury boats in the world. You see, the things we are involved in are quite separate, and to have integrity, I think everything needs to be in its own area of expertise. The only thing shared between the hotels is a family standard.' As Fabrizio Gaggio, managing director of Lungarno Alberghi, puts it: 'It's about transferring the style of the family into the hotels. This is different from what other fashion houses are doing, who are just giving their names.'

Like the Medicis, the Ferragamos understand the subtlest nuances of the commercial transaction. 'Hotels represent extreme retailing, which is a natural extension of fashion,' says Leonardo. 'There is just one critical difference. With hotels, you present your customers with a bill but they don't leave with an actual product in hand. In other words, there are no shoes in a shopping bag. All they've got to take away with them is the memory of an experience. It's a hotelier's job to make sure that memory is the very best, so they come back for more.' What is conspicuous and deliberate about the Lungarno hotels is the fact that each is different. 'We don't replicate hotels like a photocopier,' says Leonardo. 'Each has to have its own personality.'

Training a team of dedicated Lungarno staff has not been straightforward. 'It's the most difficult, time-consuming thing to transfer your vision to your staff,' says Fabrizio. For the Ferragamos, this 'vision' means an easy-going professionalism, a modern mix that puts their close-knit family approach to hotels unlike the more formal school of hospitality. Lungarno Alberghi looks set to grow and grow. 'Organically,' insists Fabrizio. 'It is the only way to do it, in order to create something like the rooms in a house and avoid it becoming a typical hotel.' To this end, the Ferragamo family consistently work with the same architect-designer, Michele Bönan. 'When we started looking for someone, we wanted an expert who made homes. That way, we could make a hotel feel like a home,' says Leonardo. 'It is vital for us to have the vision of guests rather than of managers,' he says. 'This creates a different form of hospitality. To keep this perspective, I stay in our hotels. I come with my wife and we live in them; we see how they work.'

digital designs

One of the benchmarks of a booming economy in a vibrant democracy is the way media functions and India has created enough waves in this sector. The media industry in India is undergoing a 'massive change' in terms of technology, mindset, access and the emergence of digital technologies as one of the most disruptive innovations in this sector.

Adoption of digital technology in all the areas of media industry and huge technology investments are changing the scale, scope and reach of TV channels in India now numbering over 350 and access rules through Direct to Home or DTH are changing the landscape of both diffusion of innovation adoption and the longevity of business models. The sector now offers several challenging opportunities to creative talent from India especially the designers.

The entertainment industry is one of the fastest growing segments in the economy and the Indian film industry has emerged as the leader in the world and is the largest film market with an estimated thirty-eight million viewers. The film industry produces almost a 1000 feature films every year. Hindi film industry, popularly known as Bollywood, has now expanded beyond its traditional markets to UK, the Middle East and many European countries apart from certain pockets of the USA. The animation industry is also growing in leaps and bounds, and has moved up to a second position in the world from a third and along with gaming is expected to double to almost a hundred million in the next two years. The animated feature films market, yet another growth oriented field, has grown at an impressive 56 per cent.

media & entertainment industry: gaming & animation

Let us take an indepth look at the burgeoning Indian gaming industry. It was estimated at nearly 48 million US dollars in 2006 and is expected to cross 424 million by 2010, representing a CAGR of 72 per cent over 2006-10. Currently, the mobile and console gaming together contribute nearly 77 per cent of the total gaming market in the country. The increasing mobile and broadband penetration along with the introduction of new generation consoles is expected to result in an increase of share prices of online and console gaming significantly by 2010.

Meanwhile, the worldwide gaming market – from the demand perspective – stood at 21 billion dollars in 2006. This market is expected to reach 42 billion by 2010, growing at nearly 18 per cent. Consequently, the worldwide gaming content market – from the developers' perspective – was estimated at nearly 7 billion dollars in 2006 and is expected to cross 13 billion by 2010. In the gaming market, mobile and online gaming segments are expected to grow significantly at about 30 and 25 per cent respectively, till 2010. The US and Europe remain the biggest markets for outsourcing animation and gaming related activities. Majority of the work from these markets is being outsourced to destinations in the Asia-Pacific region and Eastern Europe.

The global animation market from the perspective of demand was estimated at 59 billion dollars in 2006 and with a growth rate of 8 per cent it will reach 80 billion by 2010. Of the total revenue earned in the segment, approximately 40-45 per cent is attributed to the cost of development. According to experts, the Indian animation industry is expected to reach 869 million US dollars by 2010. Key factors driving this growth include a significant cost advantage, a large pool of English speaking manpower, improved capacities of animation studios, development of IP and an attractive domestic market opportunity.

The original content creation and offshoring are both growing at a phenomenal pace. The difference between production costs in the US and India is a major reason for opting the latter as a destination for offshoring. Many reputed studios like Sony Picture Image Works, DreamWorks, and Disney are now opening satellite studios. The animation feature value chain is also indicating that a great deal of production work is coming to India namely, character design, background creation, and visual effects. This is good news for designers and skilled technicians.

Even at these impressive growth forecasts, the Indian animation and gaming industry will account for less than 2 per cent of the worldwide market in 2010, clearly indicating a significantly larger opportunity in the days to come. Ensuring the availability of adequate, suitable manpower and a focused industry development programme can help India achieve a larger share of the pie.

Another major development is the impending growth of gaming industry. Currently, there are 150 gaming companies in India, employing about 2,500 people. This number is likely to increase at a CAGR of over 50 per cent to exceed 13,000 by 2010, with the industry revenue forecast to growth nearly tenfold and reach 424 million US dollars.

Today, animation is not just restricted to a few commercials. In India till the early 1990s, production of animation films was not so easy. Apart from the economic factors that have limited the scope of expansion, an essential missing link was to convert inputs into quality output. However, there has been a lack of vision and purposive action to leverage the inherent advantage. It is a matter of pride today that we have animated films that are based on mythological and folk characters which are exclusive to the country and contributing a great deal to the world animation industry.

The first waves of animation business was dominated by outsourcing players from the US, Canada, UK, Germany and France. Many studios opened up in India sensing new ways of generating reviews and started recruiting many art college freshers and creative individuals. But with this came the stiff challenges of maintaining the demands of global clients, competition from neighbouring countries like China for cheaper skilled labour and fast delivery of work. With the advent of digital technology and broadband communication the flatness of world brought a 24x7 work culture which demands newer visual feats for the ever demanding consumers. But unlike the film industry, the animation business has been struggling to cope with issues like lack of skilled and trained human resources, good animation schools, and government support and awareness which resulted in a mismatch of demand and supply.

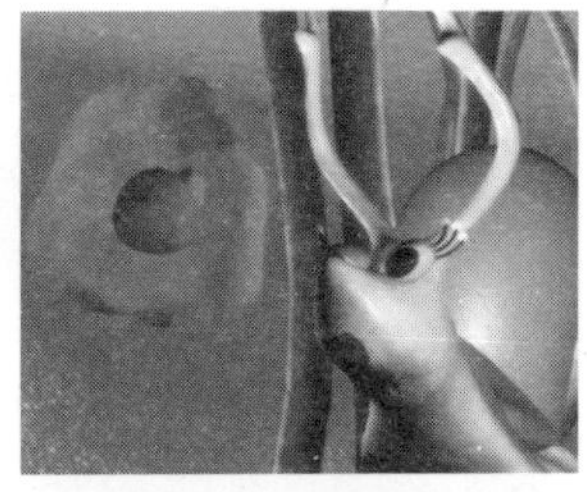

Stills from a 3D animation film, *Who Am I* by NID student, Ramneek Kaur Majithia.

However, as compared to other competitors, India has become a favoured outsourcing destination for many in the West and the reasons for this, apart from a large talent pool, are:

- English is more or less a communication medium at all social levels
- Storytelling runs deep in the Indian psyche
- Cross pollination and compatibility
- Economical and innovative
- Every state has art colleges and institutes
- Devoted film lovers across the country
- Impact of Bollywood
- Largest and stable democracy
- And a tech-savvy populace.

So the brighter side of animation and gaming are quite visible and the Chitrakatha '07 the Students' Animation Film Festival at NID brought together different generations of animators and stressed on the potential for original content creation. Even Hollywood is realizing the untapped resources of never-ending stories from India and the huge talent pool from this country. Further, with a huge youth population as the largest consumer for gaming and animated products, India is now poised for a bigger leap towards IP creation and making a mark in the global arena as a content creator from mere service provider.

Although India is already competing against the Philippines, Korea, China, Vietnam and Taiwan and has the right ingredients to stand out tall amidst competition, there are still many factors causing gaps between demand and supply chain. For example, in the initial stages of the value chain, concept creation and pre-production work, which hinder backward integration, are most striking. Several leading players have undertaken initiatives to train the talent pool available in India to create the required supply of suitable manpower. As a result, a majority of the professional talent existent today is a product of these company supported internal training programmes. This is not a scaleable solution. Though independent training institutes have also emerged, except for a few animation schools and handful of animated content providers, there is still a lack of collaboration between the industry and the training institutes. A concerted effort led by the industry, in close association with the academia and supported by the government is required to address the issue comprehensively.

transportation and automobile

India has a large and extensive transportation system and one of the world's largest railway and roadway networks, transporting millions of people every second. In a country where there is still a value base of resource conservation and a culture of adopting one product for multipurpose usage, transportation of both people and goods have many coexisting modes and it has explored all possibilities of movement viz., land, air, and water.

So far in India, transportation has been generally technologically driven with minimum or little attention paid to the user's needs in terms of comfort, safety, information and even considerations of cultural sensitivities and preferences. With new material choices available, as also the need for saving energy and other environmental concerns, optimal usage of materials, contemporary production technologies, the transport systems need strong design inputs in all the domains including public, personal and material.

In the post-liberalization era, there have been undoubtedly dramatic changes in the field of transportation. Amongst other reasons, stiff competition has brought in new dimensions due to globalization of the marketplace and easy flow of information has created an 'aware' consumer. The consumer is now looking for softer values in products that sets his product apart from others in satisfying both the physical and emotional needs. Keeping this philosophy in mind, the Automotive Mission Plan 2006-16 has recommended the following action agenda:

- Manufacture and export of small cars, MUVs, two- and

three-wheelers, tractors, components

- Negative list of items and rules of origin for FTAs/RTAs
- Appropriate tariff policy to attract investment
- Specific measures to expand domestic market
- Incremental investment of US $35-40 billion in auto industry during next ten years
- Encourage exports
- Policy initiatives for competitiveness and development of technology
- National Road Safety Board to act as the coordinating body for promoting safety
- Fleet modernization
- Time-bound implementation of goods and services tax
- A national-level automotive institute for training on automobiles as it is and automotive technical institutes
- Centres for automotive manufacturing excellence
- Adoption of ITIs and ATIs by OEMs and component makers
- An Auto Design Centre to be established at NID, Ahmedabad
- Provision of facilities for testing, certification and homologation to the industry
- Integration of IT in manufacturing and automotive infotronics
- Infrastructure development around identified auto clusters
- Closer partnership between industry, research institutions and academia for innovation and IPR to be encouraged
- R&D for product, processes and technology to be incentivised
- Continuous investments in road, port, railways and power
- Labour reforms
- Road map for Auto Fuel Policy beyond 2010

A unique achievement: Mahan Ghosh, NID student won the Alfa Romeo Jury Prize in 2007; young Indian designers are making a mark in the highly specialized field of Transportation and Automobile Design.

- Virtual SEZs and Auto Parks for auto component industry.

Design has a very important contribution to make in the way in which the objects we create in our environment work and influence our perceptions towards them.

In a bold initiative the NID has been offering since 2005 a two-and-half-year post-graduate programme in transportation and automobile design. This programme seeks to establish a credible relationship of products and services with the user, technology and environment. This programme aims to train young professionals with a thorough grounding in the systems, a holistic approach to problem-solving processes, creating a sensitivity towards the environment and addressing the needs and requirements of different user groups. The three-year-old transportation and automobile design programme has been able to make an impact worldwide with three students being selected by the FIAT Group for five-and-a-half months training in Italy from 200 design entries from eight top schools in the world (2007). The unique achievement of NID student Mahaan Ghosh winning the Alfa Romeo Jury Prize shows the possibility of young Indian designers making a mark in the global arena.

A design of stroll using steel by NID alumni, Vibhor Sogani, for Jindal Stainless Steel Ltd.

creating gennext designers

spread of quality design education

Design as a 'process' has the ability to move horizontally across all segments of industry, commerce, service and development. The twenty-first century which focuses on knowledge, dematerialization and innovations depend heavily on processes and 'intangibles' of design. All efforts, therefore, will have to be directed towards this process of integration whether in a government infrastructure project or in the creation of products, systems or services. Design plays a crucial role in today's innovation economy which in turn is driven by an unceasing struggle for achieving national and industrial competitiveness. Most importantly, the onus is on design and designers to protect and preserve culture, tradition and the crafts, and above all create a 'differential' advantage for products and services.

So the logical approach to design education in twenty-first century India should ideally reflect the aspirations of an innovation-driven creative economy and include the convergence of media, communication, entertainment and information. What was initiated in the twentieth century, led first by German and later by other European schools as the foundation of Indian design curriculum has obviously been much adapted, modified and improvised over the years. The approach, content and pedagogy needs to be reviewed continuously and more so in the context of a 'developed India'; and the reality of a global village set in an information society. Design values such as harmony, ethics, consumer delight, quality, functionality, visual culture, aesthetics and such other tangibles and intangibles can provide great value in an 'information society and creative economy' which are both somewhat impersonal. This brings to sharper focus a greater emphasis on culture, emotion, ethnicity, vernacular expression and traditions. Modern technology and engineering education need to, therefore, absorb some of the power and beauty of creative and lateral thinking emanating from art and design, especially for 'differentiation' and creation of enduring values.

For engineering and technology education in the twenty-first century, design can add value in two significantly different ways. First, in converting technologies to tangible and intangible benefits through creative problem solving and continuously innovating around the consumer. Let us not forget that while design is a synthesis of a trans-disciplinary thinking leading to a creation of products, services, experiences and a tool to communicate all these and more, innovation results in converting knowledge to wealth. Second, it is necessary to provide self-development and 'out-of-the-box thinking' tools to an engineer who already possesses a strong understanding of technology.

national design deficit

In a developing country like India, fast on its way to becoming a developed nation by 2020, design enablement at all levels is expected to add value in every link of the chain. The cost difference in design development, which India enjoys currently with the availability of creative talent, makes it necessary for us to build expertise, facilities and capabilities to nurture this competitive edge and achieve rapid 'mind to market' movement. Speed, imagination and 'time to hit' markets have become the triggers necessitating an overhaul in tools and techniques for absorbing new technologies like digital tablets for sketching, stereophotographic design visualization tools and haptic devices for modeling; Rapid Product Development (RPD) and Product Life Cycle Management tools for developing prototypes and helping in iteration, market testing and finetuning of ideas in their travel to the decisive stage of the competitive marketplace. The 'time to market' issue is a critical aspect in the times we live in with in-built obsolescence and replacement cycles. Modern design institutes need to be equipped with mind to market transformation capabilities especially for IPR-based competition globally. It was in recognition of such emerging needs that in 2003, NID's first National Design Business Incubator or NDBI was set up and later in 2005 an integrated Design Vision Centre, a most advanced 'mind to market' facility among design schools.

It is reckoned by experts that a substantial number of continuous design interventions are required in several high growth and other sub-sectors spanning different segments of industry, commerce and service sectors. The SMEs and crafts sectors also demand designers in large numbers. Other allied creative industries like cinema and TV in Bollywood for instance, require visualizers and set designers while the ever-expanding news and entertainment TV channels need animators, special-effects designers and the like. The requirements in high growth sectors like automobiles, jewellery, animation and retail may further drive the market as also the demand-supply situation in India. A rough estimate indicates that there is a need for at least 10,000 to 12,000 designers every year as against the current supply of about a 1000 designers of varying degrees in the country. Added to this, the ratio between technologists, engineers, architects and designers in the country is also highly skewed. In the US the available number of designers is around 1,80,000; UK 1,00,000; Japan 46,000 and in India it's a dismal 5,000. In America there are around 1700 design institutes, whereas China has around 400, and Korea over 300. In India, design schools with a certain threshold quality level are around 10 while there are 40 others which are also aspiring to be design schools.

Wood-in-wood inlay flooring of the reception of Petro IT office, Gurgaon, designed by KAARU.

Anomalies notwithstanding, designers will also be required for different levels of design-related work including concept design, design methodologies, and other aspects for catering to different requirements and levels of the industry. The rapid expansion of IT and other service sectors call for a new breed of designers who are equipped with competencies and attitudes such as 'learnability', 'flexibility' and an ability to be 'ambidextrous' – between the visceral and the virtual. According to an estimate by M.P. Ranjan, principal designer at NID, over 230 segments of industry, commerce and development require designers with different competencies. However, every economy has its growth engines and the numbers will only grow and, therefore, the need as well.

national design policy and spread of design education

The first National Design Policy of India announced in February 2007 proposes several steps for the spread of quality design education, which includes setting up of additional new design campuses, innovation hubs, offering design education in tertiary educational institutions and converting NID as a 'deemed to be university'.

A five-tiered approach is suggested for the spread of design education in India especially in the fields of 'IT-techno-engineering.' To quote from the policy paper:

> It is suggested that the engineering colleges which number over 1200 in the country should have exposure to design education at different levels. Tier-one institutions should necessarily have separate design schools or a centre like Industrial Design Centre (IDC) in IIT or like the Centre for Product Design and Manufacturing or CPDM at the Indian Institute of Science (IISC), Bengaluru.
>
> The second tier of institutions are those which will choose either a product design or communication design stream as per the context of the institution at an undergraduate level. It is sufficient to have a generic design programme or a product design programme in the second-tier institutions in which the accent is on design as value addition strategy enabling engineers to see beyond technologies and think more in terms of products, brands and companies.
>
> A third tier would concentrate on information, communication technology, and media institutes like the International Institute of Information Technology

Students dressed up in traditional attire for the 28th NID convocation, December 2007.

(IIIT) or other such institutes encompassing design for information societies. This is keeping in mind that India is already a 56 per cent service-led economy and on its way to becoming a 65 per cent service-led economy by 2010. There are thus huge opportunities for the software and communication sectors to encompass virtual and service design areas by incorporating information and interface design, animation and moving images by which programmes created by engineers become user-friendly and emotionally and culturally dynamic and relevant.

A fourth-tier programme will focus on offering at least two courses in the later semesters in every engineering and fine arts programmes. One called 'Design Fundamentals' and the other called 'Design Methods and Processes' by which most of the engineers and or artists could get acquainted with the need for developing another dimension to their knowledge which will come in handy at different stages of their career and also for value adding to their skill sets.

A fifth tier is introducing design in school curriculum through the existing Central Board of Secondary Examination (CBSE) or the Indian Certificate for Secondary Examination (ICSE) boards so that the availability of a creative talent pool is enhanced.

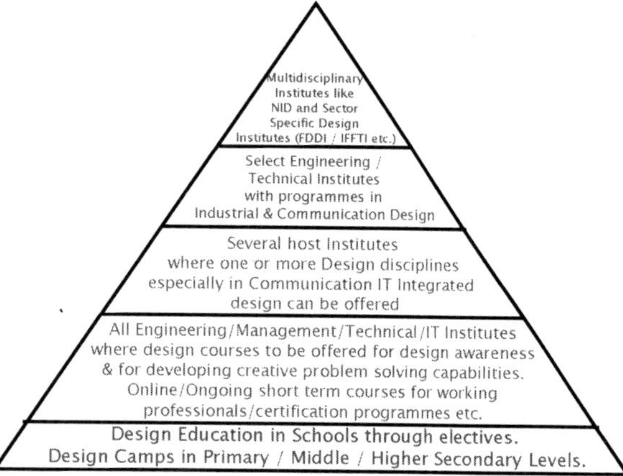

The higher education scenario in India is undergoing a rapid change and at this juncture, the time has come for design education to be part of the mainstream. This may help in design playing a crucial role as part of the four-legged modern economy, the other three being technology, management and social or environmental responsibility. NID's transformation to become India's first multidisciplinary university for design education and research is expected to be realized much before its Golden Jubilee in the academic year 2010-11.

Like in every other field of academics today, design education is also facing tougher challenges. The earlier approach of design education was more skill oriented and project based set in an apprenticeship mode. With research now becoming crucial to the profession of design, the approach to both undergraduate and post-graduate programmes needs to be evaluated and remodelled. In 2005, a major step was taken in this direction at the NID in an international conference titled *Design Education, Tradition and Modernity.* Some of the recommendations made in the Statement of Intent at this landmark conference included:

> Design education must include ways to partner with community, industry development organizations and government to promote value-based design. Design education needs to address effective ways to collaborate with the community and the potential users to ensure the positive adoption of design solutions. Educational institutions must create collaborative networks to exchange ideas and design education initiatives.
>
> There is a need to augment education of design and related human resources in all countries including different means of collaborations and "team" based creative methods and delivery systems. Design education must prepare students to be culturally sensitive and respect the local and other contexts – specific lives of people and the ecosystem as a whole.

Design education must draw upon multi-disciplinary and cross-cultural sources to facilitate originality and innovation. It should embrace valuable teaching methods like peer learning, self-learning, shared learning, and group learning to foster teamwork, developing a student and user centred approach and creating awareness of markets.

Design embraces all disciplines in its concern with innovation of forms, configurations, patterns and relationships that shape the human-made environment, responsive to our aspirations.

Design education should be geared to improve the quality of our lives through a careful consideration of physical, cognitive, social, cultural, emotional, economical and other real needs.

Design regards research as a process for empowering designers in assuring quality and achieving leadership in both cultural and global contexts. It enables bridging the gap between vision and action, to respect cultural actualizations and take responsibility for its solutions.

Design education needs a clear formalization of a flexible and updateable design curriculum with emphasis on theory, research, analysis, and synthesis ready for "realization" and "making". We recognize the need for a balancing of analog and digital approaches to problem solving depending upon the context of design.

The above points and common concerns are in concurrence with the UN declaration for the years 2005-15 celebrated as the 'Decade of Education and Sustainability'. Finally, design education needs to resist fragmentation and clearly focus on creativity, out of the box or lateral thinking and the ability to visualize, realize and think beyond the ordinary. This can only happen if design education is offered in a truly transdisciplinary context with sectoral design and domain expertise wherever required while underpinning the role of research with a balanced 'hands on, minds on' approach for the development of GenNext designers.

'Metal Petal' made from fibre reinforced plastic and aluminium sheets, designed by NID student R.S. Rajshekaran.

research-led design education

Ironically, design education not only in India but the world over has been an unintended victim of 'practice'. It was considered that continuous practice under the design faculty would make for better designers and hence an 'apprenticeship' approach was most favoured in the early days of design education well into the late 1990s – a kind of modern *gurukul*, so to speak. Fresh ideas and thoughts were hardly ever documented or published; interesting and new approaches or ideas were often scoffed at; their own expertise was guarded almost like secret mantras handed down reluctantly to the next in line!

From the point of view of advancement of design as a professional skill, this approach has succeeded to a certain extent, but from the point of view of knowledge advancement it has not. In the field of design education, the role of research, unlike in technology, engineering, and medicine, has not been sufficiently emphasized resulting in the stunted growth of a sound design education and practice. Research has been viewed and taken as a qualitative exercise based on observation and some heuristics. The expectations from design have often transcended the boundaries of disciplines and everything from bad roads and poor signages to lack of comfort and ease of a chair in a bus or airport to unaffordability of utility designs have all been attributed to design. Although a designer was perceived as someone with a 'magic wand', he or she was never given the deserved respect. The risks of the profession increased manifold even as a designer dealt with hitherto unknown tools such as new research methodologies, user-testing systems and consumer research inputs.

As a practice, a designer often borrows concepts from different knowledge domains and advocates an eclectic approach. However, this phenomenon of synthesis is not sufficiently demonstrated through everyday products and services in a way that the masses could understand and appreciate its significance. There are many reasons for this rather grim situation. For instance, books on design have tended to become philosophical or altruistic; the design profession has been fragmented with so many sub-classifications that it has become difficult for others to comprehend the full gamut; there are no more generic designers but only graphic designers, animation designers,

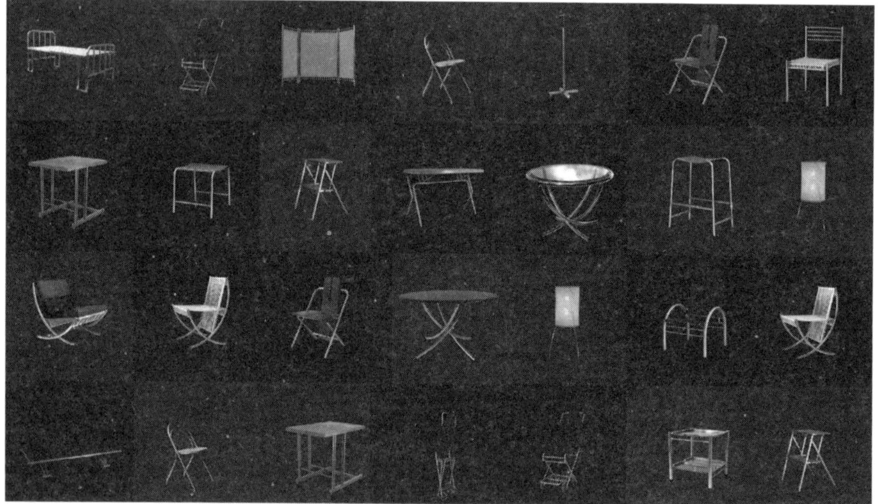

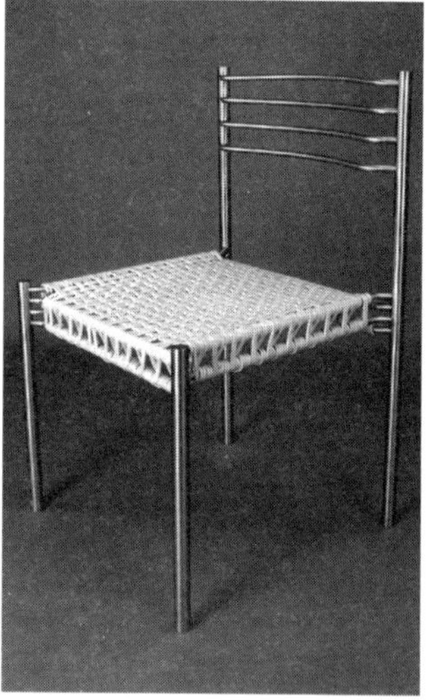

A display of stainless steel furniture and a string chair designed by Gajanan Upadhyaya, Jindal Stainless Steel Research Chair at NID.

furniture designers, product designers, interface designers, multi-media designers, new media designers, and the list goes on and on. Somewhat differently but both engineering and medicine, despite considerable specialization and fragmentation, managed to have both the mother disciplines intact as an overarching concept. There are hardly any good design case studies to show how the design process actually works and creates a new value. So the mystery continues to shroud the whole process of design.

As far as design education in India is concerned, design research has always been part of a project or process but unfortunately not considered as complementary to design education. Pushing the frontiers of knowledge through live projects has been the way with design. It may be recalled that often when somebody asks the methodology of design or how a person is going to approach the problem, there have been instances where the designer has often failed to articulate the same or resorted to clichéd methodologies. If design has not received the same importance as technology, engineering, or medicine, in the country then it is due to the fact that there have been no serious attempts to create a dependable knowledge base. For example, NID, until 2001 did not have either a post-graduate programme or research programmes to support fundamental and applied design research activities. The Advanced Entry Programmes or AEP at the NID only offered a lateral entry for engineering and other graduates but led to the same diploma at the end of the programme. There were no research chairs instituted by the industry or any other entity to support research until 2003. Compare this with other design-savvy and developed countries. At the Monash University, Faculty of Art and Design at Melbourne (Australia), a PhD is awarded to designers based on their studio work; Royal College of Art (UK), which specializes in PG programmes has set a good example of elevating design to a higher pedestal. Further, the UK Design Council having interfaced with the government, industry and academia has been playing a significant role by bringing out research papers on the economic and social impact of design regularly. Also it identifies the income impact and contribution of creative industries to the GDP which is currently estimated at 11 per cent.

The recent discussions on the changing role of design research indicates that in the 1980s the content of research in a designer's work profile was less than 20 per cent whereas today it is over 60 per cent. It is imperative for designers to understand the role of design research in order to create a symbiotic relationship between both applied solutions for industry and breakthrough innovations. The innovation may come out of a new insight into consumers' behaviour like the Thin Edge watch by Titan or it may be a breakthrough innovation as in the case of many new services offered with the assistance of technology whether it is online services like magicbricks.com, Shaadi.com, Naukri.com or NID's prototype of a storytelling box or e-Kaavad in a laptop format.

The research-based approach can be helpful especially in design for competitiveness and there are many examples where it has worked wonderfully. For example, the John Bissell Chair at NID which has focused on Nano/Plasma technology over the period 2004-07 has succeeded in developing a series of futuristic design applications; the O.P. Jindal Design Research Chair, again during 2004-07, has helped in developing over fifty innovative designs in less than three years of which eleven designs have been taken up for commercialization by the sponsor.

Yet another marvellous example is the new approach to researching Indian colour palette through 'setting up of a colour research studio' at the Bengaluru campus of the NID, sponsored by Asian Paints Ltd. This is expected to lead to greater insights about Indian colours and colour preferences as also applications. Therefore, the marriage of design and research should be encouraged and the latest PG programmes at NID are mandated to have a higher research content of upto 30-35 per cent or more in the coming years.

charting a new vision

Liberty and freedom came at a very heavy price for this country and post-Independent India had to contend with the trauma of Partition, overburdened exchequer, poverty and unemployment. For those born in the 80s and 90s all that is just a footnote in history for they witnessed a growing economy flush with a bludgeoning middle class with enough confidence to engage the world on equal terms. Especially with successes in sectors like communication and Information Technology, India's self-confidence and motivation has grown in leaps and bounds. The time is here and now to sustain this growth, to be anything but complacent and go that extra mile in whatever field and I would like to focus here on the one thing which concerns me most – education, and then design education.

My preoccupation with the NID has been since the turn of the new century and there was a time, not long ago, when the educational infrastructure at the institute was obsolete with very few students that too only for undergraduate programmes with few AEP students and just a single campus in Ahmedabad. It was indeed a huge and rather risky path I had to tread to lead a transformation in the early part of the twenty-first century.

I was clear about one thing: NID has to become a global leader in design education and research and should become a trendsetter and thought leader. Putting systems into an institution built on 'past legacies' and an informal approach for years was no mean task and some of that involved contemporarizing educational infrastructure, rekindling a spirit of adventure and discovery among the faculty and students, inducting and training a new generation of faculty members, commencing sector-specific PG programmes, introducing Academic Credit Evaluation System, developing stronger international ties across the world, achieving sound financial health and reaching out to other parts of India to become truly national.

The core objectives of NID right from its formative years of pursuing educational excellence and design practice have not really changed but have been re-focused to meet the challenges of the knowledge economy which includes a greater focus on research-led design education, global positioning and design innovation for creation of wealth through original Intellectual Property like patents and designs. In this emerging context, NID needed to be strengthened and more importantly, reoriented to meet new challenges and suitably positioned to become a 'Global Leader in Design Education and Research.'

The institute's greatest strength was the 'Foundation Year' programme very relevant to Indian needs especially for craft sector and SMEs; as was really intended in the *India Report* of the Eames'. But even this required major overhauling and till date this has been a moving target. Over the last five decades in NID, design education has been finetuned many times through trial and error and immense contribution by different members of the initial faculty cadre to respond to emerging needs and global trends. As was expected, NID graduates in the past mostly looked at design as a tool for development as India was still under the siege of a protected economy. One of the new age entrepreneurs once said about NID graduates, 'Six out of ten became design activists who wanted to change the world and the rest practised in traditional sectors or freelanced for several years in multiple areas.' This abiding image, I feel has to change. Another big challenge in this regard has been the need to convert good ideas and concepts which were accumulated in plenty into viable economic products and services. To the credit of NID, it has been the constant endeavour at the institute to predict and realize the needs of Indian society, while searching for an Indian idiom in design.

What started out as a mission bore fruit, albeit slowly, and change in NID began showing – the NID Forward Plan 2002-07 had very clearly proposed certain physical and intellectual targets and it is heartening that the targets have not only been achieved, the outcome and results are far above what had been anticipated. There is now an increasing acceptance of design as an integral part of corporate strategy, it is recognized as the new dynamic field of education, research, employment and entrepreneurial activity. Efforts towards creation of a critical mass of designers by increasing the numbers marginally at the undergraduate level and seventeen PG programmes has shown results as the total number of graduates passing out in the first decade of the twenty-first century would exceed the total number of graduates in the preceding four! The seventeen sectoral PG programmes introduced over the period 2000-07 has already enhanced the numbers by five times apart from developing more active industry constituencies for design. The bold step of introducing a Strategic Design Management Programme for the first time in the country in 2004-05 is now being emulated by both management and design schools which have graciously acknowledged NID's leadership.

Amongst several other things, what makes NID truly contemporary is the setting up of India's first R&D Campus for Design at Bengaluru signifying the arrival of design research in the country as also the full-fledged research-based PG education campus at Gandhinagar, twenty-five kilometres away from Ahmedabad. This fifteen-acres of prime land will eventually house all PG programmes by integrating course and research work so that new design knowledge and breakthrough innovations are created. From the current indications based on the work of students and faculty, this campus will definitely create new vistas in the next few years.

There is no doubt that these two will set an example for the world in showcasing India as a global leader in design education and research.

Individual and collective efforts notwithstanding, the government also has ambitious plans for the National Institute of Design. For example, the Tenth Five Year Plan helped in strengthening NID's educational infrastructure and financial position. Sample these – a New Media Lab (2002), a contemporary Knowledge Management & Information Services Centre (KMC, 2003), an IT Centre, Film & Video studios (2003), Textile CAD/CAM labs (2003), and LAN network (2004). The Rapid Product Development and Design Vision Centre (2005) have already resulted in turning NID into one of the most well-equipped institutes. The eleventh Five Year Plan (2007-12) is even more ambitious and projects a greater vision with a 150 per cent increase in total outlay. The interim plan meanwhile includes the setting up of a Faculty Development Centre (FDC), initiation of National Entrance Exam for Design (NEED) and the rapid scaling up of key disciplines. In addition, NID in collaboration with Birmingham Institute of Art and Design, UK (BIAD) has implemented a major initiative titled SEED (System of Excellence in Education in Design) to ensure that the institute's educational system of selection of students, faculty development, pedagogy, course structure, delivery, evaluation, research and course certification practices are benchmarked globally on a continuous basis.

In order to develop financial self-sustenance, NID has also been organizing, streamlining and extending the reach of consultancy and outreach activities and these have indeed paid rich dividends. One very vital issue is, of course, the strategic thrust of design for the development of crafts, Khadi, rural and needy sectors, and the International Centre for Indian Crafts (ICIC) at the NID, is expected to play a key role in taking design interventions in the crafts sector forward. And there are several other feathers in NID's cap – programmes and projects set up to form a closer nexus with the industry and to provide revenue streams and they have indeed registered a steady progress.

At the end of a day, design is about defining and solving a problem and creating opportunities for both industrial and social sectors. NID's objective is to create world-class design professionals through education, research and training and to reap IPR value through design innovations. The new role for NID encompasses several

NID R&D Campus, Bengaluru.

avatars and there is little doubt that it is 'the catalyst' for design education, research and promotion in the country. The first National Design Policy 2007 provides NID with an unprecedented opportunity in becoming a 'deemed to be' design university apart from contributing to the expansion of design education as also articulating and orchestrating a design movement in India. It may be recalled that internationally, the *Businessweek*, in 2006 and 2007 placed NID as one among the top design schools in the world!

the national inspiration of design

Any institute, especially a design education institute, becomes a vibrant place because of its people especially students, for the ideas they generate, the products and services they design, and the activities that the staff and faculty take up from time to time. However, another very important dimension is the quality of the visitors to the

NID Heritage Campus, Ahmedabad.

campus including the visiting faculty, off-campus faculty and occasional lecturers. I believe, that if an institute attracts top-caliber visitors who bring their worldview, experience and wisdom – however intangible – it contributes a lot to the overall intellectual growth of an institute and its people and the convocation speakers at NID over the last twenty-eight convocations have truly provided considerable intellectual churning from time to time.

In 2001, Narayana Murthy, recalled at NID that India has the third largest pool of world-class scientists and engineers and has gained self-sufficiency in foodgrains, in addition, to building dams, rockets and satellites. However, he also pointed out that there is still not a single field where we can confidently say that we are the best in the world. Perhaps many in the audience would have thought that it is the same story in design as well! An important observation Narayana Murthy made was, 'The ongoing convergence of IT and consumer electronics portends the emergence of various user-friendly intelligent goods. Therefore, design will continue to play an important role in the technology driven world.' He then quoted the nineteenth century American clergyman, Henry Ward Beecher: 'Hold yourself responsible for a higher standard than anybody expects of you. Never excuse yourself.' Referring to Canadian politician Harold Taylor, Murthy said, 'The roots of true achievement lie in the will to become the best that you can become.'

In 2002, Adi Godrej, chairman of Godrej Group, pointed out in the convocation address at NID that economic progress comes from a single source of increased efficiency or productivity. He underlined that design together with technology and management is a determinant to progress. It is true that although we have become 'design centric', it is still not relevant to other areas like technology and management. In a country like India it is imperative that products and services are customized for the Indian consumer at affordable costs leading to 'serving the poor profitably' as Prof C.K. Prahalad argued in his book and thus creating more employment and sustained wealth creation for the growth of the country. Peter Butenshcon, a Norwegian and former President of *ICSID*, in his address at the *CII*-NID Design Summit in December 2002 questioned whether we are really pursuing the right goals as a community. He said, 'We privatized the water post, from the yard to our own kitchen sink. We split up the public bath and put it in our bathroom. We took the collective washing machine from the cellar upto our own washing room. The cinema was put into our TV room, the public playground into kids room, the park into our own garden. We left the bus to take the car and we even moved a music from the concert hall to gramophone player and straight to our own protected ear through the walkman and ear plug. We are proud of these advances.' This indeed is a wake-up call to developing economies like India.

In January 2003, NID had the privilege of yet another distinguished visitor, Ratan Tata, chairman of the Tata Group, who observed that the NID vision was indeed set in the right direction. He also urged the faculty to rediscover NID's relegated capabilities of model-making, sculpting, visualization and representation and other such precious skills.

I also remember vividly how a team from World Bank on their visit argued for design and how it was not in the agenda of either technology institutions, government, or management institutes. They felt that design brings objective focus and can play a very significant role particularly in the case of corporate social responsibility (CSR) and the 'three bottom line' approach of environmental, social and economic achievements. However, Paul Braund, renowned architect and an award-winning industrial designer made a very significant observation – the failure of design, said Braund, was that it lived in the realm of abstractions without clearly delivering value and thus became a 'feather on the table' of CEOs and other decision-makers. Will the 'feather' be blown away by a small breeze through the window without serving the purpose, is the question?

Carving in stainless steel and sandstone for Radisson Hotel Gurgaon, designed by KAARU.

Renaming the National Institute of Design as the 'National Inspiration of Design', Ad Guru Alyque Padamsee said that it is necessary to put design in a certain context to leave a lasting impression especially on the emotional retina. He also pointed out 'design is not what happened yesterday, but what happens tomorrow. A design should affect the emotional retina of a person, which, in turn, will help remember it for a long time.'

One of the most unforgettable experiences was to have His Excellency, President of India. Dr APJ Kalam at the 25th convocation of NID in 2005. He said:

> Competitiveness has three dimensions: quality of the product, cost effectiveness and supply in time. Indeed this dynamics of competitiveness in marketing of products by developing and developed countries is called the law of development. The students of the National Institute of Design have a very important role to play in improving the quality of the product by injecting aesthetics, user friendliness, promoting cost reduction techniques through the use of locally available raw material and creating designs using existing processes.
>
> Indigenous design and development capabilities are the keys to gaining a competitive edge. The competitive edge is governed by low-cost, high quality and superior performance, and timeliness that will bring customers delight which is a function of design and development, manufacturing and service.
>
> The nation's strength in the design and development of high technology products and product engineering will also increase exports. It is therefore important that the Indian R&D sector, design centres, and industries recognisze this dimension of technology.
>
> During my visit to the northeastern states particularly to Arunachal Pradesh and Nagaland, I found in every village, even every house has a unique pattern of life. They hand weave their dresses and dye it themselves with beautiful colours. They make their own headgears. A design organization like yours can visit and study this traditional craftsmanship capability and hand weaving capability for further augmentation through technology and design, so that, we can enrich the people of Arunachal Pradesh and Nagaland.

Adi Godrej, chairman of Godrej Group lighting the lamp at NID's convocation, 2002.

beyond the glass ceiling: future of design education

Design is now being increasingly recognized as a value adding link between culture and products, services and experiences and between businesses and customers. As a problem defining and creative solution-seeking discipline, design has immense potential to foster partnerships with governments, target industries and other stakeholders not only to provide a leading edge in the marketplace but also to develop a better quality of life. For instance, the community partnership driven, DOTT 07, a project in north-eastern England realized by the Design Council of UK and the Doors of Perception is a good example of such a participatory approach which could be a major tool in sustained economic and social development.

The new millennium has heralded sweeping winds of globalization, aided by converging technologies and 'ideas driven' economy. Although globalization has opened doors of economic prosperity to the 'majority world' it has also raised the issues of sustainability, appropriate technology, culture-centric preferences, survival of local arts and crafts, like never before. The challenge before design education is, therefore, to proactively respond through curriculum, pedagogy and new approaches. This calls for revamping design education and adopting collaborative practices, establishing international linkages and partnerships by drawing up a fresh design pedagogy based on time tested traditions of design education which mostly emanated from Bauhaus, Ulm and some of the Scandinavian countries, while absorbing the convergent and ubiquitous new media and collaborative tools being adopted by some of the new age design schools around the world especially in the US, Australia and UK.

Ad guru Alyque Padamsee addressing the students at NID's 27th convocation in 2006.

The issues of tradition and modernity have, therefore, perhaps never been more relevant to design education than in the twenty-first century where the dynamics of globalization and its socio-economic consequences have prompted educators and thinkers to critically appraise the role of design in enhancing and delivering the quality of life in a more accessible and inclusive manner. Whilst many traditions in design education continue to incorporate regional aspirations, many design educators, students and researchers are breaking regional barriers and are crossing continents in search of new sensibilities, alternative methodologies and collaborative opportunities, and these 'glocal' tendencies are likely to continue and expand in future.

Technological leapfrogging, especially in the IT and communication sector, has done a lot of good to developing economies like India which is fast becoming a service driven economy. In the context of the creative economy, understandably, there is a growing appreciation of the value adding and even intangible role that design can play in accelerating a harmonious economic growth, upgradation of quality of life and in developing uniqueness and differentiation.

It is noteworthy that most successful economies of the West have long and varied footprints in design education and practice. The onus is now increasingly on institutes of design education to create Gen Next designers for emerging economies that have swiftly progressed from the industrial age to the innovation age, characterized by breaking down of the glass ceiling and boundaries – for example, between, products and services and services and experiences. This will help to shape design professionals who are capable of identifying problems seeking solutions and solutions seeking markets. The solutions for the changing world need to transcend the physical spaces and products and connect the images and experience to create new values to go

Narayana Murthy, former chairman of Infosys, lighting the lamp at NID 2001 convocation.

beyond the glass ceiling. The new designers have to constantly challenge themselves and upgrade competencies to contribute, push the envelope and prolong their careers. Design education has to instill in potential students the ability to stay the course and pursue dreams and most importantly nurture creativity and passion.

designing the future

It is a brave New World out there spawned by convergence of technologies and rapid transition from analog to digital and all of us inhabit a 'global village' linked through internet connectivity on a real time basis. We witnessed the stirrings of a knowledge economy for quite some time since the last decade of the twentieth century. However, as we move closer to the finishing line of the first decade of the new century, it looks as if knowledge economy is in the process of morphing into a vibrant creative economy fuelled by speed – of ideas primarily. The mind to market travel of ideas has to be at a blitzkrieging pace. Designing the future and designing for future are the two most important tenets that designers have to keep in mind. As Alan Kay, the American computer scientist once said: 'The best way to predict the future is to invent it.' The *Time* magazine in its 13 December 2006 issue articulated this by putting 'YOU' as the 'person of the year' on its cover.

The recognition of the 'web' population, the growth of user-generated content and the dominance of cyber space has finally arrived. In a list of influential brands released by an international survey recently, ideas won the pride of place: Google beats Apple for top slot, video sharing website YouTube debuts at no. 3 followed closely by Wikipedia at no.4. This paradigm shift clearly demonstrates that a new sort of 'creative destruction' is going to be part of the unfolding new deal. Ideas, products and services usher in with a predetermined 'expiry date' dictated by technologies.

In the case of India, the transition from agrarian economy to industrial economy which hopstepped to a full-fledged service economy is now morphing slowly but surely into a creative economy. Innovation is becoming the new buzzword and the roles played by tools such as creativity and design are beginning to take centre stage. Creative and innovative brains are in demand all over. As Tom Kelly of IDEO says: 'Innovators don't just have their head in the clouds. They also have their feet on the ground.' Companies hunt for this particular group and designers who are able to crystal-ball-gaze the future and see the evolving innovation terrains and landscapes of products, technologies, brands, are the ones who are likely to succeed in a fiercely competitive marketplace. The new age designer balances precariously on this quicksand of contexts and consumers and only the brave hearts who have no fear will make it back.

Those who learn will have to adjust to a continuously changing teaching-learning space, straddling both the present and future. And those who teach will have to exist in a spectrum of technologies to make the best use of the new processes in education. As a result, pedagogy will undergo dramatic changes in the not too distant future. Discontinuous innovation in education is at our doorstep.

The *Horizon Report* 2007 recognizes the winds of change in the use of educational technologies over the next five years in leading education and research campuses worldwide. The report indicates several incisive directions for educators to ponder over. A key direction is the role of 'user-created content.' It is very important that teachers and students realize the immense potential of user generated content as demonstrated by YouTube and Wikipedia in the creation of content which then could become future learning materials. Another key direction is the power of 'social networking' wherein connecting with total strangers is being encouraged through web-based media. In the case of knowledge sharing, this is certainly an emerging pattern where experts who are strangers to the realm of the 'teacher and the taught' could be part of chat groups or

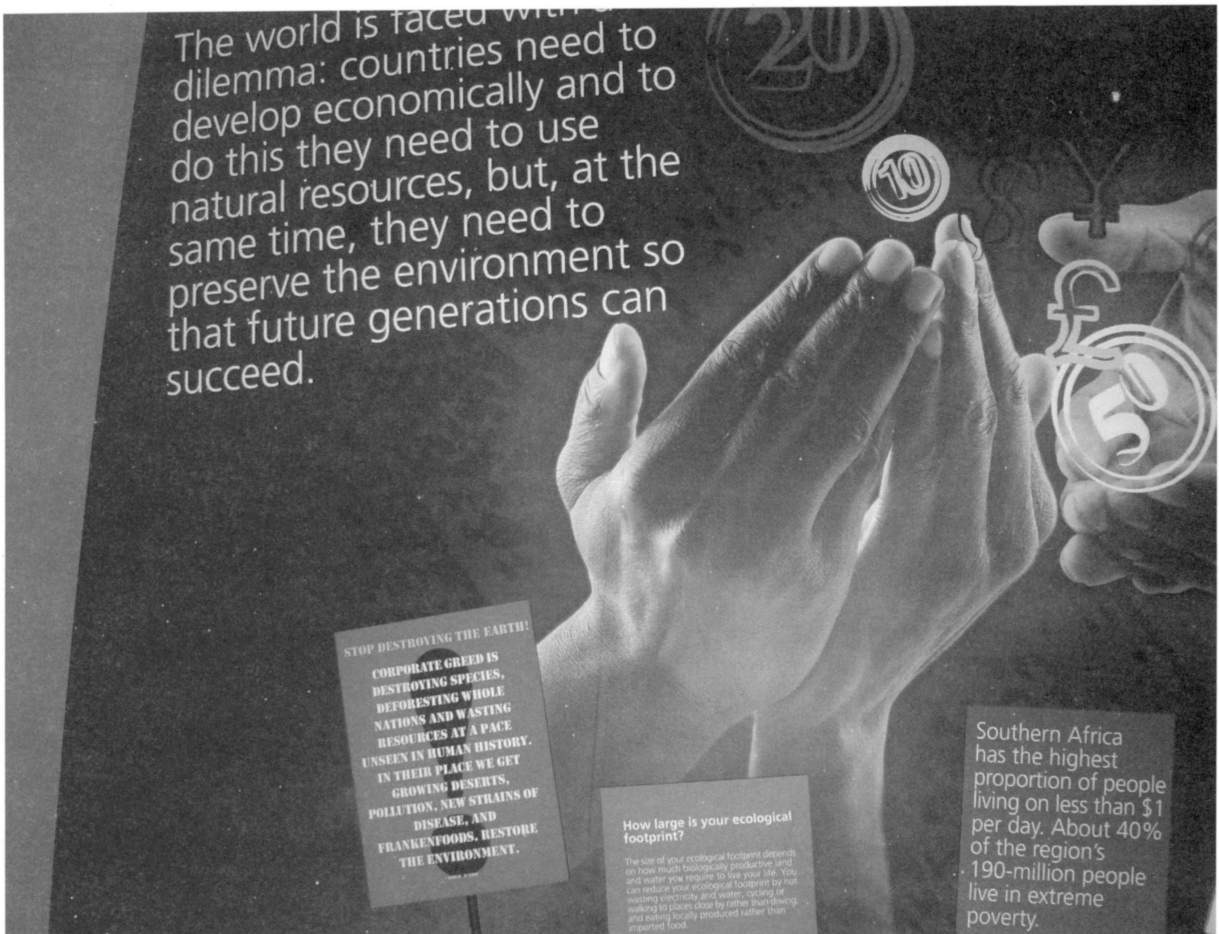

Newer technologies are being used by education and research institutions worldwide.

subscription groups for sharing information and keeping themselves updated. For example, design CORE.77 and the blogs by Bruce Nussbaum of the *Businessweek* have already made a great impact.

The next trend is that of mobile phones, digital devices and screens becoming the critical components of teaching-learning situations. Recently a visiting faculty teaching in Apparel Design informed me that while he was teaching, the students were using wi-fi to access online knowledge resources to ask relevant questions. Interactive White Boards and Courseware management systems like Black Board are already in use in a number of leading campuses. Yet another learning tool is that of Virtual Worlds like the Linden labs' 'Second Life' which enables immersive experience to the user. It is possible that online education even for design would become effective with a combination of technologies especially with the help of the new media. The virtual worlds could become a discontinuous innovation not only affecting education but also the social lives of people. Another trend outlined in the *Horizon Report* is that of 'new scholarship and emerging new publications.' There was a time when only the 'erudite' could provide solutions or write books, whereas in the new age these distinctions are blurring and a different type of nascent scholarship is emerging. The last direction underlined is about 'massively multi-player educational games'. According to the report, this may be in the long term incubation of five years or more, but are clearly the result of the advancing gaming technologies. Educational technologies may marry gaming approaches to become realistic and emotionally engaging.

Personally I think that despite the overwhelming presence of new-age technologies and tools, students and teachers in India perceive it differently and the onus is on educational institutes to correct this anomaly. Design education basically revolves around three critical faculties viz., conversion of 2D understanding to 3D spatial thinking; foresight to see ahead of the bent and an ability to synthesize. What is of course most important is the transition particularly from the traditional Indian mindset (TIM) to an emerging Indian mindset (EIM). It is very important, at this stage, to strengthen creativity and innovation through integrated design thinking in the minds of the students so that they are constantly able to innovate and challenge existing stories, ideas and solutions. Nineteenth century Danish philosopher, Soren Kierkegaard's view about standing on the 'edge of possibility' is becoming the hallmark of new age designers. It is very important to have the courage and conviction to stand up and deliver so that Indian design can emerge victorious. As Winston Churchill said long ago, 'We shape our buildings and our buildings shape us.' In the present case, we create designs and then the designs shape us and we are going to hear about it a lot more in the twenty-first century.

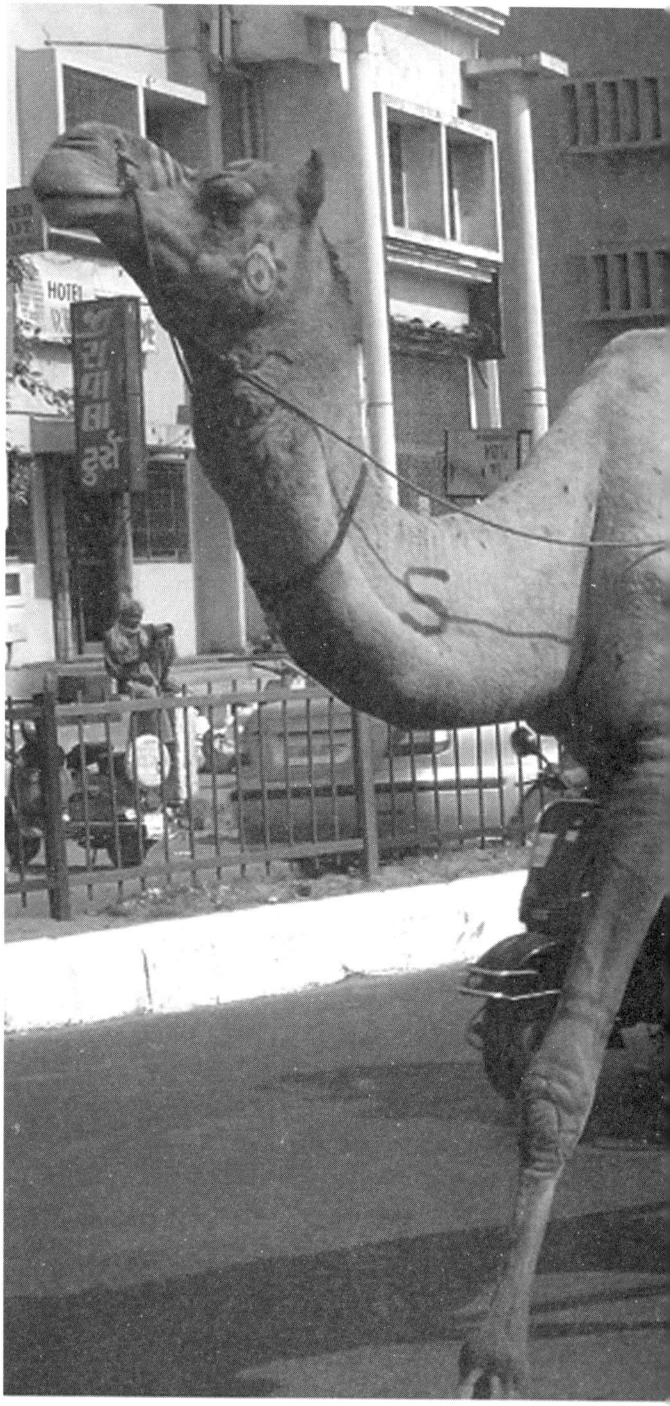

A camel cart being used as a mode of advertising in this modern age of electronics.

discover the
three-way advantage
savings • growth potential
accident death insurance cover
Reliance
Tax Saver (ELSS) Fund
utual Fund

TATA nano

towards a design-enabled india

As a concept, acceptance of design has been gaining momentum globally and one of the main reasons for this is its ability to leverage innovation-led enonomies around the world. The World Competitiveness Yearbook (IMD WCY) Scoreboard of 2007 shows Luxembourg and Norway lead the ranking in per capita income at number one and two generating 88,294 and 72,163 US dollars, respectively. On the other hand Indonesia, the Philippines and India at fifty-three, fifty-four and fifty-five positions account for 1643, 1318 and 726 US dollars, respectively, which underlines yawning gap between the 'developed, and the 'developing' countries and the inequities prevalent in highly populous countries.

There is also a flip side to this. According to the WCY 2007, the low demography in Europe, Japan and Russia takes a toll on the dynamism of the respective economies. It has been projected that in 2050, Europe will account for

Nano: India's first affordable car for the masses by the Tata Group.

628 million people, having shrunk by more than a hundred million in fifty years. The WCY 2007 under The Competitiveness Roadmap: 2007-2050 also indicates that the absolute level of poverty (one US dollar a day at 1996 prices) has been drastically reduced. It has decreased from 15.4 per cent to 5.7 per cent of the world population between 1970 and 2006. However, inequalities of incomes among world population increase in a sustained fashion. The richer become even richer and social stratifications become deeper. The divide between the 'information-rich' and 'poor' is also increasing although in countries like India, mobile telephony is helping to reduce this gap.

The major design concerns for tomorrow are going to be driven by allocation of scarce economic and natural resources to an increasing global population especially in Asia and Africa, the impact of convergent technologies and a deteriorating environment. It is quite clear that design policies and promotion will need to address not only the rapid impact of globalization but also the growing divide between 'information rich' and 'information poor'. In a world dominated by the affluent 'minority', design is more often viewed from an 'incrementalism' perspective than true innovation. The disadvantaged majority on the other hand look for innovation in design for addressing real and often basic and primary needs, to bring about a substantial upgradation in the quality of life.

The world bodies are also beginning to see the change. The ICSID, which was set up fifty years ago, has also undergone change both from ideology and operational points of view. To quote from part of an ICSID document '... traditional professional borders are breaking down: the design of products become the design of services: and the design of strategy and experiences.'

Indian culture has a long history of 'aesthetic sensitivity' and a fascinating visual language of colours and even geographical areas within a state have varying hues, structure and form which can be seen in myriad rituals, objects, art forms and performances. For a common man design often represents what appeals to the eye and at tactical levels it does deal with the visible aspects of a product, its aesthetic layer and so on. But this is often misunderstood as 'the' only significant contribution of design and, therefore, needs a relook.

This is especially critical for long-term manufacturing competitiveness as well as for the knowledge-based service economy where leadership issues in the marketplace are determined by a complex set of attributes that need to be synthesized into emotionally satisfying products and services. The rate of change in the marketplace of a globalized economy is so high that it needs a long term commitment and involvement from both the Centre and the states.

There is no doubt that periodically the government does initiate several plans and projects with a view to advance the country in a growth trajectory. But how relevant are these initiatives and in what context, are questions which need to be answered. Let us take a look at India's Science and Technology Policy of 1987 and although it has been two decades, it is relevant here to revisit it. It said: 'Technology must suit local needs and to make an impact on the lives of ordinary citizens, must give constant thought to even small improvements which could make better and cost-effective use of existing materials and methods of work. Our development must be based on our own culture and personality.' If we go by this statement, it is clear that the objectives cannot be achieved either by technology or science alone. Design, being an integral part of product development process, should have been incorporated into the policy statement.

India has an estimated seven million engineers and technologists while the number of trained professional designers from leading institutes are reckoned to be only around 5000 out of which those practicing would be considerably less, which leads to insufficient creative outcomes. While the IITs, the IIS and other premier national institutions together admitted an estimated 1,50,000 students in technology or science or engineering programmes in 2006-07, in major design institutes like the

NID, IDC of IIT and IIS only about 500 students were admitted for professional design education. Thus the gap between ideas, innovative concepts, technology and real products or services in the marketplace is widening rapidly resulting in insufficient indigenous brands on the shelves. This calls for a clear framework for a design policy which will connect technology and design as also brands and design while setting forth a clear agenda for using design as a 'horizontal force' across different sectors with a clear focus of adding value and upgrading and improving the quality of life.

The framework for a comprehensive design policy and promotion in a rapidly developing economy like India with a 1.1 billion population will need to connect the following stakeholders:

- The government
- National design promotion organizations
- Industry and design-led companies
- Design educational institutions
- Design professional associations
- Design users or consumers
- Design houses as service producers to industry/commerce/developmental sectors
- World bodies like ICSID, ICOGRADA and IFI
- Developmental organizations and NGOs.

The government which is one of the prime stakeholders for initiating and implementing a National Design Policy ought to and can create a climate to facilitate design activities in improving functions, enhancing communication, simplifying manufacturing methods, simplifying user interface while preserving cultural traditions, and utilizing them to create long-term sustainable advantage.

The next important links for the effective implementation of design policy in the country are industry and design-led companies. As we have seen earlier, Indian industries which take design seriously are very few and can be counted on one's fingertips – automobiles and two wheelers, watches, lifestyle products, jewellery and the nascent IT sector. Auto companies are clearly reaping in benefits of their design and product development initiatives: according to figures released by the Society of Indian Automobile Manufacturers (SIAM), car sales in 2006 stood at 8,82,094 units against 8,20,179 units in 2004-05. The success of India's own car, Indica and Indigo from Tata Motors is a great example and the success of multi-utility sports vehicles like Bolero and Scorpio, from Mahindra & Mahindra is also noteworthy. The dream car for the masses, Nano, from the Tata's stable with a price tag of one lakh, which has surpassed all expectations in design is expected to create a paradigm shift towards 'affordable design' for the masses. In the *Newsweek* of February 2008, Millie Richardson says, 'I would look at it as a disposable car. We have so many things in our lives now that are disposable – why not disposable cars? It would be so cheap, you could always afford a new one.' To quote from the same source, 'This is not a fad,' says Dave Schembri, president of Smart, USA. Meanwhile, John Wolkonowicz, auto analyst of *Global Insights* says, 'The Nano will put the Third World on wheels, and that will have far-reaching implications. Its going to affect every citizen of the world.' The Boston Consulting Group predicts, 'By 2015, 100 million households in the developing world will be able to afford cars priced between the Nano and the $6,000 Renault Logan.'

So far as two-wheelers are concerned, motorcycles have continued to blitzkreig as the sales soared by 17 per cent in the domestic market and touched 58,15,417 units as against 49,64,753 units in 2004-05. Overall, the two-wheeler segment, including scooters and motorcycles, grew at 14 per cent.

A company like TVS refocused on product development and strengthened the mobike portfolio by raising fuel efficiency and relaunching MAX100 and also introduced the Samurai and Shogun. 'Scooty', also by TVS, is a new category which falls between a scooter and moped and combines the lightness of design with a ruggedness associated with bikes and what is most fascinating is the way in which interesting graphics and silhouettes add to its fuel-efficient, functional design.

Design application in watch and jewellery products have truly been revolutionary. The success stories of Titan (Raga) watches and Tanishq jewellery are good examples of fusion in Indian design of ancient skills and modern science. The Raga range of watches, conceived as jewellery for women's hands, are inspired from traditional Indian motifs. The Tanishq jewellery on the other hand is trendy, innovative with new concepts like 'jewellery for working women'. The success of the above industries in fending off global competition augurs well for the future of design in India.

As we have seen earlier, whether it is a three wheeler or vehicles for mass transportation, or transport for the rural areas or the elderly, the design challenge in a country like India is enormous. An articulated design policy can attempt to encourage design solutions rooted in Indian culture rather than a force-fit approach often adopted by many Indian manufacturers.

Design helps in building human capabilities especially in a vastly changing technological environment. For instance, new media technologies can connect a farmer in a remote village through information kiosks, offer primary education to school kids or run programmes for eradicating illiteracy through use of visual language. Well-designed products and services are tools of human development that enable people to enjoy a better quality of life. The new technologies are pushing forward the frontiers of how people can use convergence to create new possibilities for improving health and nutrition, expanding knowledge, stimulating economic growth and empowering people to participate in their communities. At the end of the day, design is not just about achieving industrial competitiveness but also about maintaining the quality of life, enhancing societal development and creating an environmental balance.

design for health

An effective design policy for the times should address the grave deficiencies which ails India's health-care system. While private nursing homes boast of good medical facilities with hi-tech imported equipments, they are just beyond the reach of the majority needing health care in a country like ours. A simple design solution in terms of appropriate utilization of space – like enough beds for the ill – can ease the hardships patients undergo in generally overcrowded hospitals. Yet another simple system designed to eliminate errors while drying X-ray films could be of enormous benefit in primary health-care system as a study by one of the designers pointed out.

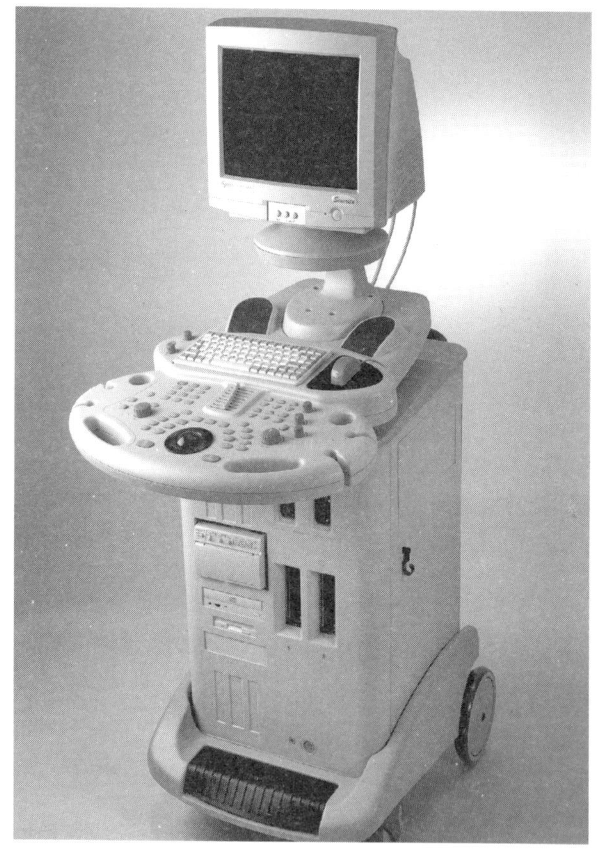

Similarly, most of the products used today need considerable redesigning for making it inclusive for the elderly and challenged. It is imperative for the state-run health-care units to provide proper facilities and there is a need to encourage and support indigenously developed medical equipments and physical aids particularly for disabled persons. Different types of disabilities (visual, hearing, speech and loco motor) affect about fifty million persons in India which is approximately 5 per cent of the total population. The disabled deserve an active participation in all the spheres of life and smart design applications in developing appropriate physical aids for the challenged can help them to join the mainstream.

design against disasters

Natural disasters are not humanmade and, therefore, perhaps inflict maximum damage on human lives and I have dealt with NID's experience during the 2001 earthquake and the 'Design after Disaster' postscript which also needs to be rephrased into 'Design before Disaster' as a motto. India had to contend with several in recent years – the earthquake in Latur, Maharashtra, Bhuj in Gujarat, or the dreaded tsunami which ravaged several parts of coastal India and other parts of the world. The lack of preparation to cope with such natural calamities

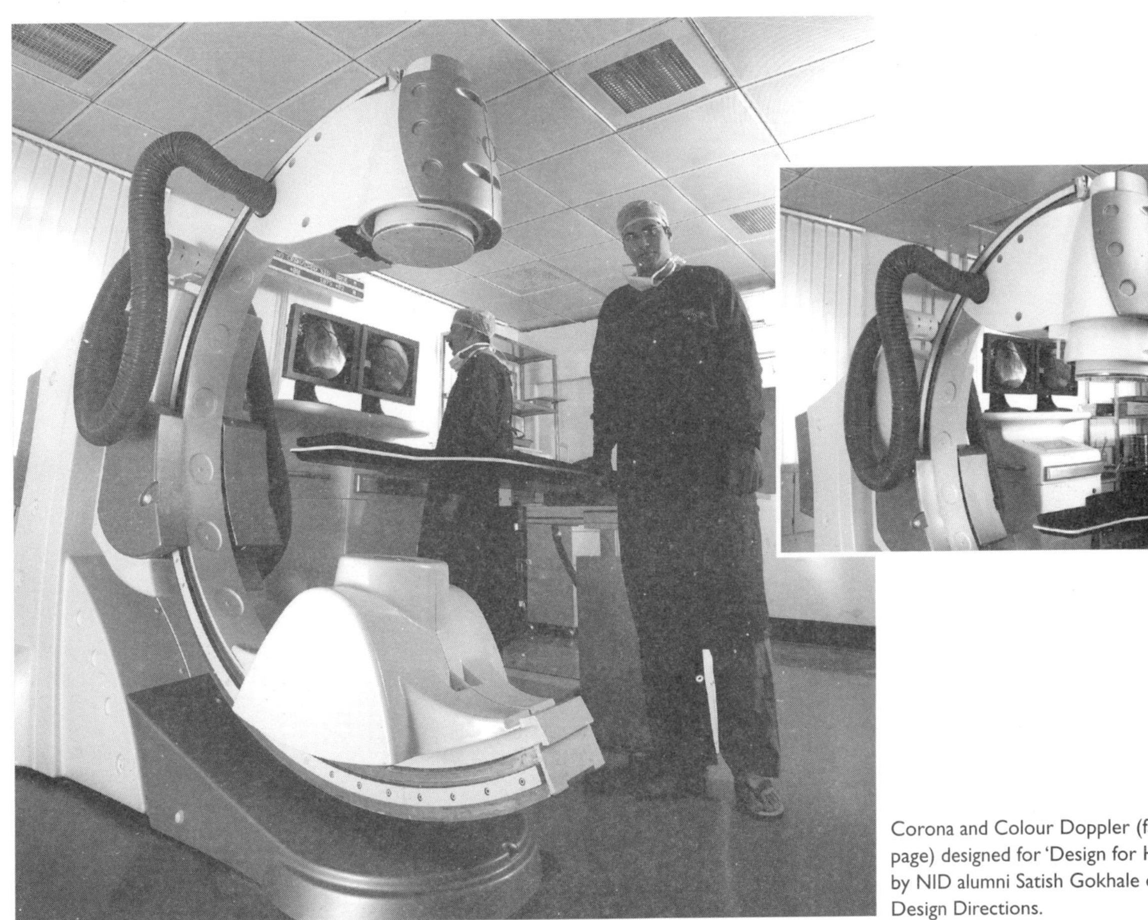

Corona and Colour Doppler (facing page) designed for 'Design for Health' by NID alumni Satish Gokhale of Design Directions.

and disasters has been poignantly brought to light again and again. The role of design and designers in developing innovative concepts in mitigating disasters can be a great boon to humanity in this context. Dr APJ Abdul Kalam, in his Convocation Address at NID in 2005 said this about design and disasters.

> India has various forms of disasters ... landslide, earthquake, floods, cyclone and tsunami. Why not generate designs of location specific options of habitats of various types and sections of people so that loss of lives is reduced. Also of options of designs for structures in sea coast which can minimize deaths and property loss.
>
> There are yet unconfirmed reports that the tribal population and animals including cattle were not affected by the tsunami as much as the other population.
>
> We must work towards learning the right lessons even from this disaster so that our future can be safe. The fishermen of late seem to have been pushed to live closer to the sea shore than ever before due to the demands placed by tourism and urban development. I strongly feel that this trend should be reversed and the law that human habitats should be at least be 500 meters away from the sea should be strictly enforced. Inspite of various precautions, disasters and accidents happen. Often we do not handle crisis systematically. For example there are high rise shelters in areas, often prone to floods or cyclonic rise for people to stay for a few days till floods recede. Even fast evacuation system can have designs without stampede which cause death. World over designers apply their mind to these practical issues.

design for the economic uplift of rural/tribal societies

If design has to play a role in improving the standard of living of the people of the country, the problems of more than 75 per cent of the total population, living in rural and tribal areas, have to be addressed effectively. A socially responsible design policy can bring about the change by introducing better designs in terms of improved equipments and tools used in agricultural activities, low cost housing structures for farmers, and sanitation facilities in rural areas. Design can actually revolutionize the system of disseminating the required information for farmers in India by fusing communication design with Information Technology.

design for literacy and primary education

In a country where more than 35 per cent of the population still remains illiterate, and many children in the rural and tribal areas tend to dropout at the primary level itself, an effective use of communication design or international design for e-learning can help to create a sustained interest in education among these sections.

Water embroidery in stainless steel thread in fabric designed by KAARU.

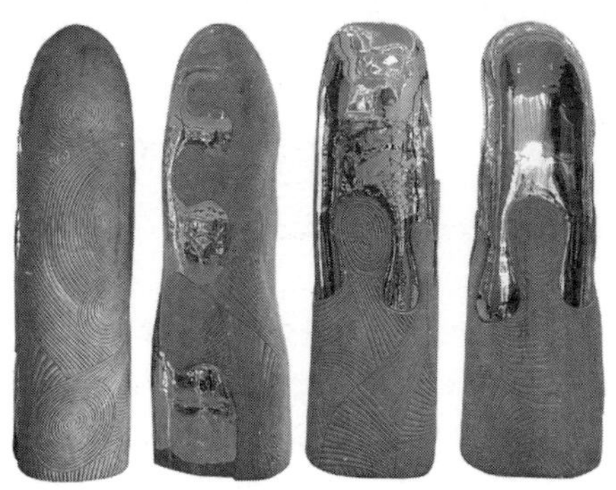

Stainless steel and stone sculpture for Radisson Hotel designed by KAARU.

design for small and medium scale enterprises

The SME sector in India is the backbone of the manufacturing economy churning out almost 7500 products, while contributing substantially to the industrial manufacturing to the extent of 45 per cent or so while accounting for 35 per cent of total exports. Most importantly, it provides employment to over seventeen million people. Due to several economic reasons, the SMEs get stuck with obsolete designs and outdated technologies. An appropriate action plan which emphasizes on 'design clinics' and other models of design interventions can assist in developing competitive edge for SMEs.

design for preserving culture/ identity

I think the biggest challenge for design in India lies in its very diversity – 18 major and 1,600 minor languages and dialects, 6 major religions and ethnic groups, 52 major tribes, 6,400 castes and sub-castes, living in 29 states and 6 union territories celebrating 29 major festivals. This is indeed unmatchable and mind-boggling! A responsive design policy could help foster the cultural identities of different regions, states and communities and preserve what is unique and vibrant in the world's largest democracy.

design for environment

Global warming is the latest scare making countries around the world paranoid. The Nobel Peace Prize to Senator Al Gore for his film *An Inconvenient Truth* and TERI's Rajendra Pachauri and his team for heading the UN Panel on Climate Change and espousing the cause has brought the issue to the forefront even further. There is a greater need for creating greener products in the face of this global threat and the ever increasing problems of pollution. Design solutions have to make concerted efforts to zero-in on environmental factors now as development and progress has brought along with them an imbalance in nature with deteriorating natural resources. As design has a seamless role to play in the future, it needs to find solutions and innovative remedies to protect and save the planet from an ecological disaster for future generations.

towards a 'glocal' design view

With the emergence of a borderless society around the world, a 'glocal' design view needs to be articulated – an idea which accommodates and meets the specific needs of different regions with respect to economic and cultural realities. The 'glocal' design view should attempt to harness the latest technological transformations as tools for creating well-designed products and services by marrying global design directions and local consumer requirements.

One can suggest and recommend several methods by which design can lead to the overall prosperity of any country, notwithstanding its relative small size in the global power structure. For instance, an article by Dong-Sung-Cho of Korea in the *Design Management Review* in 2004 highlights the fact that in order to accomplish economic development, some countries in the West had taken around 200 years while Korea achieved it in a matter of just four decades. Amongst several other factors, the author also attributes this to the adoption of design as a tool for strategic advantage and long-term competitiveness and the result: brands from Korea like LG and Samsung have replaced many well-known global brands around the world. In the case of UK, governmental support has not only contributed to the country becoming renowned for design consultancy services but also has succeeded in positioning UK as a cutting edge 'Design Hub.'

promoting a design wave

It is well known that for every idea to get into the top of the mind recall, gain acceptance, to be followed, extended and extrapolated, some stages have to be traversed in order to acquire a critical mass. A significant corollary to design education is promotion and design promotion has adopted the following formats in countries across the world:

- Setting up of a design council (UK, Malaysia, Australia)
- Initiating design awards and setting up design centres (Germany, Japan, Hong Kong)
- Holding of international design conferences, exhibitions, fashion shows, seminars, and several design competitions

It was not fully realized at different points of inflection of development that without a design promotional infrastructure, designers would not get opportunities in the industry or elsewhere to use their skills and knowledge effectively. At home in recent years, especially 2001 onwards, the holding of CII-NID Design Summit, the *Businessworld*-NID Excellence Awards since 2003, the Design Broadband Competition, commencing of NIDUS (NID's own Design Shoppe), the Graduate Show of NID, IDC (IIT, Delhi and Mumbai), SRISHTI, NIFT, have enabled designs to acquire a bigger presence and awareness.

The real beneficiary of design promotion is design education because closer collaboration with industry and target groups help in redefining education and in pushing the frontiers of design. Design creates, connects and cares for people. Design has also a magical quality of anticipating the future. As Sir Terrance Conran, the renowned British designer once said, 2 per cent of magical and aesthetic quality of design combined with 98 per cent of common sense is what improves the 'quality of life.' In the days to come, affordable design for masses shall become a primary concern for industry, recognizing design opportunities at the 'bottom of pyramid' thus advocating 'design for everyone.' Designers, who are generally not overwhelmed by constraints, can play a pivotal role in shaping India's present and future. The proactive role of designers in Beijing Olympics 2008 is illustrative of the possibilities. The Canadian IDM's example of providing subsidy to SME enterprises for employing designers has already succeeded in placing hundreds of designers at different levels of the industry.

Talking of designers getting their due, despite their so-called 'abstract' profession in popular perception, it is not as if they are unsung and not celebrated. For example, Raymond Loewy the famous industrial designer appeared on the cover of *Time* magazine way back in 1949, heralding the ascent of industrial design in the US. Alvar Aalto, the architect-turned-furniture designer from Finland appeared on a currency note in their country. The need to promote and celebrate design is now being increasingly recognized by the stakeholders in India as well. Many private initiatives like the Jindal Steel Excellence Awards, Elle Décor Awards and the Zee TV awards for architecture, interiors, indicate a growing awareness about design not only as a value add but also as a strong strategic force.

The first time an Indian designer was recognized through a Design Excellence Award in India was in June 2003 when *Businessworld* or BW and NID joined hands to institute the BW-NID Design Excellence Awards. The cover page of the magazine carried the photograph of the 'Best Indian Designer of the Year', Satish Gokhale. It was a watershed event in the history of Indian design and since then Indian designers along with the overall design scene have gained in many tangible and intangible ways. First of all, it has become clear to most that awards are an important ingredient for the design movement to gather momentum dovetailing other essential components viz., design promotion and good design mark. It is probably not coincidental that only after *Businessworld* and NID started this award that our own designers began to get invitations to be on the juries of international design competitions whether in the US or elsewhere and the design consultancies in India began to scout overseas for strategic alliances and broader relationships. When we compare the aggressive foray of Asian countries in design promotion and the huge progress they are making in creating an Asian 'design identity', it does hurt to see that India has virtually no presence in the arena and this needs to be addressed collectively.

When we compare the success and scale of the Hong Kong Design Week or the Singapore Design Festival by Design Singapore; our weaknesses become more stark. A country like Singapore places their design services as a gateway between two mammoth markets, namely, China and India. The Taiwanese are branding Taiwanese design, celebrating the manufacturing competence along with creativity and culture. It is amazing that the city of Turin in Italy, which was nominated as the World Design Capital for 2008 by ICSID has brought out a wonderful magazine illustrating the quintessence of Italian design.

Design education in all these countries is also exploding with facilities and new programmes and thousands of designers are ready to take on challenges of not only their markets but others as well. With Indian markets opening up, the designers from Asia and Europe are getting alternative slices of the Indian market and the competition is hotting up. Only the fittest and most savvy will survive in this battle. Team work, technological competence, marketing insights and above all a good hold on design visualization and realization will give the winners an edge. If Indian designers and the design fraternity do not shift gears and work closely for the design movement, then in all likelihood it will once again be the oft-repeated story of having missed the bus.

My years on the executive board of the World Apex Body for ICSID over three terms – 2001-03, 2005-07 and now for 2007-09 has exposed me to many design promotion efforts across the world. I am particularly impressed with the efforts made by Korea, Taiwan, Singapore and Japan while almost overawed by the aggressive efforts of China. The hugely expensive campaigns carried out by countries and cities for winning the bids for the headquarters of ICSID/ICOGRADA/IDA as also for the World Design Congress and World Design Capital are lessons which indicate how India lags behind in projecting a united front, supported by vision and sufficient funds to make 'Designed in India' stand head and shoulders above others in world arena! Of course the promise needs to be converted to real design achievements on the ground.

The only viable mantra to achieve what has been done by our peers around the world is through a sustained collaborative effort and the day is not far when India will become a major influencer in both Asia and the world.

Beaten stainless steel fruit bowl on carved gray stone base for Jindal Steel Exhibition designed by KAARU.

strategic perspective of the first national design policy

In the context of India, we have already seen how several factors if synergized with design can create wonders. However, it is not enough to just formulate a National Design Policy and be complacent in the thought that it is the destination. In this context, co-creation and co-operation are more than just buzzwords if participatory design processes have to be set in motion. It is more important to evolve an acceptable definition of design which captures the role, and the processes of design. Noble Laureate Herbert Simon defines design as the process by which we devise courses of action aimed at changing the existing state of affairs into a more preferred one. According to experimental art theorist, Ken Friedman, 'Robust design requires more than artistic insights and ethical concerns. Today's designers are called upon to solve problems that require knowledge and preparation.' Richard Buchanan, professor of design theory, on the other hand defines design as 'the human power of conceiving, planning and making products that serves human beings in the accomplishment of their individual and collective purposes.'

A comprehensive definition also comes from the ICSID and it says: 'Design is an activity whose aim is to establish the multi-faceted qualities of objects, processes, services and their systems in whole life-cycles. Therefore, design is the central factor of the innovative humanization of technologies and the crucial factor of cultural and economic exchanges.' While primarily the National Design Policy has to addresses industrial and communication design, it could also recognize the roles of 'services' and 'experience' in an economy like India which is rapidly moving towards becoming a service-led economy.

An overview of economic achievements of design policy and promotion in some parts of the world can be summarized as follows:

Satish Gokhale, NID alumnus at the BW-NID Design Excellence Awards 2003.

US — Holder of maximum number of global brands and patents.

UK — Leader in design consultancy services and creative industries, with focus on design education from school level onwards.

Japan — Pioneer of hi-tech design culture and good design award system leading to quality and design upgrdation of Japanese products.

Taiwan — Developed design to overtake Japan in electronic goods and redefined value price proposition globally.

China — Global leader in low-cost manufacturing. Actively taking to design promotion, design education and development of power brands.

Thailand — Design for export of manufactured goods and crafts.

India does not feature in the table but I am sure that in a conducive atmosphere such as today's in the country, it can aspire to be in a commanding or atleast influential position.

As with any plan, a strategic perspective has to be evolved by the stakeholders to operationalize the National Design Policy with a timeline for accomplishments. In order to make India a design-enabled country by the year 2020, the following action points need to be stressed upon:

One of the best insights into Indian design came surprisingly from the minister of Commerce and Industry, Kamal Nath, at the 4th CII-NID Design Summit in 2004. In a very focussed speech, he began by saying, 'Design is often misunderstood to be more ornamentation, trimmings, beauty. Nothing could be more inaccurate. While aesthetics is certainly an essential component of design, when we speak of design in the industrial context we mean much more.' Nothing could be nearer to what I have been saying right at the beginning of this book as to how design actually acts as a good socio-economic indicator of an economy. And for a thriving economy such as India's, the critical role of design, also endorsed by the minister, has to be recognized particularly by the industry, sooner rather than later. Here Kamal Nath quoted an instance – 'Just four years ago, if you recall, the Indian manufacturing industry was facing a severe crisis. Big automobile companies had made unprecedented losses. And then, last year we witnessed a qualitative turnaround in the manufacturing sector. A significant reason for this was that these companies started vigorously investing in product development and innovation, pursuing design strategies and creating internal capabilities.'

We can argue endlessly about the merits and demerits of it but we have to accept that there is a visible paradigm shift so far as the economy is concerned and slowly but

Bottom of the Pyramid Model:	Design for masses, source of innovation and wealth
Thrust towards quality of life:	Design for development
Brand & Design:	Creating Indian brands for global arena
Perception of the whole country/industry	
Identifying groups of industries through which Design can add value	Assessing impact, role and value of creative industries
Demonstrating: 'design as strategy' through design-led companies	Innovation driven value chain
Revival of manufacturing sector including SME enterprises	Design as tool for competitiveness (i.e. toy sector) and for enabling enterprises to compete on value
Rejuvenation of traditional sectors like handloom, handicraft through design intervention programmes	Design for cluster/growth centres
Technology/engineering chain for sustainable advantage	Achieving synergy to drive value design – management
Public sector enterprises	For pursuing competitiveness
Infrastructure design:	Public Spaces/Heritage Conservation and urban design
Design of services:	Public Utilities, Delivery of Public Services and IT Technology enabled Services
Outreach:	Artisanal development/micro-enterprises sector

surely it's getting to be more service-driven. And in his speech the minister focused on this aspect by saying, 'Services is an area where India is bullish. We are aggressively targeting exports of services. Our burgeoning middle class is itself a growing consumer of services, and the demands for "quality" in service is rapidly increasing. It is design that can bring in this quality.'

There is no gainsaying that many Indian companies are now comparable to international conglomerates in terms of their size, policies, strategies and the huge numbers or profitability. But design which is at the core of brands is given a shoddy treatment by many of these corporate giants. There is this complacency bordering on a lackadaisical mindset when it comes to giving design its deserved position. Considering I head a design institute, this may sound like a bit of an exaggeration but Kamal Nath pretty much said the same thing: 'It is disappointing that a lot of Indian companies have no in-house design facilities or formalized design capabilities. There is also great potential in offering design services from India to MNCs and overseas clients, and India can emerge as a 'design hub' in the Asian region. I call upon industry to step up its investment in design to see that original designs of India come up to the global arena so that, along with "Made in India" and "Served by India", "Designed in India" also becomes a reality soon.'

So far as creativity goes, design evolves its own idioms in different cultures and therefore nations. I am not for a moment suggesting that for designers in countries as homegenous as say America it must be easy to create but then India is a diverse entity and also ancient. Therefore for an Indian designer the challenges are mammoth. Amongst other things, the country is on a threshold of vast technological and communication overhaul which means that a designer apart from creating and delivering in his profession also has to have an holistic approach to improve the quality of people's lives through products and services. In this context, opined: '... Design has the power and potential to link India's strong competencies and the rural crafts and traditions to the new high-end products and services to project India's unique capability. Design has the power to touch lives, to change lives. The "social" role of design still lies untapped. Public services, public utilities, education and health-delivery systems – all these can be significantly improved through design.'

So the time has come for design to work in close association with various other segments and get systematized wherein it could get a direction and fixity of purpose. In the Indian context, whenever there is talk of government policies and reams and reams of paper devoted to it, the common response is one bordering on cynicism. That is because often policies remain on paper and never get implemented. But there is hope and Kamal Nath articulated the same when he announced the intent of the government to come out with the first National Design Policy: He said ' . . . And so we have decided to come with a National Design Policy. But this policy would have no use or meaning if it were devised solely in the cubicles of Udyog Bhawan. If it is to be useful and 'owned' by practitioners, then all stakeholders have to be consulted.'

The policy also has a special relevance for NID as it echoed the institute's need to have a national design policy way back in the mid seventies and again in the beginning of the twenty-first century. I recall that in the first issue of *Design Plus*, the in-house magazine of NID I had said: 'NID wants to strengthen its new design satellites to act as heads fountainheads of design movement and provide inputs to Government for formulation of National Design Policy while working closely with industry apex associations like CII to help industry to use design as a strategic tool to build competitive advantage.' The foundation had thus been laid and later in the same year in the first CII-NID Design Summit held in 2001 in Bengaluru, the need for a National Design Policy was emphasized and included in the 'Road map' for Indian design. Subsequently, as explained earlier, in the fourth CII-NID Design Summit, Kamal Nath, announced the government's intention as well.

Finally, on 8 February 2007, the government announced the long awaited National Design Policy. This landmark step has established beyond doubt that design has become a national priority now and will soon become integral to our agenda for industrial and societal development. For design, growth of which is so closely linked with that of the industry and economy as a whole, this is quite a favourable moment as there are abundant opportunities available. The design policy though in its very early nascent years promises to usher in a new chapter of development and brings hope and cheer to the design community which should rise up to the occasion to make use of this unprecedented opportunity. Some important parts of the first National Design Policy are excerpted below:

> Strategic importance of design for national and industry competitiveness is now universally recognized. Value addition through innovations in deigns can play a pivotal role in enhancing the competitiveness of both manufacturing and service industries.
>
> Realizing the increasing importance of design in economic, industrial and societal development and in improving quality of products and services, the Government of India had initiated a consultative process with industry, designers and other stakeholders to develop the broad contours of a National Design Policy. The vision behind initiating a National Design Policy is to have a "design enabled Indian industry" which could impact both the national economy and the quality of life in a positive manner.
>
> Preparation of a platform for creative design development, design promotion and partnerships across many sectors, states and regions for integrating design with traditional and technological resources;
>
> Presentation of Indian designs and innovations on the international arena through strategic integration and cooperation with international design organizations;
>
> Global positioning and branding of Indian designs and making "Designed in India" a by-word for quality and utility in conjunction with "Made in India" and "Served from India";
>
> Promotion of Indian design through a well defined and managed regulatory, promotional and institutional framework;
>
> Raising Indian design education to global standards of excellence;
>
> Creation of original Indian designs in products and services drawing upon India's rich craft traditions and cultural heritage;
>
> Making India a major hub for exports and outsourcing of designs and creative process for achieving a design-enabled innovation economy;
>
> Enhancing the overall tangible and intangible quality parameters of products and services through design;
>
> Creation of awareness among manufacturers and service providers, particularly SMEs and cottage industries, about the competitive advantage of original designs;
>
> Attracting investments, including Foreign Direct Investments, in design services and design related R&D; and
>
> Involving industry and professional designers in the collaborative development of the design profession.

The strategy to achieve this vision would focus on strengthening quality design education at different levels, encouraging the use of design by small scale and cottage industries and crafts, facilitating active involvement of industry and designers in the development of design profession, branding and positioning of Indian design within India and overseas, enhancing design and design service exports and creating an enabling environment that recognizes and rewards original designs. And nothing, I believe, is impossible. The journey towards a design-enabled

visions for design leadership

shaping designpreneurs

Dr APJ Abdul Kalam inaugurating the Design Vision Centre (DVC) at NID Ahmedabad in 2005.

One of the most significant aspirations of design is to strengthen the hands of those who create it. Although the twenty-first century has ushered in considerable opportunities for Indian designers to commence their own enterprises, there is no system for supporting designer-entrepreneurs either through Venture Capital or incubation. Finally, after several presentations and discussions, the Department of Science and Technology agreed to provide a window of opportunity for design as part of the Technology Incubator Scheme and the National Design Business Incubator or NDBI after nearly two years of ground work since 2003 was formally inaugurated at the NID on 15 February 2005. An old building hitherto used as a storage was converted into an airconditioned studio space, offices and common facilities thus realizing a determmined step towards converting ideas to wealth.

The NDBI stresses on the need to achieve design-technology leadership for the country by realizing the dream – 'Designed in India, Made for the World'; to foster successful 'Designpreneurship' and develop an intrinsic capability among the industry to deal with design and other related areas. Thus NDBI attempts to inculcate a spirit of entrepreneurship in the creative minds of young designers, so that their ideas get transformed into new products or services capable of being marketed and sold. NDBI is thus a comprehensive, all inclusive (technology, design, materials, processes and business plan) one-stop innovation and product/concept development nodal centre.

Incubatiosn is a versatile combination of business development processes, infrastructure, and people, designed to nurture and grow new and small businesses by supporting them through the early stages of development and change while absorbing certain risks. A budding designer or a design-led entrepreneur can approach NDBI at NID for seeking incubation support in:

- Converting product concepts/ideas into commercializable products
- Directly getting (without any lead time) feasible product ideas
- Having ideas assessed for feasibility and fast track implementation
- Product design audit from both user and manufacturers' perspective.

Design-based business incubators based on the relative success of NDBI at the NID so far have the potential to become strategic tools for creation, sustenance, survival and growth of new innovation-led enterprises. They also facilitate speedy and risk reduced commercialization of research outputs. The NDBI deliverables could be summarized as follows:

- Making a product failure proof: on an ongoing basis, NDBI evaluates the pros and cons of each and every step in the product development process to ensure that the product and the idea are free from major risk factors. This analytical approach will help to develop successful product development strategy, which can be used in training and education pedagogy.
- Need to face global competition: NDBI helps design products that are comparable and competitive not only with global products in Indian markets but also with global products in overseas markets. This will help to increase the export potential of the country and position 'Designed in India' impactfully.
- Need to know the market trends: since the NDBI is in close touch with the latest in design and technology, it may be able to forecast market trends and consumer aspirations to help develope products that are more commercially viable.

Apart from the NDBI, which encourages young designers to manage their own businesses, yet another platform was needed to take the good ideas to

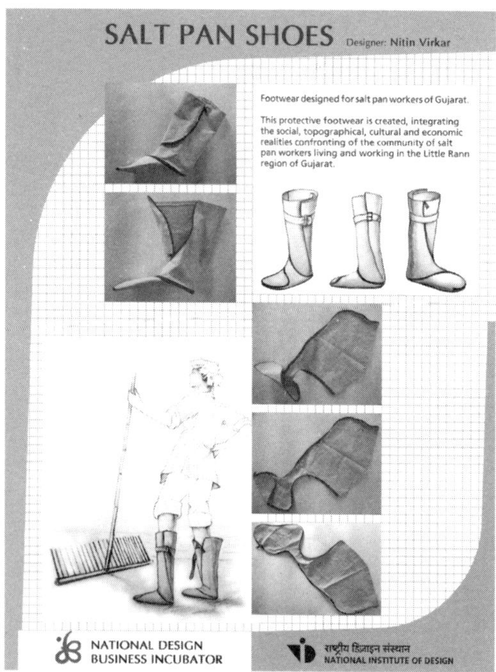

Footwear designed for the salt pan workers of Gujarat by Nitin Virkar.

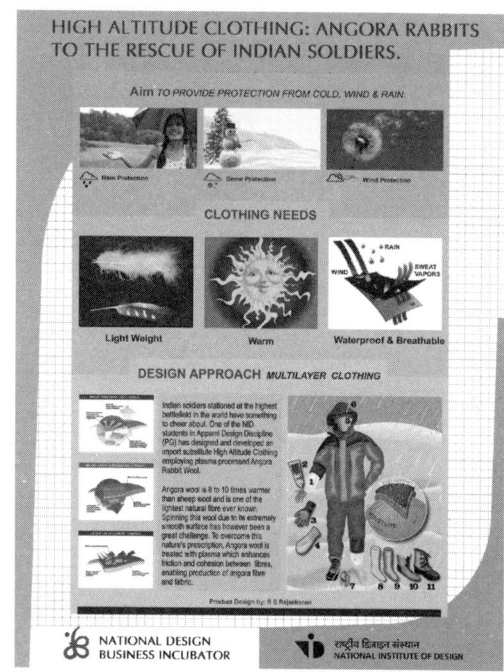

High altitude clothing for soldiers by NID Apparel Design & Merchandising student R.S. Rajshekaran.

entrepreneurs so that they could in turn explore the marketability of such thoughts. Design Idea Fair or DIF was, therefore, conceived in 2006 for the first time in Delhi and again held in 2007 during the 7th CII-NID Design Summit in Bengaluru where design-led innovations, ideas, concepts and services were showcased to the industry to facilitate trade and exchange of IPR. In the first fair, around thirty-five and in the second forty-six innovative ideas were on display. There is a great deal of interest at such a confluence where exchange of ideas between designers and entrepreneurs take place for creating new opportunities for success.

Design ideas if taken up by imaginative entrepreneurs can create successful enterprises provided they work in close collaboration with the designer as design is an iterative process and needs responsive and continuous innovations to remain afloat. The success stories of three incubates in recent times at the NID, namely, Rahul Misra, Samar Firdos and Deepti Toor indicate the great potential of incubating talented designers by providing them with entrepreneurial exposure and some financial and marketing support.

The talented duo of Rahul Misra and Samar Firdos, part of an Outreach Programme Project at NID, created a fascinating collection of garments from the fine Balarampuram (Kerala) fabrics and called it – 'The Ray of Light'. This was further taken up as an incubation project for over a year at the NDBI. The basic idea behind the project was to use traditional Kerala handloom textiles in a contemporary style targeting tourists visiting God's Own Country, Kerala and to bring back a thousand-year-old craft into the mainstream. Most often tourists want to taste the local flavours of a place and apart from food, there could be no better way than to wear the traditional outfits of a region.

'Reversibility' formed the second key factor of the

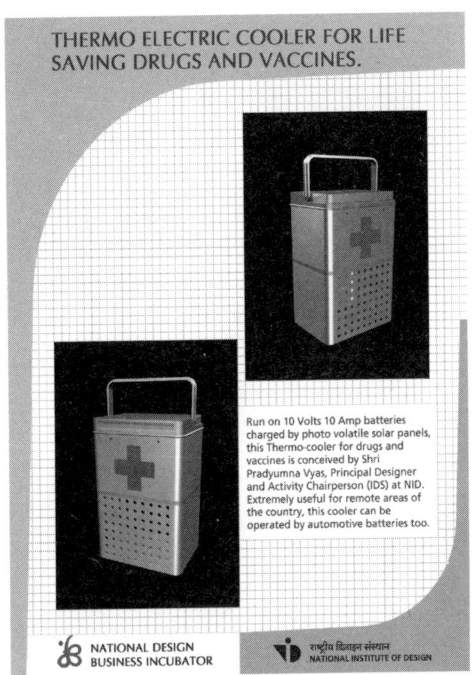

Thermo-electric cooler for life-saving drugs and vaccines by NID faculty Pradyumna Vyas.

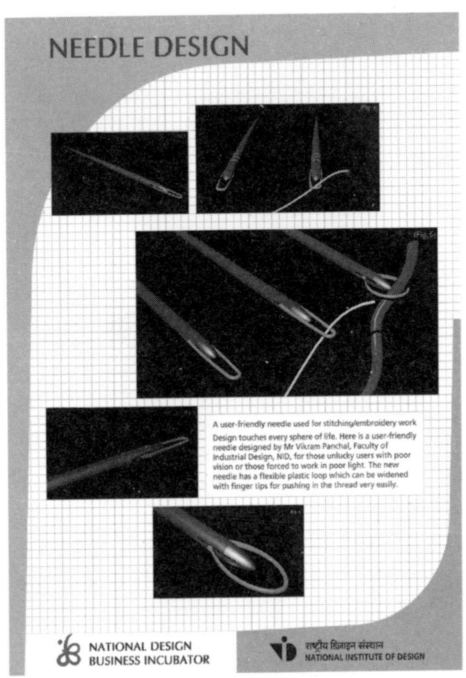

A user-friendly needle designed by Industrial Design faculty Vikram Panchal.

collection, where a complete new look unfolded on reversing the garment, which included change of colour, texture and also silhouettes. The problem of carting heavy luggage in the hot and humid weather of Kerala was solved through the 'reversibility' feature of the collection as a single garment gave tourists a dual option. And so far as the maintenance of the outfit was concerned, the collection was made out of cotton (hundred counts) and on washing dried faster. Also because it was double layered, it didn't get crushed easily – yet another boon for those living out of suitcases! By and large tourists visiting India love our attires – a sari or a dhoti – but find the drapes unmanageable, whereas in this case, the drapes were easy to handle and the dress could be fastened in no time.

The collection went on to create rave reviews for the two designers at the Lakme India Fashion Week in Mumbai in 2005. Subsequently, Rahul Misra and Samir Firdos became young entrepreneurs, encouraged as they were due to the great exposure and feedback in the Gen Next and 'Emerging Designers' segment shows at the Lakme Fashion Week in Mumbai.

The third young and talented incubate, Deepti Toor also made a great impact at the Lakme Fashion Week where she showcased the miniature painting style of Indian art in her comfortable and chic styles. Thus three 'designpreneurs' have actually arrived on the scene and their success is sure to boost the confidence levels of many more incubates at NDBI.

There is yet another success story but this time of a member of the faculty incubate at NID – Pradyumna Vyas who designed a portable thermo cooler for vaccines and life saving drugs. Vyas later found an entrepreneur who took up the mass marketing of his product to the health-care sector especially in the rural areas. After successful field tests, the manufacturer now awaits orders from the Ministry of Health for various state's primary health-care centres.

Such successes though modest, point to the need for setting up a customized Rolling Venture Capital Fund for designpreneurs in India. The reasons: by and large incubates implement their business plan in 12-18 months which is indeed short. They need quick financial support process so that they can spend time effectively on developing new products. Most of the financial institutions or venture capitalists do not support young and fresh incubates from academic institutions as they are often first generation entrepreneurs. Further, venture capitalists do look for higher investments and may not show interest in incubates where the investment is mostly up to of fifty lakhs only.

Institutes are 'repositories of ideas' but once outside the ambit of creativity, these need to be translated into viable products in a fiercely competitive marketplace. Technological tools like Rapid Product Development and visualization can be of great assistance for the travel of ideas from mind to market. The design incubator should, therefore, ideally be able to provide adequate R&D and visualization facilities including adequate financial support and linkages to markets for developing a generation of designpreneurs who will call the shots in the unfolding design scenario in India.

managing as designing

Let me tell you a story about a rabbit which was excellent at hopping around happily. One day an expert was brought in and he felt that the rabbit needed to be taught swimming as well so that it could multi-task. Obviously the rabbit could not swim even after very strenuous lessons and in the process also found it very hard to hop around gracefully as it used to do before the swimming lessons! The tale exemplifies the inherent conflict of interest in the two professions: managing and designing. The discussions about how designers need to become managers and vice-versa constantly remind us of this dilemma.

By and large, managers definitely stand to benefit by an exposure to the process of designing especially in a creative economy, as the key to it lies in releasing the embedded or acquired knowledge into products and services for the customers in the shortest possible time. However, it needs to be clearly understood that first-rate designers cannot necessarily become first-rate managers and the reverse also holds true. Designers have to first fully develop their innate creativity to become top notch professionals who can dream, imagine, visualize, represent, prototype and above all create. If they are not good at these essential elements of design, then making it to the next level would not be easy. In all likelihood, three types of creative practitioners are likely to emerge in the coming decades. Imagineers (or blue sky visionaries), ideators or innovators (thinkers, 'out-of-box' designers) and finally designers (who can both visualize and realize).

I believe that managers attempting to become designers and its reverse is quite like the fox in the folktale which tried to paint itself white to get an entry into a flock of sheep. The make-over doesn't really help and in the

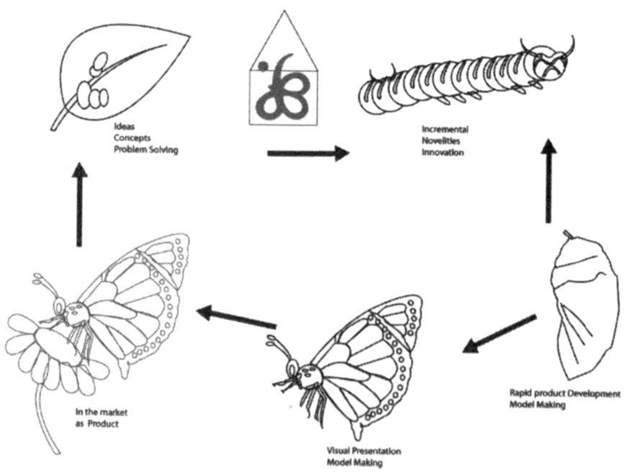

National Design Business Incubator System: A schematic view.

Deepti Toor (left), NID student incubatee walking the ramp in the Lakme GenNext show in Mumbai.

process, the credibility of the respective professions might take a beating. Design expression is related to the creative quality of mind which connects the rational to the 'emotional' domains of one's psyche. Designers have a key role in dovetailing culture and nature with finished products and services and in also taking the business to customers. The roles of managers and designers are, therefore, very distinct though it is also true that many successful leaders and managers do have a high level of creativity and innovation. They are somewhat like 'thought designers' who allow the 'head' to take a lead in decision making and mix the left brain with right in good measure. In this case, the 'head' and 'heart' are in that order of vertical hierarchy in the decision making process. Designers obviously are more likely to allow the 'heart' to rule over the 'head.' However, there isn't really a hard and fast rule to this as several successful designers do appreciate the value of proper marketing and design research along with awareness about winning strategies in the market place.

In recent times, some of the overseas management schools have set up design schools in India in response to an emerging creative economy. While there is obviously nothing wrong with such a practice, it is important to recognize clearly the objective of such a step and the rigorous processes involved in shaping a high quality designer. There is no point in creating a breed of disgruntled 'design managers' or 'manager designers.' The attempts of running 'Design Management' or 'Business of Design' courses are no doubt experimental but have to be handled with great sensitivity and care.

I am in no way undermining efforts made by engineering and management schools to absorb design into their system. For example, as mentioned earlier in this book, Samsung's design approach, which believes in marrying technology and design in the right proportion, is one of the ways forward. At Samsung, the value of retaining the mysteries of consumer behaviour at the level of heuristics rather than conversion to algorithms which formed the basis of the twentieth century approach for creating products for mass consumption as in the case of Ford Cars, Frito Lays or McDonalds and hundreds of such examples, has been well recognized and this approach has made them a design-led corporate in the early part of the twenty-first century. Designers with the creative ability to imagine well, connect dots and synthesize will be in great demand in the times to come and managers who comprehend and appreciate design may strike better success rates for sure.

We have enough examples to show how designers are chosen by companies not for their managerial abilities but for their 'out-of-box' lateral thinking, blue sky vision and the right attitude for teamwork. However, the one thing which often creates barriers between a designer and the rest of the team is a common malaise which afflicts most adults – ego. A designer may often act reluctant in accepting other's ideas or concepts even if he or she knows that its probably the best way forward. Although ego is part of any personality, the scope of its 'size' should be curtailed for achieving goals within a team. This is how a flexible mind with a high level of creativity can remain relevant and fertile year after year.

However, its not as if the twains shall never meet – managing can be viewed from the perspective of 'designing', as the American architect Frank Gerhy explained, provided the essential difference between 'managing' and 'designing' is well understood. Managing demands fast crystallization of ideas and decisions while 'designing' requires considerable 'non-crystallized' liquid stage of existence in prototyping and iteration. Often the initial concept is mistaken by others as the final design whereas it's only a 'design direction.' Through a conceptual discussion and numerous interactions, a designer arrives at the final design and therefore remains in a 'liquid' stage for a long time. Designing as a process is almost like being in a 'liquid' form as it reaches the freezing point slowly. If these rather dichotomous approaches are dovetailed, then managing can become more like designing wherein solutions are found through appropriate creative and often iterative processes.

design speaks: 'designed in india, made for the world'

A book brought out by the Domus Academy titled, *Design Parla Italiano* (Design Speaks Italian), is a bold and proud statement from a country which has in different periods of its rich and vibrant history expressed, promoted and absorbed art, culture and design in its entirety. The Domus Academy represents what Bauhaus (1919-33) and the Ulm School (1955-68) stood for in their times. There was a period till 1986 when except for the Domus Academy there was no other school in Italy which taught industrial design. Design was treated as part of architecture. It was only in 1997 that the Politecnico di Milano set up its faculty of design.

In contrast, India set up the NID with separate industrial design and communication design education programmes way back in 1961 and the government actually commissioned a prior study by the legendary designer couple, Ray and Charles Eames which came to be known as the *India Report* in 1958. In restrospect, this was indeed remarkable considering that India was still a nascent republic and design was not a dominant influence. However, the irony is that even after fifty years of the *India Report*, Indian design still struggles to find its feet. I wait for the day when we will be able to say – 'Design speaks Indian (languages)' – with tremendous amount of confidence and élan. One way perhaps is to have a Common Maximum Programme (CMP), like major Indian political parties do, endorsed by design educators, policy makers, design faculty, students and industry leaders and other stakeholders with a level of consensus on the road map. Even if plans and projects didn't come to fruition, the one thing which hurts and has done so for a very long time is the baseless and uninformed criticism, an indifference to truth as opposed to perceived truth, emotional response to every issue concerning design and a total lack of empathy resulting in many missed opportunities for creating that 'one voice' for Indian design, on both national and international platforms.

I have in this book quoted the Italian design experience several times and will continue to repeat it for its relevance in the Indian context. The truth is that Italy has indeed been a shining example and as mentioned earlier in this book, particularly in the area of exclusive luxury brands which truly reflect Italian style and culture. And unlike in India or even other countries, there's a method to this process. These world-class brands are represented by an association called Altagamma which promotes the Italian culture of excellence as the highest value add of Italian lifestyle. The result: if you take a look at the world consumption of high end design products, such brands amounted to over 75 billion euros which is equivalent of 85 billion US dollars. Out of this, Italy has a market share of 19.9 billion euros followed by France with 16.4 billion euros, Switzerland and the US come third and fourth with 14.6 billion and 10.5 billion euros respectively. The rest are quite small compared to the four giants above. It is clear that Italy which holds a 27 per cent market share dominates the mindspace of high end design products especially in textile, apparel, soft goods, perfumes and accessories.

Let's accept it – somehow good design and fashionable products seem to have become synonymous with Italy. In design furniture – Alessi, Artemide, Capellini, Cassina; in fashion – Gianfranco Ferré, Guccio Gucci, La Perla, Missoni, Salvatore Ferragamo, Valentino, Versace, Zegna; in jewellery – Bvlgari; and in automobile and boats – Ferrari, Riva. Indeed all of them are today giant global brands but amazingly most of these began as SMEs. In fact, design drives the brand in most of these cases and in these companies, innovation focuses majorly on design.

With a burgeoning middle class, impressive kitty of disposable incomes, and a brilliant talent pool, the obvious question is: if Italy can do it, then why not India? For one, in India the SMEs fear to tread the path of innovation and have been mostly satisfied with a 'me-too' or 'wannabe' syndrome. By and large, somehow designers have not been able to make the desired impact with SMEs and in comparison have been more effective in the traditional handloom and handicrafts sectors. In general, there is a widespread lack of understanding of how design and brands are intrinsically related and how original designs can provide an impetus to create original brands. The story is no different in large enterprises who also display a very limited understanding of the power of design. They often relegate design to an auxiliary role or treat it as an afterthought. From a study on the cluster models in Italy which talks about the methodology for design-driven innovation transference to SMEs, there are some key observations: focus on an entire industrial cluster to bring in design culture rather than on single companies; encourage companies to 'try', 'touch', and 'taste' design rather than 'to just listen about,' design institutes, designers' associations and apex industrial bodies, Chambers of Commerce and other stakeholders need to act as facilitators of such a convergence processes.

For India, the way ahead is both full of challenges and immense opportunities. Even if all the roadblocks are cleared and one gets an opportunity to start afresh, it is finally 'our' mindset which will decide the future of Indian design.

towards design democracy

Developed economies around the world have now mostly become service-driven economies. What this means is that service sectors contribute to the larger share of their GDP, far exceeding manufacturing and agriculture. US for example is a 70 per cent service-driven economy with a larger part of its GDP coming from various services and allied activities, including IPR. As mentioned before, in recent years, India is also on its way to becoming a service-led economy with nearly 56 per cent of its GDP now being generated from service sectors and is slated to reach over 65 per cent by 2015.

The paradigm shifts in the early twenty-first century are analog versus digital, global versus local, tradition versus modernity, fragility versus sustainability, visceral versus virtual, and utilitarian versus experiential. The shift over from analog to digital has already changed the way the world functions and the one tussle that continues is between tradition and modernity.

One of the reasons for this perhaps could be that the frenetic pace of our globalizing world often leaves people confused about their identities and often tradition provides them with a soothing touch. The juggernaut of dematerialization has stream rolled many known human activities and service economies are more about dematerialization. Artists are worried about the manner in which computers generate New Media Art works where there are really no originals as the computer can create hundreds of so called originals. It is in situations like these that artists feel distinctly fragile about the digital world which makes people look at more sustainable models which includes handcrafted, hand-painted work and such other manifestations which are not duplicated with the help of algorithms. The most important change of the cascading impact is reflected in spaces and products becoming inseparable just like images and products in as much the same way as products and services morph into experiences in the minds of consumers. This is indeed a major transformation as products by themselves are not able to satisfy customers without converting themselves into tangible services with intangible experiences. In other words, 'experience prototyping' and 'storytelling' skills will now lead to products and services based on new concepts rather than the other way round.

We are all aware that culture was always a part of design. As the famous writer Aldous Huxley observed, 'Culture is like the sum of special knowledge, that accumulates in any large united family and is the common property of all its members' and this was captured in all culturally cohesive societies. Renowned scholar on classical Indian dance and art, Kapila Vatsyayan in another context had said, 'In each of these culturally cohesive societies, "creativity" was recognized as a quality, as essential and ordinary as the act of breathing. Art – creations of things and products were intrinsic to the act of living. From birth to death, life was punctuated with key moments of time when objects and products created were given meaning and significance as "signifiers" and symbols beyond their form. These ranged from the objects, processes and expressions in all "media" from song to movement, from floral design to floor and mud paintings, to mobile toys, to the making of rattles and "cots". All sense perceptions came into play and a totality was created by cultivating distinctive sense of sight, hearing, scent, touch and taste.'

The new age brand guru, Martin Lindstrom, who is known for some very revolutionary ideas in advertising, recently observed, 'Vodafone owns the red colour and not Coca-Cola. Coca-Cola has not been consistent. Coca-Cola's new colours are green, yellow and many other different shades in different countries of the world. Today, Pepsi owns the colour blue. Pepsi took it away from IBM. Branding is all about consistency. If one wants to secure ownership, then one needs to stick with it. Memories get activated and drive brand choice. Our memories are like an untidy, overstocked cupboard. Everything is recalled at once. Senses are the keys to unlocking the cupboard. Experience creates and confirms expectations. Appealing to all five is likely to double brand awareness and strengthen the impression a brand leaves on its audience.' Well said, indeed!

Even sounds have a lot to do with creating multi-sensory perceptions and in this context Lindstrom says, 'Microsoft Windows has become the owner of its signature tune. About 62 per cent consumers are aware of it. Similarly, Nokia has patented its own tune which is easily recognizable. It was invented around nine years ago.'

It is clear that as service economies become more and more dematerialized, they need to discover the true import of cultural nuances and sensory experiences through brands to make a positive impact on people's minds. There is a strong connection between design democracy and service economy. Design democracy is about empowering people through design which is often delivered through service interfaces with the help of modern technologies. At the end of the day, it does help people to lead a better quality of life and this has become possible only because of the emergence of new information and communication technologies, user-generated content, web-based systems and hand-held devices. I recall one craftsperson at a seminar in NID ruefully commenting about how all the government policies in the past sixty years did not help him as much as the mobile phone which empowered him to connect to the markets. This response is a typical spin-off of service-led economies in which services are seeking to become 'designed experiences; For instance, the mobile phone, as eulogized by my craftsman-friend, is today seen as part of a person's identity cutting across caste, income barriers, vocation, social status, and all such existing discriminating factors. This palm sized device has delivered a whole new world to ordinary consumers especially in large populated countries like India and many parts of Asia and Southeast Asia. I have been repeatedly exploring democratization of design through technology-enabled services which enable the movement towards true design democracy. Therefore, design for the elite, as it was viewed in the twentieth century, has given way to design for everyone, everywhere in the twenty-first century.

designing services

I believe that our designers and students of design have been too immersed in designing products and systems in place of services. Afterall a successful economy is about empowerment and that can be seen in the number of technology-enabled 'solutions' around us. Most importantly, these technologies have become very affordable whether it is a mobile phone, skype, e-banking, e-auctions, matrimonial or job sites, e-ticketing, e-greetings or hundreds of other services available at the click of a mouse. So, it's a perfect setting for design democracy to flourish wherein not just the affluent but even ordinary folks are together pushing the envelope of experiences and therefore, services. Well-known American economist and author of *Rise of the Creative Class*, Richard Florida underlines the quest for experience, but of a different kind, by the creative class. 'On many fronts the creative class lifestyle comes down to a passionate quest for experience ... and the kinds of experiences they crave, reflect and reinforce their identities as creative people.' In a manner of speaking, the service economy, which is experienced by both the common people as well as the creative class, would want designers to come out with new ideas to change or add more value to their lives. Just as e-mails have helped the young to search for new jobs and find life-partners, digital music and moving images are able to provide us instant entertainment while enabling real time need gratification. Innovation-led service economy revolves around new services and memorable experiences. This reality unveils a new way of life bordering on the unreal which means that one plane of existence is on the visceral while the other is on virtual or digital. The challenge of designers is to ensure that the experiences derived from the new vehicles of service, whether it is an ATM, kiosk, GPS or a mobile phone, are true to life.

When we look at designing of services, the new realm of strategic design is bound to have far reaching impact on the lives of people. In the book, *Designing Interactions* edited by IDEO's co-founder, Bill Moggridge, service design is defined as the design of intangible experiences that reach people through many different touch points which happen over time. For service design to be effective, it needs to have a service ecosystem and designing interactions refer to a term 'service ecology' to denote thinking which acknowledges multiple service providers, and partners in a way a product doesn't. 'A service ecology is a process to establish a systematic view of the service and the context it will operate in.' In order to make such service successful, there would have to be several such touch points. In order to design such touch points, 'experience prototyping' with the help of 'storytelling' is now resorted to. Therefore, telephone, transport, taxi, retail, entertainment, maintenance, banking, and public civic services are all which call for 'taking people seriously' as the Netherlands design approach indicates, to design for them. Most of the new services are enabled by technologies and, therefore, just as technological products are designed by multi-disciplinary teams, services also need to be designed as experiences which will encourage the participation and empowerment of people. Two schematic models below explain this concept of 'designing of service experiences' to improve the quality of life.

Let us look at some international examples which demonstrate the success of design democracy through service design. The i-mode service, which is an internet-based service, created a mobile internet which successfully introduced the internet way of thinking rather than the telecom way to implement the i-mode strategy at NTTDOCOMO, Japan. As it is summed up in the book,

Designing Interactions: 'The challenge of design and services are mostly about this sort of complexity, where no single organization has direct influence of entire experience.' This kind of a service had a huge impact on massive segments of the population and truly represented the power of design democracy by service design. At home, the electronic voting machine in India, for which research work was done at the NID in 1988, went on to create a massive impact on the process of adult franchise as voting and election procedures became a more credible and transparent exercise in this complex country.

Service design and design democracy also need to be placed in the context of the pressing need for societal innovation. It is societal innovation which is alluded to in the 'bottom of the pyramid' concept propagated by Prof. C.K. Prahlad where the bottom of the pyramid which has 700 million people in India becomes not only a source of wealth creation but also one of tremendous 'bottoms up' innovation. If a massive democracy like India can unleash the potential of innovation by people using the models of service design, there will be great surge forward from 'individual innovation' to 'societal innovation' which creates a better quality of life for all. By this I mean those who are impacted more by personal compulsions first and economic constraints later. Nelson Mandela had once said, 'The greatest single challenge facing our globalized world is to combat and eradicate its disparities.' The old models of societal transformation need to be reassessed as 'design for better quality of life' has now become accessible and possible through design of service which truly represents the emergence of design democracy in an equitable and non-discriminating world. The pictures in this section capture the diverse services being offered with the help of technology and how the common people benefit from such innovations.

I find that there is a bridge which is waiting to be built to create designed experiences and services which truly democratize design, making it more inclusive and affordable. Affordability has many models today as proven through Google's services, and design practitioners need to take note of the enormous possibilities which will influence the twenty-first century probably the most.

Kaji Prasad uses his mobile as a torch while repairing a car. The mobile, a mode of communication, has multiple uses for people from all walks of life.

design leadership in a creative economy

Designing Quality of Life

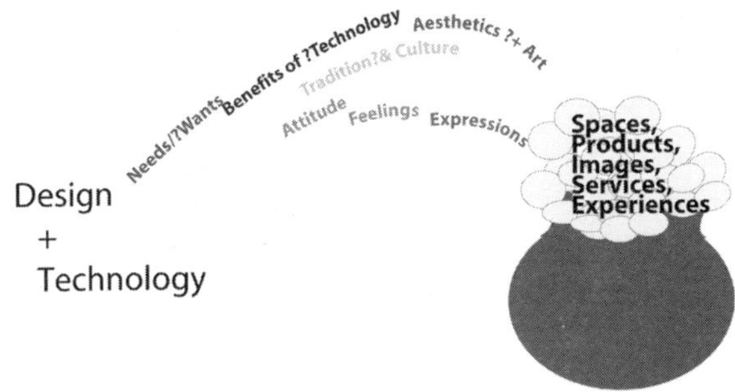

The world has changed, probably less under our feet and more before our eyes. Creative economy is spreading its wings rapidly in a convergent world, and like several other fields, design as a profession is also witnessing a period of watershed. The one word which dominates our everyday existence today is 'change' and as a result of which, existing tenets and paradigms are being subjected to considerable pressures and are being increasingly defined and redefined. This is because people in general, and users in particular, have become more empowered; organizations across the world are networked at a faster pace, and the new-found connectivity holds out an option of establishing multi-layered dimensions of living. Real time communication through fibre optical networks which deliver terabytes, e-mail and voice-mail, lead to instant need gratification and this constantly brings up the requirement of real time design, as predilections and aspirations keep altering. Design essentially is about creative problem solving, sometimes in the most complex of circumstances but finally aspires for an outcome that is simple, aesthetic, and if possible with a surprise element, as well as time and cost-efficient.

As the world struggles to find a fine balance, coping with hands-on and minds-on, there is naturally an expectation from the new breed of designers to achieve breakthrough innovations. Creating and designing new experiences in all spheres and walks of life through a deep cognitive understanding of the interfaces is an emerging challenge. It wouldn't be incorrect to say that digital economy is virtually challenging and pushing design into new frontiers.

Whenever and wherever there is change, there is bound to be a difference of opinion and a demarcation of who is 'for' and 'against' for the reasons and results of change. In the new digital-driven world as well, the one major demarcation is between what is defined as quality of life and quality of experience. Concerned as we are with the design profession, the careful straddling of the so-called twin worlds puts enormous pressures and responsibilities on the profession. What is a holistic experience in a world seen through a convergent technology screen, is often a mystery. The need to humanize technology in order to avoid the impersonal ways of living that might envelope and overwhelm the digital world, is a tantalizing problem for both young and experienced designers. The stratification of the world into information-poor and information-rich is even scarier than the divides and strifes of the last millennium. The new designer will have to concentrate all his energies to bridge this gap through constant design innovation.

It's not as if I am painting a situation which seems rife with insurmountable problems. We need to constantly remind ourselves that design is truly an integrating and harmonizing force. From concept to consumer, design provides companies the cutting edge in a marketplace; brands are made in the minds of consumers through perceptions and experiences; design plays a crucial role in brand strategy as it helps in communicating through semiotics and other such nuances, which make the products worth buying, possessing, consuming and exhibiting. Design thus acts as an integrating rather than a peripheral intervention. While many countries in Europe and the Asia Pacific are busy projecting themselves as the creative hot shops to the rest of world, Indian design community cannot just be enjoying the spectacle and later wake up to ask, 'And what on earth happened to us?'

Designers as people and professionals are extremely connected to the urges, aspirations and angst of human beings. While adapting to a new world where daily lives focus more on a technology-driven world, designers with considerable support from industry and media, as it happened in the fashion world, will have to necessarily work towards realizing the various dreams of mankind, while upholding human dignity, ecological sensitivity, thus ensuring a better quality of life. Anticipating the future is a magical aspect of design which therefore can play a pivotal role in this quest. For many decades, visionaries of industry and society have used design as the lingua-franca to translate dreams and words, to deeds and reality. The role of design as a 'synthesist' is yet to be fully explored for addressing the real problems of humanity and for creating new opportunities towards sustainable existence and growth. Some of the major visions for design leadership not only for India but around the world ought to include:

Designing Quality of Life

Creative Services

↓

Services Experience
(Experience prototyping)

↓

Empowering People

↓

Impact on Society

↓

Better Quality of Life

- Expanding the horizons of design to delve into diverse societies, cultures, countries and regions to create a repository of locally evolved good designs as an inspiration for designers to discover their own roots while searching for harmony in the context of digital divide, stratification and alienation.
- A 'design-led' approach rather than a 'designcentric' approach not only for designers, but design promotional organizations, education institutions, government and NGO networks. Design-led approach maximizes the impact of design while working in co-creation mode with scores of other knowledge domains. This can lead to innovative solutions for 'bottom of pyramid' issues faced by developing countries like illiteracy, poor sanitation and physical disabilities. The lessons learnt are universally applicable especially when it comes to certain problems like disaster mitigation and prevention of crimes and conflicts.
- Encouraging businesses to use design for Corporate Social Responsibility (CSR) which are qualitatively different from the concerns of the twentieth century. Also adapting a new approach for the twenty-first century urging businesses to use design in a proactive strategic mode of 'people first'.
- Urging designers to explore connectivity of products, services and images for creating humane experiences rooted in people's emotional and cultural contexts, in a clearly 'ambidextrous' manner, for both visceral and virtual worlds.
- Enabling the young and also children to discover the joy of creative problem solving in local situations for releasing their full potential through a participatory model.
- Using national design policies especially in developing countries as an instrument to cut across differences and to synergize action.
- To democratize the power of design especially through 'affordable designs for masses' and 'technology enabled service designs' to really make a difference in the quality of life of people at large.

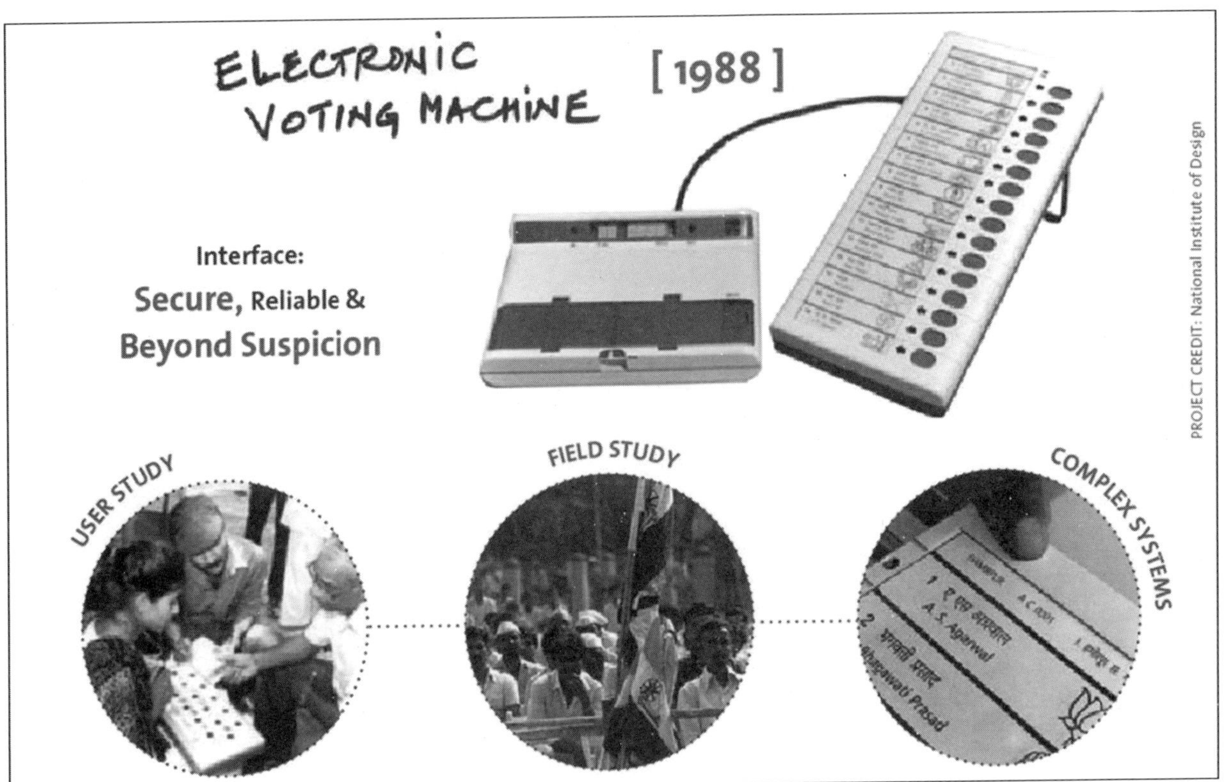

Electronic voting machine researched at NID (1988).

The journey from 'designs for a privileged few' to 'design for everyone, everywhere' will not only be fulfilling for designers but also for countries and communities around the world. Such a journey requires creative leadership and tremendous courage and to quote Steve Jobs who once said in a different context, 'Your time is limited, so don't waste it living someone else's life. Don't be trapped by dogma – which is living with the results of other people's thinking.' Dr Kalam, the then president of India had also put it succinctly in his Convocation Address in 2005 at NID, said:

> There are 540 million youth below 25 years in the population of a billion people. The nation needs young leaders who can command the change for transformation of India into a developed nation embedded with knowledge society ... The leaders are the creators of new organizations of excellence. Quality leaders are like magnets that will attract the best of persons to build the team for the organization and give inspiring leadership even during failures of missions as they are not afraid of risks. One of the very important ingredients for success of the vision of transforming India into a developed nation by 2020 is the evolution of creative leaders. I am giving a connectivity between developed India, economic prosperity, technology, production, productivity, employee role and management quality, all of which are linked to the creative leader. Who is that creative leader? What are the qualities of a creative leader? The creative leadership is exercising the task to

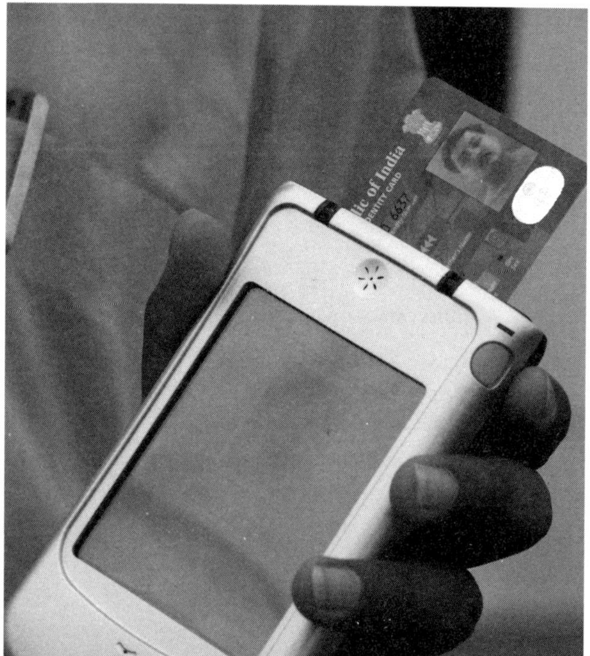

Multi-purpose national identity card designed by Rupesh Vyas and Pravin Nahar, faculty members at NID.

change the traditional role from commander to coach, manager to mentor, from director to delegator and from one who demands respect to one who facilitates self respect. The higher the proportion of creative leaders in a nation, the higher the potential of success of visions like developed India?

In order to have a 'design enabled' India as part of a developed India as envisaged in Vision 2020, there is a need for creative leaders of this kind in the government, among policy makers and captains of industry and most importantly among designers, design academia and the GenNext design students. The Indian design edge can become a reality only by 'leadership through design' and all those concerned about making 'Designed in India' a buzz-word for Indian creativity and pride of heritage need to gear up to face the challenges ahead.

leadership through design: next bold steps

The National Design Policy announced in 2007 is indeed a significant landmark, a definite enabler and a major beacon for the design movement in the country but will require considerable action on the ground by the stakeholders. The success of Indian design will depend on energizing a design movement which has an expansive vision and an action plan. Tracing back the journey in the last decade, the holding of the first CII-NID Design Summit in 2001 against heavy odds was an important milestone in laying out a blueprint for Indian design. Of course, there was the background of the 1979 UNIDO-ICSID Declaration but all that was in the past and much forgotten. As far as I am concerned, the efforts to revive the National Design Policy agenda was almost like fighting a guerrilla warfare. With the amount of hostilities and cynicism that I had to face and contend with, I am sure that even the most committed soldier would have shown his back to the battleground! I am glad and thankful that along with a few other colleagues from NID, I stuck to my ground. By the end of 2006, the design community had already begun to rally around these initiatives and finally the announcement of the National Design Policy in 2007 vindicated my efforts.

However, going by the rather slow progress made over the past seven painstaking years, it is clear that only bold and imaginative steps can now raise the level of Indian design and that too by making up for the time lost in the previous decade during which competing countries in the Asian and South-east Asian regions have made rapid progress. A serious minded collective effort is now required to accelerate the Indian design juggernaut. There is a lot on our table and requires immediate attention: the Golden Quadrilateral Project, the makeover of airports, the expansion of Metro Rail, the malls and condominiums, the flyovers and underbridges, the increasing pace of urbanization in metros and mini-metros and several other concurrent public and private initiatives – all influencing the trajectory India is likely to take for the next 10-15 years. And the National Design Policy of 2007 can be used as a platform to catalyze concerted action provided different ministries and states get actively involved to give it the necessary momentum.

However, the most important aspect of this entire spectrum is to strategize design and for starters, this thought needs to be internalized by policy-makers, corporate leaders and people who matter in the twenty-first century. One of my biggest predictions, if I am allowed to use that word, in this book is about services dominating the economic landscape of India and for design this is the time to go all out and do the best it can. Let's turn to the proof of the pudding, so to speak that is, numbers – in India designing of services offers a big opportunity as by 2015, services would become nearly 60 per cent of the GDP, close to USA which is at 70 per cent.. This is very different from China and, therefore, while China will have to depend on design and product development to advance in the manufacturing sector, India needs to use design and technology together to spawn relevant services and emerge as a dominant force. This will open up avenues for true dominance through design democracy. With India's first rate software/IT leadership, this seems achievable even if designing of services will have to piggyback on it.

The marriage of design and technology has to stop at being one of convenience. The example of SBI's mobile ATM and Airtel's mobile telephone booth for the disabled and hundreds of such good examples are around us to see and it is apparent that designers are not sufficiently engaged in the creation of such service embedded products mainly because of the disconnect between technology and design.

The Indian manufacturing and retail sectors are desperately in search of brand leadership and considering both generate immense employment opportunities, design can play a key role towards strengthening both. There is a disconnect between designs and brands in India

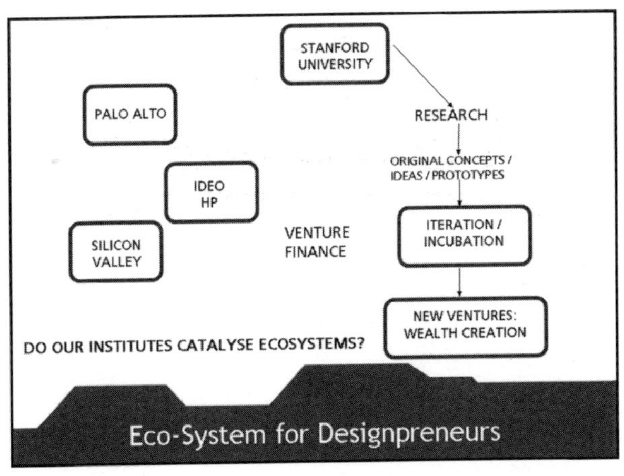

and afflict both the corporate leadership as well as the designers themselves. Design should ideally move into a strategic position to fuel the dream or the new fanged desire for building Indian brands. The private labels in big retail organizations provide great opportunities for design-led brand building. The activities of the Future Group have taken a cue in this regard by setting up 'Idiom', a creative hot shop to help in developing ideas to reach the market place. The new branding as we have seen for the Mumbai airport, Chhatrapati Shivaji to Airtel, also indicates design's great potential of occupying the centre stage of brand building.

I wonder why innovation is treated like the panacea by many even before design starts making an impact. This is a knee jerk reaction. Innovation is nothing but the essence of technology-design fusion strategy and the results of which may take some time. Design is the application of creativity in the process of innovation and in the realm of IT-enabled and web-based services, there are applications galore which beg for designers' attention. 'Designing experiences' by combining spaces, products, images, and services is probably closer to the core of design now. But it needs to be kept in mind that experience is only a vehicle to deliver the service and much focus has to be laid on designing the services by both technologists and designers in a co-creation mode.

A collage of various images to elucidate service design. This image showcases various uses of mobile phone, mode of advertisement, Mumbai dabbawalas, SBI Mobile ATM Services, Eco Milk Van – are some of the examples of service design in India.

Like in any other field, design in India today is screaming for efficient leaders. The profession of design has to define change, design change and help the business leaders to manage change. In India, often several among the design community fail to read the future as they perhaps fear the reality of contending with change. If design leadership has to become a reality there is a need as Steve Jobs said to have 'the courage to follow your heart and intuition.' The ability to cope with massive change and to accept change as the raison de'tre have become pre-requisites for modern day designers.

Indian design cannot expect to innovate or celebrate major breakthroughs unless or until it invests in original design research. Design education in India has not measured up as traditionally it has focused more on producing students with a high level of skill sets and never bothered to push for new knowledge creation. There is no great urgency, as is usually shown by design institutes, to enable designers to connect the dots and think laterally. The result of this attitude would end up in original creative designs and innovative outcomes being inversely proportional to the time spent on the campus of many design institutes! The new students often imbibe frozen energies very quickly and tend to miss the oppourtunities ahead by being too preoccupied with the past or present. Designers beign emotional are prone to develop high resistance to change though change is the *raison de etre* of design.

It's often said that its not just enough to cook a great meal but a great-looking meal. India has just moved into a period of talent crunch in several fields and mediocrity will rule if we turn complacent. The country requires a huge talent pool of design technicians and those associated with trade skills to accomplish good design ideas with superb execution. More importantly, in India the mind to market travel is cumbersome and time consuming. Only in recent times, after showing much resistance, designers have taken to technology for model building and visualization. When I had initiated the setting up of a Design Vision Centre, a first of its kind in a design institute, way back in 2004-05, the cry of opposition had become a shriek so intense that the weak-minded would have fallen by the way side. Today, the Design Vision Centre at NID with its mind to market facilities including Rapid Product Development, 3D Scanners, Laser Engravers and Super Graphic Computing for visualization, have transformed the way students think and work. The fact that an NID student could win an international Concept Car

Competition shows that these technological tools are imperative to achieve shorter product development cycles. Similarly, an affinity towards research-led education and 'self-learning' as in other advanced disciplines need to be inculcated in young designers and the R&D campus of NID in Bengaluru and PG campus in Gandhinagar exemplify this futuristic vision of bringing research and technology closer to design. Again, the short sightedness of many among design fraternity place hurdles in acclerating these visions. Time has become an essential dimension in design and the design leadership today rests as much on time as on creativity. Indian design community has to imbibe the value of competing on time and I strongly suggest that our design consultancies either 'shape' up or 'ship' out in double quick time, or else face what some advertising agencies in India did. The writing is very much on the wall.

While India takes great pride in its premier and world class educational institutions like the IITs, IIMs, and even NID since the late fifties, it has somehow not succeeded in developing an ecosystem for driving innovation and design in the right direction. A visit to Stanford University provides an insight as to how critical it is to develop an eco-system with a strong institute-industry nexus. The combination of research and teaching, creation of ideas and knowledge, setting up of creative hot shops, and availability of venture capital support have led to an eco-system around Stanford for wealth creation through new enterprises which includes the Silicon Valley, Palo Alto, IDEO and HP. Apart from the limited success of incubators in some of our IITs, I find a complete void of such eco-systems anywhere.

As late as 2008, following the announcement of the National Design Policy in 2007, the ground reality is that while the government has made a massive allocation in the eleventh Five Year Plan for education in technology, management, agriculture etc., it has completely missed out on design which is in fact the true enabler of an emergent creative economy.

True design leadership is a moving target. As Indian design gears up to look at the challenges ahead, in India's neighbourhood – Korea, Taiwan, Singapore and China – design is reaching new heights. With Indian economy on an upsurge, and Indian markets attracting huge Foreign Direct Investment inflows, the time for Indian design is here and now. The government, industry, design educationists and designers need to move fast and to echo Alice from *Alice in Wonderland*, 'we have to run as fast as we can, even to remain where we are ...'

To echo Swami Vivekananda, when I look at the long road ahead, I do realize that what has been achieved is far too little. However, the acceleration and momentum now witnessed in Indian design makes me very optimistic about its future. The design community has to clearly see the goal and opportunities rather than the obstacles on the way. As the famed *India Report* of 1958 completes fifty years and NID moves towards its Golden Jubilee in 2010-11, the design movement in India is showing signs of a surge and energy which can certainly put Indian design and 'designed in India' on a very strong wicket. At the end of the day, what is even more important is the way in which design changes the lives of the ordinary Indian and puts a smile on his face and a song on his lips.

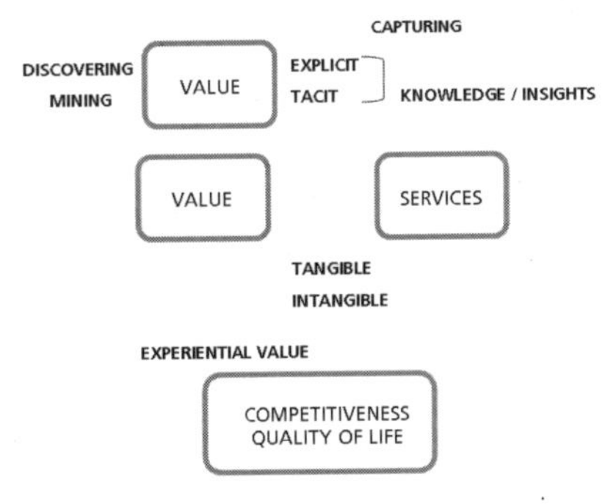

LEADING EDGE DESIGN RESEARCH

select bibliography

Books

Anderson, Chris, *The New Economics of Culture and Commerce: The Long Tail, How Endless Choice is Creating Unlimited Demand*, Random House Business Books, New Delhi, 2006.

Balaram, S., *Thinking Design*, National Institute of Design, Ahmedabad, 1998.

Bijapurkar, Rama, *We are like that only: Understanding the Logic of Consumer India*, Penguin, New Delhi, 2007.

Blanchard, Ken, *Leading at a Higher Level*, Dorling Kindersley, New Delhi, 2007.

Bruce Sterling, *On the Next 50 Years, Military Economies* (MIL), pp. 172 & 173

Chakravorti, Bhaskar, *The Slow Pace of Fast Change: Bringing Innovations to Market in a Connected World*, Harvard Business School Press, USA, 2003.

Demetrios, Eames, *An Eames Primer*, Thames & Hudson Ltd., London, 2001.

Falabrino, Gian Luigi, *Design Speaks Italian: Domus Academy Story*, Libri Scheiwiller, Milano, 2004.

Fletcher, Alan, *The Art of Looking Sideways*, Phaidon Press Limited, New York, 2001.

Florida, Richard, *The Flight of the Creative Class: The New Global Competition for Talent*, Harper Business, New York, 2004.

Florida, Richard, *The Rise of the Creative Class*, Basic Books, New York, 2002.

Forbes, Naushad and David Wield, *From Followers to Leaders: Managing Technology and Innovation*, Routledge, London, 2002.

Godin, Seth, *Survival is Not Enough: Zooming, Evolution and the Future of your Company*, Simon & Schuster UK Ltd, Great Britain, 2002.

Gopalakrishnan, R., *The Case of the Bonsai Manager: Lessons from Nature on Growing*, Penguin, New Delhi, 2007.

Joshi, Kiran, *Le Corbusier from Marseilles to Chandigarh 1945-1965*, Chandigarh Administration, 2007.

Kaplan, Robert S. and David P. Norton, *Strategy Map, Converting Intangible Assets into Tangible Outcome*, Harvard Business School Publishing Corporation, USA, 2004.

Kelley, Tom, with Jonathan Littman, *The Art of Innovation*, Doubleday, USA, 2001.

Khandwalla, Pradip N., *Management of Corporate Greatness*, Dorling Kindersley, New Delhi, 2008.

Koshy, Darlie O., *Effective Export Marketing of Apparel to the US, EU & Japan*, Global Business Press, New Delhi, 1995.

Koshy, Darlie O., *Garment Exports: Winning Strategies*, Prentice-Hall of India Pvt. Ltd., New Delhi, 1997.

Kotler, Philip & Nancy Lee, *Marketing in the Public Sector: A Roadmap for Improved Performance*, Pearson Education, Inc., New Delhi, 2007.

Leonard, Dorothy & Walter Swap, *When Sparks Fly: Igniting Creativity in Groups*, Harvard Business School Press, Boston, 1999.

Mau, Bruce, *Massive Change and the Institute without Boundaries*, Phaidon Press Limited, London, 2004.

Mote, V.L., *Textiles and Fashion: Challenges and Strategies for the Industry*, Tata McGraw-Hill, New Delhi, 2000.

Morris, Steve, Graham Willcocks & Eddy Knasel, *How to Lead a Winning Team: Realise your Full Potential & Develop your Leadership Skills*, Pearson Education Limited, Great Britain, 1995.

Pande, Pete and Larry Holpp, *What is Six Sigma?*, Tata McGraw-Hill, Delhi, 2002.

Peter Zec, Peter, Designing *Success: Strategies, Concepts, Processes, Design*, Zentrum Nordrhein Westfalen Edition, Essen, 1999.

Postrel, Virginia, *Substance of Style: How the Rise of Aesthetic Value is Remaking Commerce, Culture & Consciousness*, HarperCollins, New York, 2003.

Pottruck, David S. and Terry Pearce, *Clicks and Mortar: Passion Driven Growth in an Internet Driven World*, Jossey-Bass, San Francisco, 2001.

Rivkin, Steve, and Fraser Seitel, *Idea-Wise: How to Transform Your Ideas into Tomorrow's Innovations*, East West Books (Madras) Pvt. Ltd., Chennai,

Roberts, Edward B., *Innovation, Driving Product, Process, and Market Change*, Jossey-Bass, San Francisco, 2002.

Robinson, Ken, *Out of Our Minds: Learning to be Creative*, Capstone Publishing Limited, UK, 2001.

Roodhouse, Simon, *Cultural Quarters: Principles and Practices*, Intellect Books, UK, 2006.

Schmidt, Klaus and Chris Ludlow, *Inclusive Branding: The Why and How of a Holistic Approach to Brands*, Palgrave Macmillan, New York, 2002.

Sheth, Jagdish N., *Chindia Rising: How China and India will Benefit your Business*, Tata McGraw Hill Publishing Company Limited, New Delhi, 2008.

Singh, Khushwant, *Train to Pakistan*, Lotus Collection, New Delhi, 2006.

Syrett, Michel and Jean Lammiman, *Successful Innovation: How to Encourage and Shape Profitable Ideas*, Profile Books Ltd., London, 2002.

Taleb, Nassim Nicholas, *Fooled by Randomness*, Random House, New York, 2004.

Zaltman, Gerald, *How Customers Think: Essential Insights into the Mind of the Market*, Harvard Business School Press, USA, 2003.

Periodicals

Cartier Art Magazine, Number 18, 2007, London.

David Kester, *Design Council*, Issue 1, Winter 2006, UK, www.designcouncil.org.uk.

Edward de Bono, *The Economic Times*, New Delhi dated Tuesday, 18th September 2007.

The New Logo unveiled by Ray and Keshavan for Mumbai airport, Source: *Business Standard* of Thursday, 20 September 2007, Ahmedabad.

Websites

CLE website Link: http://www.leatherindia.org/statistics.asp

http://www.designdb.com/english/kidp/policy/policy.asp

http://www.prague-shopping.cz/photo/parizska/salvatore_ferragamo.jpg

IMD World Competitiveness Yearbook 2007

Source: http://www.iloveindia.com/economy-of-india/india-gdp.html)

Statistics reference: Indianembassy.org

Tables and Charts reference: http://www.factbook.net/leather_introduction.php

WIPO Statistics, April 2006, http://www.wipo.int/ipstats/en/statistics

www.filgifts.com/.../Salvatore-Ferragamo.jpg

www.malaysiadesigncouncil.gov.my

www.culturelink..or.kr

http://www.nmc.org/pdf/2007_Horizon_Report.pdf.

Other Sources

Case Study of 'Solemates' designed by Satish Gokhale.

Case Study of Hidesign: Website of Hidesign.

Case Study of Tata Leather: Website of Tata Leathers.

Case Study Onio Design Pvt. Ltd. is one of leading Design & Branding Studio by Manoj Kothari.

Case Study: Differentiate by Design – the Infosys Approach, Source: As told by author by Sridhar Marri, Vice President and Head – Communication Design Group Infosys Technologies Limited.

Case Study: Neelam Chibber, IndusTree Success.

Case Study: Sanjeeb Chatterjee & Anjali Wakanker, KAARU.

CII India Design Resource Book 2008: Go Beyond Success, Confederation of Indian Industry, 2008, Dr Darlie O. Koshy, Design in India, pp.4-6.

David Kester, The Business of Design: Design Industry Research, UK Design Council, 2005.

Design for New Coin Series in India by Anil Sinha, Graphic Design Faculty, NID.

Designing Demand: Make design deliver lasting success for your business, Design Council 2007, UK.

Ezio Manzini, Francois Jégou, Sustainable Everyday: Scenarios of Urban Life, Edizioni Ambiente, Milano.

Leading Lights on Design, A Compilation of 23 NID Convocation Addresses, 2004, National Institute of Design, Ahmedabad, India.

Luca Berchicci, *The Green Entrepreneur's Challenge: The Influence of Environmental Ambition in New Product Development*, DFS Publication, Delft University, The Netherlands.

Mishra Anu, Phad Baanchna, A Tradition of Storytelling: A Craft, Documentation by NID Student, Guide: Errol Pires.

P.B. Jhala, R.M. Sankar, Information Technology in Textile and Clothing Industry: State-of-the-Art, ITCTI Monograph, ATIRA, 2004, Ahmedabad, India.

Rai Namrati, Ganjifa – A Craft Documentation of the Playing Cards in Sawantwadi by NID Student, Guide: Errol Pires.

Ravi Sawhney – A designer's experience protecting IPR, From the presentation of Ravi Sawhney at CII-NID Design Summit at New Delhi, 2002.

Report on the Design for Development, Lekgotla 2006, A Publication of the SABS Design Institute, 2006, Dr Darlie O Koshy, National Design Interventions for Development in India, pp.15-16.

Stainless Steel products Art d'nox by M/s Jindal Stainless.

Statistics reference: Annual Report of Bata.

Study on Animation and Gaming Industry in India, A Report by NASSCOM, New Delhi.

'Study on Animation and Gaming Industry in India', NASSCOM 2006; 'Indian Entertainment and Media Industry: Unraveling the potential', Price Waterhouse Coopers Pvt. India, 2006.

Symphony Presentation at IPR Seminar in NID by Achal Bakeri, March 2007.

The Story of Edge: Strategic Design in Action, as told Michael Foley to the author, Titan's Chief Creative Associate (Previously).

Titan Heritage: Confluences of culture and time, as told by Abhijit Bansod.

Vijay Singh Katiyar, Shashank Mehta, Scholastic Papers from the International Conference, Design Education, Tradition and Modernity, DETM '05, Section 6, Envisioning the Future, Dr Darlie O Koshy, Towards a National Design Policy and a Multitiered Approach to Spread of Quality Design Education, pp. 490-92.

World Design Forum Proceedings, Design Policy and Global Network by ICSID, Seongnam, 2002, Dr Darlie O Koshy, Broadbanding Design Policy & Promotion: Focus on the Region and India, pp. 141-59.

Index

175
indian
design
edge

photo credits

Tata Motors, KAARU, Vijay Kumar Arumugam, Chitra Sarwara, Ramesh Gound, Piyush Sharma, Tobias, Abhijit Bansod, Keyur Zaveri, Uzma Ahmedi, Narayanan Rajagopalan, Yusuf Manan, Ajit Kirkole, Chandrasekhar Badve, R.S. Rajasekaran, Amaresh Panigrahi, Abhimatha Kala, Karma Bhutia, Jasleen Bindra, Sharat Chandra Parsa, Kavita Singh, Ranveer Singh Sahmbi, Achal Bakeri, Srinivas Pattur, Michael Foley, Altagamma, Namrati Rai, Anu Mishra, Aditya Vikram Sengupta, Sushant Jena, Vikram Panchal, Ramneek Kaur Majithia, Mahan Ghosh, Vibhor Sogani, Maropeng Museum in South Africa, Praveen Nahar, Satish Gokhale, Nitin Virkar, Pradyumna Vyas, Vikram Panchal, Deepti Toor, Shivanjali Tomar, Praveen Nahar, M.P. Ranjan, Rupesh Vyas, Roli Books, and NID.